THE PARADISE WITHIN

Studies in Vaughan, Traherne, and Milton

THE PARADISE WITHIN

STUDIES IN

VAUGHAN, TRAHERNE,

AND MILTON

by Louis L. Martz

NEW HAVEN AND LONDON: YALE UNIVERSITY PRESS

1964

For Bernard Schilling

ACKNOWLEDGMENTS

FOR THE PAST several years I have been quarrying in the rough manuscript of this book, in order to provide materials for lectures on various occasions. Condensed versions of the first five sections in the study of *Paradise Lost* have been delivered as lectures at Oberlin College (1958), the University of Manchester (1963), and the University of London (1963). The study of *Paradise Regain'd* was presented, in a version close to its present form, as a lecture before the Tudor and Stuart Club of The Johns Hopkins University (1959); this was published in *ELH* (September 1960). The essential materials in the study of Vaughan were first presented as a Lilly Endowment Lecture at Saint Mary's College, Notre Dame (1961), and, in revised form, as a lecture at New York University (1962); the study was published in substantially its present form in *PMLA* (March 1963). I am grateful to these institutions for the occasions and the subsequent discussions that have brought parts of this book into better form than would otherwise have been achieved. I am also grateful to the editors of *ELH* and *PMLA* for permission to reproduce here materials that have previously appeared in the pages of those periodicals.

I am deeply indebted to the Bodleian Library for permission to study the manuscripts of Traherne in its possession, and to reproduce here a page from the manuscript of the *Centuries;* I should like to thank the staff of the Bodleian for many courtesies extended to me during a year's residence in Oxford, 1962–63. I am equally indebted to the Master and Fellows of University College, Oxford, for permission to reproduce the windows of their splendid chapel, and also for the unfailing hospitality of their Senior Common Room. I am particularly indebted to Peter Bayley, Praelector in English at University College, for many conversations concerning the chapel windows. Miss Helen Gardner's courtesy and conversation have also helped this visitor in many generous ways.

I am grateful to Miss Carol Thomas and Mrs. Joyce Brewster for indispensable help in preparing the manuscript for press; to my wife for her expert aid in correcting proofs; to David Horne for his constant encouragement; to Miss Crimilda Pontes for her interest in the book's design, both physical and mental; to Miss Marjorie Wynne for frequent help in connection with the rare books of the Yale University Library. My friends John Smith and Maynard Mack have both read portions of the manuscript of this book, and I am grateful to them for many valuable suggestions.

To my friend James Osborn I owe the privilege of studying the hitherto unknown manuscript of meditations by Thomas Traherne that has recently become a part of his distinguished collection; an account of this important discovery appears in the Appendix to this book.

In dealing with the massive output of Miltonic studies, I have tried to include in my footnotes every study to which I am conscious of having some specific debt, along with a few other studies that have some particular interest within a certain context. But my references are highly selective; my general indebtedness to the work of Merritt Hughes or Douglas Bush, for example, must be taken for granted. I should like to take this opportunity to mention one recent study which appeared after the manuscript had been completed: Anne Davidson Ferry's admirable *Milton's Epic Voice* (Cambridge, Mass., Harvard University Press, 1963), which bears closely upon the point of view developed in the opening section of my study of *Paradise Lost*.

I wish to thank the following publishers for permission to

quote from their authoritative editions. The Clarendon Press, for quotations from *Thomas Traherne: Centuries, Poems, and Thanksgivings,* ed. H. M. Margoliouth (2 vols. Oxford, 1958), and from *The Works of Henry Vaughan,* ed. L. C. Martin (2d ed. Oxford, 1957). The Westminster Press, for quotations from *Augustine: Earlier Writings,* ed. J. H. S. Burleigh (Philadelphia, Westminster Press, 1953), and from *Augustine: Later Works,* ed. John Burnaby (Philadelphia, Westminster Press, 1955); these volumes, in The Library of Christian Classics, were published simultaneously in London by the SCM Press. The Bobbs-Merrill Co., for quotations from *Saint Bonaventura: The Mind's Road to God,* trans. George Boas, copyright 1953, by The Liberal Arts Press, Inc.; quotations reprinted by permission of the Liberal Arts Press Division of The Bobbs-Merrill Co., Inc. Appleton-Century-Crofts, for quotations from *The Student's Milton,* ed. Frank Allen Patterson, copyright 1930, 1933, by Frank Allen Patterson.

The dedication expresses my gratitude to Bernard Schilling for his vigilant and witty insistence on the writing of "his book."

L. L. M.

Saybrook College
Yale University

CONTENTS

CONTENTS

Chapel of University College, Oxford. Windows by Abraham Van Linge, 1641
(Photograph by Edmark, Oxford)

PREFACE

THE FOLLOWING studies approach a group of works by Vaughan, Traherne, and Milton from the standpoint of the Augustinian concept of interior "illumination." In Augustine's writings this concept is not advanced primarily as abstract doctrine: it is rather a conviction demonstrated through a lifetime's exploration, an experience considered in many different contexts, an insight partially expressed in many different metaphors and nowhere comprehended in any single statement. From the beginning to the end of his career, Augustine's efforts to define "illumination" may be summed up in his words: "We have found, not the thing itself, but where it is to be sought; and that will suffice to give us a point from which a fresh start may be undertaken."[1] Such inquiry "concerning the incomprehensible," he declares in the last book of his treatise on the Trinity, "is justified, and the enquirer has found something, if he has succeeded in finding how far what he sought passes comprehension. Comprehending the incomprehensibility of what he seeks, yet he will go on seeking, because he cannot slacken his pursuit so long as progress is made in the actual enquiry into things incomprehensible: so long as he is continually bettered by the search after so great a good—both sought that it may be found, and found that it may be sought:

1. Augustine, *De Trinitate*, 8.13, in *Later Works,* trans. John Burnaby, Library of Christian Classics, 8 (London, SCM Press, Philadelphia, Westminster Press, 1955), 55. Quotations from this series are made by permission of the Westminster Press.

xiii

still sought that the finding may be sweeter, still found that the seeking may be more eager."[2]

Augustine's incessant search for ultimate truth derives from a conviction that the intellect of man is an indestructible inner "light," which works toward knowledge through the guidance of a higher "Light" that is always present to the mind, even when the mind is not conscious of its presence. Discovery of truth consists in the operations of man's intellect, working within the "illumination" granted by divine power. To define the manner of this interior working, Augustine says, "We must find, in the rational or intellectual soul of man, an image of its Creator planted immortally in its immortal nature." Even though "reason and understanding may at one time be dormant" in the soul, "and at others appear either small or great, the human soul is never anything but rational and intellectual; and for that reason, if its making in God's image represents its power to use reason and intellect for the understanding and the beholding of God, we may be sure that from the first beginning to be of so great and marvellous a creature, that image always remains, whether it be so faded that scarcely anything of it is left, whether it be obscured and defaced, or clear and fair."[3] That is to say, as Burnaby points out,[4] the image of God is manifested not in the mere passive possession of certain qualities but in the *action*, the *power to use* reason for its proper ends. The mind, even in its fallen state, is thus conceived as a center of power, a source of creative activity: "Human nature is a great thing, but because it is not the highest it was liable to spoiling; and although liable to spoiling because it is not the highest, yet because it has a capacity for the highest and is able to become partaker in it, it remains great."[5]

Here is a basis in Christian tradition for the powerful

2. Ibid., 15.2, *Later Works*, p. 129.
3. Ibid., 14.6, *Later Works*, pp. 102–03.
4. *Later Works*, p. 103 n.
5. *De Trinitate*, 14.6, *Later Works*, p. 103.

optimism of Thomas Traherne: a side of Augustine that is sometimes overshadowed by discussions of his influence upon seventeenth-century views regarding predestination and man's depravity. Augustine's view of the mind as a center of indestructible power is of course related to his Platonic and Neoplatonic heritage, to which he pays tribute throughout his career, not only in the early *Soliloquies* and in the reminiscent *Confessions* of his middle years, but also in the later *City of God,* a work which contains some of his darkest utterances concerning man's corruption. Here, for example, is what Augustine finds it possible to say of the Platonic philosophers, at the opening of the tenth book of *The City of God:*

> But we and those great philosophers have no conflict about this question; for they well saw, and many of them plainly wrote, that both their beatitude and ours had its origin from the participation of an intellectual light, which they counted God, and different from themselves. This gave them all their light, and by the fruition of this they were perfect and blessed. In many places does Plotinus explain Plato thus—that that which we call the soul of this universe has the beatitude from one fount with us, namely, a light which it is not, but which made it: and from whose intellectual illustration it has all the intelligible splendour. . . . So (says the great Platonist) the reasonable or intellectual soul . . . has no essence above it, but only God's that created both 'it and all the world . . . herein truly agreeing with the scripture, where it is written: 'There was a man sent from God whose name was John. The same came for a witness to bear witness of the Light, that all men through him might believe. He was not the Light, but came to bear witness of the Light. That was the true Light which lighteth every man that cometh into the world': which difference shows, that that reasonable soul which was in John could not be its own light, but shone by participation of another, the true Light.[6]

6. *The City of God,* 10.2, trans. John Healey (1610), rev. R. V. G. Tasker (2 vols. London, Everyman, 1945), *1,* 275.

In his earliest writings, as Gilson says,[7] Augustine in places expressed his doctrine of "illumination" in terms of something very close to the Platonic theory of reminiscence, whereby the soul retains and recovers memories of an earlier existence. Thus in the early *Soliloquies,* he concludes his exploration of the ways in which truth "dwells in you" by assuming a Platonic principle that he later retracted: "I said that those who are educated in the liberal arts doubtless, in learning them, draw them out from the oblivion which has overwhelmed them, or dig them out, as it were. I do not approve of this. When even untrained persons, suitably questioned, are able to return correct answers about some of the arts, a more credible reason is that they have according to their natural capacity the presence of the light of eternal reason. Hence they catch a glimpse of immutable truth. The reason is not that they once knew it and have forgotten, as Plato and others like him have thought."[8] It may be that a few traces of this old Platonic theory of *anamnesis* can be found even as late as the *Confessions;* at least William Watts, his translator of 1631, thought so, for at one point during Augustine's exploration of the memory, in Book 10, Watts added the marginal note: "He appeares to be of the *Platonist* mind, and that to *Know* was nothing but to *Remember.*"[9] If Watts felt this implication, Traherne and Vaughan, rightly or wrongly, may have felt it too. But there can be no doubt that, on the whole, Augustine's discussion of the memory in the *Confessions* is in accord with the final view that emerges in the *De Trinitate,* where Augustine takes special care to deny any possibility of truth in the Platonic theory of reminiscence.

7. Etienne Gilson, *The Christian Philosophy of Saint Augustine,* trans. L. E. M. Lynch (New York, Random House, 1960), pp. 71–72, 284.

8. Augustine, *Retractations,* 1.4.4; *Soliloquies,* 2.33–35; *Earlier Writings,* trans. John H. S. Burleigh, Library of Christian Classics, 6 (London, SCM Press, Philadelphia, Westminster Press, 1953), 18, 60–62.

9. Augustine, *Confessions,* trans. William Watts (London, 1631), Bk. 10, ch. 11.

Augustine's mature view of the power of the memory lies in his belief that the inner light comes from God, as Creator, Redeemer, and Sustainer of life: creating man first with the natural light of reason, restoring that native light by grace through the sacrifice of Christ, and, beyond this, enlightening the mind by the rays of a supernatural light that shines within the human memory—memory conceived as a storehouse of potential forms. Vaughan, with his various images of light, including the light of childhood, and Traherne, with his extensive use of the symbolism of childhood memories, are not moving beyond the range of possibilities contained within this central Augustinian view. It is, indeed, within this view that their strong Platonic and Hermetic interests cohere. Augustine, to be sure, had little interest in infancy or childhood: his concern lay with the operation of the mind's mature powers. In the first book of the *Confessions,* where he deals briefly with his own childhood, he devotes his pages largely to an account of his sinfulness; yet at the very close of this account he utters a powerful testimony to his belief in the goodness of the essential qualities granted to man, in words that in themselves are not far from the thoughts of Vaughan and Traherne concerning childhood:

> But yet, O Lord, thanks have been due to thee, our God and most excellent Creator, Governor of this universe, although thou hadst not been pleased to have brought me any further than the age of childhood. For even then a Being I had, yea Life and Senses; even then I had a care of mine own well being, which is an impression of that most secret unity of thine [*vestigium secretissimae unitatis*], whence I had my being; in my inward sense preserved I the entireness of my outward senses; even in these little things and in reflecting on little things, was I delighted with the truth. I would not willingly be deceived; a fresh memory I had; in forms of speaking I was well tutored; by friendly usage I was made tractable. I avoided all sadness, dejectedness, and ignorance; in such a little creature, what was there not admirable, not

commendable? But all these are the gifts of my God: for I bestowed them not upon myself. Good endowments they were; and all these was I. Good therefore is he that made me; yea, he is my good, and to him will I rejoice for all my good gifts, which of a child I had.[10]

With Milton, however, the doctrine of "illumination" does not involve these problems of the memory and childhood: his two poems of Paradise tend rather to find their center in the view expressed in Augustine's late summation of his views, in Book 14 of the *De Trinitate,* where he takes pains to remove any implication of Platonic memory:

To a mind inclining to take pride in a good supposed of its own making, the truth is told by the apostle: "What hast thou that thou hast not received? and if thou hast received, why dost thou boast thyself as though thou hadst not received?" But when it duly remembers its Lord, it receives his Spirit, and becomes fully conscious of the truth learnt from the indwelling Teacher, that it can rise only by his undeserved goodness, even as it could have fallen only by its own voluntary default. It has indeed no memory of its own blessedness; for that was once and is no longer, and the mind has totally forgotten it, so that no reminder can bring it back. It can only believe, on the faith of the Scriptures of its God, written by his prophet, the story of a happiness of paradise and the account conveyed in narrative form of man's original good and evil. But it has the memory of the Lord its God. For he ever is ... And he is everywhere in his wholeness; so that in him the mind lives and moves and has its being, and therefore has the power to remember him. Not that it recollects having once known him in Adam, or anywhere else before this bodily life, or at its first making and planting in this body. Of none of these things has it any memory whatsoever: all of them are buried in oblivion. But it can

10. *Confessions,* 1.20; in the corrected version of Watts's translation published in the Loeb Library edition of the *Confessions,* ed. W. H. D. Rouse (2 vols. London, 1912); I have also used this edition for quotations from the Latin text.

be so reminded as to turn again unto the Lord, who is the light by which even in its turning away from him it was still somehow touched.[11]

This Augustinian principle of "the indwelling Teacher," then, provides the central approach for the following explorations into the style, the organization, and the meaning of four literary works composed, approximately, within the same quarter-century: the first edition of Henry Vaughan's *Silex Scintillans* (1650), the *Centuries* of Thomas Traherne, apparently composed between 1670 and 1674, and Milton's *Paradise Lost* (1667) and *Paradise Regain'd* (1671). The studies were conceived, and for the most part composed, in the sequence in which they here appear. Each of the four parts, I think, will make sense if read separately; yet each study is designed to throw some light upon the study that follows; and all four, I hope, will work together to suggest a central principle prevailing in English religious literature during the middle years of the seventeenth century. In my own mind the studies have come to assume a form somewhat analogous to that of a musical suite. At the same time I find, on looking back now, that the book has been unconsciously or half-consciously influenced by Augustine's way of carrying on an inquiry into the incomprehensible.

L. L. M.

Oxford
August 1963

11. *De Trinitate*, 14.20, *Later Works*, pp. 118–19.

I

HENRY VAUGHAN
The Caves of Memory

Yet doubt not but in Vallie and in Plaine
God is as here, and will be found alike
Present, and of his presence many a signe
Still following thee, still compassing thee round
With goodness and paternal Love, his Face
Express, and of his steps the track Divine.

—*Paradise Lost,* Book 11

Grant I may so
Thy steps track here below,

That in these Masques and shadows I may see
Thy sacred way,
And by those hid ascents climb to that day
Which breaks from thee
Who art in all things, though invisibly . . .

—Vaughan, "I walkt the other day"

1. Modes of Communion

IN THE YEAR 1649 Richard Crashaw died in exile at Loreto,
a little more than six months after his master King Charles
died on the scaffold at Whitehall. An era had ended for English political and religious institutions, and also for English
religious poetry. With Crashaw's death the power of liturgical
and eucharistic symbols died away in English poetry of the
seventeenth century: the symbols earlier celebrated by South-
well, Alabaster, Donne, and Herbert. These poets had their
doctrinal differences, and I do not wish to minimize those differences; but they had something more in common: a devotion
to the mysteries of the Passion and to a liturgy that served to
celebrate those mysteries. All five of these poets entered into
holy orders; all five would have agreed with George Herbert's
vision of "The Agonie":

> Who knows not Love, let him assay
> And taste that juice, which on the crosse a pike
> Did set again abroach; then let him say
> If ever he did taste the like.
> Love is that liquour sweet and most divine,
> Which my God feels as bloud; but I, as wine.

In 1650 Andrew Marvell wrote his famous "Horatian Ode"
in honor of the man who

> Could by industrious Valour climbe
> To ruine the great Work of Time,
> And cast the Kingdome old
> Into another Mold.

3

And in the same year appeared the first edition of Henry Vaughan's *Silex Scintillans,* a volume that, along with Milton's miscellaneous *Poems* of 1645, marks the emergence of the layman as a central force in religious poetry of the period. Vaughan's volume, though written by a staunch Royalist and Anglican, nevertheless stands as a sign of a profound mutation in human affairs. Without neglecting the highly individual qualities of Vaughan's vision, I should like here to consider his volume of 1650 as the symbol of a vital transformation in the religious outlook of the age.

It is important to look closely at *Silex Scintillans,* 1650. For Vaughan's enlarged volume of 1655, with its second part and its greatly expanded opening matter, presents a modified outlook, a less consistent fabric, and a weaker body of poetry, despite the fact that seven or eight of Vaughan's finest poems did not appear until the 1655 edition. The common charges against Vaughan's poetry—that his poems often begin with a flash of power, but then dwindle off into tedious rumination, that he works by fits and starts, that he cannot sustain a whole poem—these charges find their chief support in Book II of *Silex,* which reveals many signs of a failing inspiration. There is a greater reliance on the ordinary topics of piety, especially in the many labored poems based on Biblical texts; there is a marked decline in the frequency of Herbertian echoes, and a corresponding rise in the use of conventional couplet-rhetoric, after the manner of the Sons of Ben Jonson: a school to which Vaughan showed his allegiance in his undistinguished volume of secular poems in 1646. At the same time the crabbed and contentious Preface of 1655 strikes a tone quite out of line with the dominant mode of the poems in the 1650 volume, here bound up as the first "book" of what has now become a religious miscellany.[1] But the volume of 1650 is a whole, like

1. The unsold sheets of the 1650 volume, with two canceled leaves, were bound up with new materials and a new title page to form the 1655 edition of *Silex Scintillans;* the engraved title page of 1650 and the Latin poem facing the engraving were omitted in 1655: see *The Works of Henry*

4

Title Page, *Silex Scintillans*, 1650 (Yale University Library)

Herbert's *Temple;* and indeed there are many signs that the volume was deliberately designed as a sequel, a counterpart, and a tribute to Herbert's book.

Vaughan's subtitle is exactly the same as Herbert's: "Sacred Poems and Private Ejaculations"; but the main title represents a vast difference, enforced, in the 1650 volume alone, by the engraved title page presenting the emblem of the Flashing Flint—the stony heart weeping, bleeding and flaming from the hand of God that strikes direct from the clouds, steel against flint. Furthermore, a careful look at this flinty heart will reveal something that I never noticed until my friend Evelyn Hutchinson, examining this title page with his scientific eye, asked, "Do you see a human face peering forth from within the heart?" It is certainly so: a man within can be clearly seen through an opening in the heart's wall.[2] And facing this we have, again in the 1650 volume only, an intimate confession in the form of a Latin poem, explaining the emblem. Perhaps a literal version of this cryptic Latin will show how essential this poem and this emblem are for an understanding of the 1650 volume as a whole:

The Author's Emblem (concerning himself)

You have often touched me, I confess, without a wound, and your *Voice,* without a voice, has often sought to counsel me; your diviner breath has encompassed me with its calm motion, and in vain has cautioned me with its sacred murmur. I was deaf and dumb: a *Flint:* You (how great care you take of your own!) try to revive another way, you change the Remedy; and now angered you say that *Love* has no power, and you prepare to conquer force with *Force,* you come closer, you break through the *Rocky* barrier of my heart, and it is made *Flesh* that was before a *Stone.* Behold me torn asunder!

Vaughan, ed. L. C. Martin (2d ed. Oxford, Clarendon Press, 1957), p. xxiv.

2. The profiles of at least two human faces may also be seen along the outer edges of the heart; the whole heart, then, is animate: the stone has been made flesh, as Vaughan says in his Latin poem facing the emblem.

and at last the *Fragments* burning toward your skies, and the cheeks streaming with tears out of the *Adamant*. Thus once upon a time you made the *Rocks* flow and the *Crags* gush, oh ever provident of your people! How marvellous toward me is your hand! In *Dying,* I have been born again; and in the midst of my *shattered means* I am now *richer.*[3]

Authoris (de se) Emblema.

Tentâsti, fateor, sine vulnere sœpius, & me
  Consultum voluit Vox, *sine voce, frequens;*
Ambivit placido divinior aura meatu,
  Et frustrà sancto murmure præmonuit.
Surdus eram, mutusq; Silex: *Tu, (quanta tuorum*
  Cura tibi est!) aliâ das renovare viâ,
Permutas Curam: Jamq; irritatus Amorem
  Posse negas, & vim, Vi, *superare paras,*
Accedis propior, molemq;, & Saxea *rumpis*
  Pectora, fitq; Caro, *quod fuit ante* Lapis.
En lacerum! Cœlosq; tuos ardentia tandem
  Fragmenta, *& liquidas ex* Adamante *genas.*
Sic olim undantes Petras, Scopulosq; *vomentes*
  Curâsti, O populi providus usq; tui!
Quam miranda tibi manus est! Moriendo, *revixi;*
  Et fractas *jam sum* ditior *inter* opes.

At once, after this story of a sudden, violent illumination, comes the short and simple poem headed, like the opening poem of Herbert's *Temple,* "The Dedication";[4] it contains a number of verbal echoes of Herbert, and the whole manner of the poem represents a perfect distillation of Herbert's intimate mode of colloquy:

3. I am indebted to the Rev. Marcus Haworth for suggesting some of the phrases in this translation.
4. In 1655 this fourteen-line poem becomes the first part of a poem in 46 lines, with the elaborate dedicatory heading: "To my most merciful, my most loving, and dearly loved Redeemer, the ever blessed, the onely Holy and Just One, Jesus Christ, The Son of the living God, And the sacred

Some drops of thy all-quickning bloud
Fell on my heart, these made it bud
And put forth thus, though, Lord, before
The ground was curs'd, and void of store.

These three elements, then: engraved title page, Latin confession, and Herbertian Dedication form the utterly adequate preface to *Silex Scintillans*, 1650. They introduce a volume that will have two dominating themes: first, the record and results of the experience of sudden illumination; and second, a tribute to the poetry of George Herbert, which, it seems, played an important part in cultivating Vaughan's peculiar experience. Thus, toward the middle of Vaughan's volume, after hundreds of unmistakable echoes of Herbert in title, phrasing, theme, and stanza-form,[5] Vaughan at last openly acknowledges his debt by accepting the invitation of Herbert's poem "Obedience," where Herbert offers his poetry as a written deed conveying himself to God, with this conclusion:

He that will passe his land,
As I have mine, may set his hand
And heart unto this Deed, when he hath read;
And make the purchase spread
To both our goods, if he to it will stand.

How happie were my part,
If some kinde man would thrust his heart
Into these lines; till in heav'ns Court of Rolls
They were by winged souls
Entred for both, farre above their desert!

Virgin Mary." The added lines of 1655 are plodding couplets of conventional piety.

5. Most of the important echoes have been listed in the notes to Martin's second edition of Vaughan's *Works*. The echoes have been perceptively discussed by E. C. Pettet, *Of Paradise and Light: A Study of Vaughan's Silex Scintillans* (Cambridge University Press, 1960), ch. 3. See also the helpful article by Mary Ellen Rickey, "Vaughan, *The Temple,* and Poetic Form," *Studies in Philology*, 59 (1962), 162–70.

Vaughan, in "The Match," answers in Herbert's own mode of familiar address:[6]

> Dear friend! whose holy, ever-living lines
> > Have done much good
> > To many, and have checkt my blood,
> My fierce, wild blood that still heaves, and inclines,
> > But is still tam'd
> > By those bright fires which thee inflam'd;
> Here I joyn hands, and thrust my stubborn heart
> > Into thy *Deed* . . .

As we look back, this joining of hands and hearts between Vaughan and Herbert is almost equally evident in the opening poem of the volume proper: "Regeneration." Here the allegorical mode of the painful quest, the imagery of struggling upward toward a "pinacle" where disappointment lies, the sudden cry mysteriously heard upon this hill, and even some aspects of the stanza-form—all these things show a poem that begins by playing variations on Herbert's poem "The Pilgrimage," which leads the speaker through "the wilde of Passion" toward the hill suggesting Calvary:

> When I had gain'd the brow and top,
> A lake of brackish waters on the ground
> > Was all I found.

> With that abash'd and struck with many a sting
> > Of swarming fears,
> > I fell, and cry'd, Alas my King!
> > Can both the way and end be tears?
> Yet taking heart I rose, and then perceiv'd
> > I was deceiv'd:

> My hill was further: so I flung away,
> > Yet heard a crie
> Just as I went, *None goes that way*

6. The allusion was pointed out by Elizabeth Holmes, *Henry Vaughan and the Hermetic Philosophy* (Oxford, Blackwell, 1932), pp. 12–13.

And lives: If that be all, said I,
After so foul a journey death is fair,
And but a chair.

But Vaughan's pilgrimage has quite a different theme: in the fourth stanza the Herbertian echoes fade out, as Vaughan's pilgrim is called away into an interior region of the soul, here imaged with the combination of natural and Biblical landscape that often marks Vaughan at his best:

With that, some cryed, *Away;* straight I
Obey'd, and led
Full East, a faire, fresh field could spy
Some call'd it, *Jacobs Bed;*
A Virgin-soile, which no
Rude feet ere trod,
Where (since he stept there,) only go
Prophets, and friends of God.

The allusion to Jacob's vision and journey toward the East (Genesis 28:10–22; 29:1) is only the first of many such allusions by Vaughan to the "early days" of the Old Testament; here the scene begins an allegorical account of the mysterious workings of grace; the pilgrim enters into a state of interior illumination, where he is prepared to apprehend the presence of God and to hear the voice of the Lord. In the remaining six stanzas the setting mysteriously changes to another landscape, a springtime scene, where a grove contains a garden with a fountain; the state of grace is imaged by combining the natural imagery of spring with subtle echoes of the most famous of all spring-songs: the Song of Solomon. The key to these stanzas is given by Vaughan himself in a verse from the Canticle appended to the poem: "Arise O North, and come thou South-wind, and blow upon my garden, that the spices thereof may flow out." It is the Garden of the Soul: one of the great central symbols in the Christian literature of meditation and contemplation. For Vaughan's poem here we need to recall especially

9

the four verses of the Canticle (4:12–15) that immediately precede Vaughan's citation:

> A garden inclosed is my sister, my spouse; a spring shut up, a fountain sealed.
> Thy plants are an orchard of pomegranates, with pleasant fruits; camphire, with spikenard,
> Spikenard and saffron; calamus and cinnamon, with all trees of frankincense; myrrh and aloes, with all the chief spices:
> A fountain of gardens, a well of living waters, and streams from Lebanon.

So in Vaughan's spiritual landscape "The aire was all in spice," while

> Only a little Fountain lent
> Some use for Eares,
> And on the dumbe shades language spent
> The Musick of her teares;
> I drew her neere, and found
> The Cisterne full
> Of divers stones, some bright, and round
> Others ill-shap'd, and dull.
>
> The first (pray marke,) as quick as light
> Danc'd through the floud,
> But, th'last more heavy then the night
> Nail'd to the Center stood;

Vaughan is developing his favorite image-cluster of light and darkness through symbols that suggest one of his favorite Biblical passages: the third chapter of St. John's gospel, where Nicodemus hears the words of Jesus by night:

> Except a man be born of water and of the Spirit, he cannot enter into the kingdom of God.
> That which is born of the flesh is flesh; and that which is born of the Spirit is spirit.

So in Vaughan's allegory, the spiritual part of man is here reborn, made bright and "quick" as light; while the fleshly part remains dull and heavy, nailed to the earth. Much the same significance is found in the following scene, where in a bank of flowers, representing his own interior state, the speaker finds

> Some fast asleepe, others broad-eyed
> And taking in the Ray . . .

And finally, all the images and themes of this poem coalesce with a three-fold allusion to the "winds" of grace: the "rushing mighty wind" of Pentecost (Acts 2:2), the winds that are prayed for in Vaughan's quotation from the Canticle, and the wind described in the words of Jesus to Nicodemus: "The wind bloweth where it listeth, and thou hearest the sound thereof, but canst not tell whence it cometh, and whither it goeth: so is every one that is born of the Spirit." And so the poem concludes:

> Here musing long, I heard
> A rushing wind
> Which still increas'd, but whence it stirr'd
> No where I could not find;
>
> I turn'd me round, and to each shade
> Dispatch'd an Eye,
> To see, if any leafe had made
> Least motion, or Reply,
> But while I listning sought
> My mind to ease
> By knowing, where 'twas, or where not,
> It whisper'd; *Where I please.*
>
> Lord, then said I, *On me one breath,*
> *And let me dye before my death!*

So the poem,[7] like dozens of others by Vaughan, begins with echoes of George Herbert, whose simplicity of language and intimacy of tone pervade the whole poem and the whole vol-

7. This brief account of "Regeneration" deals only with those aspects important to the present study; for more detailed interpretations, differing

ume of 1650; but, like all of Vaughan's better poems, "Regeneration" moves away from Herbert to convey its own unique experience through its own rich combination of materials, in which we may discern three dominant fields of reference: the Bible, external Nature, and the interior motions of the Self. There is in "Regeneration" not a single reference that could be called eucharistic. Yet Herbert opens the central body of his poems with an emblematic Altar, typographically displayed upon the page, and he follows this with the long eucharistic meditation entitled "The Sacrifice," where he develops the meaning of the Passion through a variation on the ancient Reproaches of Christ, spoken from the Cross as part of the Good Friday service. Nothing could speak more eloquently of the vast difference between these two poets.

In accordance with his central symbols, at the outset of his *Temple* Herbert gives seventy-seven stanzas of epigrammatic advice on how to lead a good life, under the title, "The Church-porch"; these stanzas form a preparation for the mental communion that constitutes the heart of Herbert's central body of poetry, "The Church," as he makes plain by these lines on the threshold:

> Thou, whom the former precepts have
> Sprinkled and taught, how to behave
> Thy self in church; approach, and taste
> The churches mysticall repast.

Now Henry Vaughan also has a group of stanzas in this epigrammatic form, under the title "Rules and Lessons"; they come exactly in the center of the 1650 volume, as though the advice there given formed the center of the volume's devotional life. But Vaughan's advice bears no relation to any ecclesiastical

---

in some respects from my own, see the illuminating studies of this poem by R. A. Durr, *On the Mystical Poetry of Henry Vaughan* (Cambridge, Mass., Harvard University Press, 1962), pp. 82–99; by Ross Garner, *Henry Vaughan: Experience and the Tradition* (University of Chicago Press, 1959), pp. 47–62; and by Pettet, pp. 104–17.

symbolism: it is as though the earthly church had vanished, and man were left to work alone with God.[8] Vaughan's rules and lessons for the devout life lay down, in twenty-four stanzas, certain ways of individual communion with God in every hour of the day, from early morning, through the worldly work of midday, and on through night, until the next day's awakening: one couplet gives the essence of the rules:

> A sweet *self-privacy* in a right soul
> Out-runs the Earth, and lines the utmost pole.

Man's duty is to cultivate the inner self, using as aids the two "books" that we have seen in "Regeneration": the Book of Nature, and the Book of Scripture, as Vaughan suggests in his advice for morning devotions:

> Walk with thy fellow-creatures: note the *hush*
> And *whispers* amongst them. There's not a *Spring,*
> Or *Leafe* but hath his *Morning-hymn;* Each *Bush*
> And *Oak* doth know *I AM;* canst thou not sing?
> O leave thy Cares, and follies! go this way
> And thou art sure to prosper all the day.

> Serve God before the world; let him not go
> Until thou hast a blessing, then resigne
> The whole unto him; and remember who
> Prevail'd by *wrestling* ere the *Sun* did *shine.*
> Poure *Oyle* upon the *stones,* weep for thy sin,
> Then journey on, and have an eie to heav'n.

Note the rich and curious complex of the Biblical and the natural: the allusion to the bush from which Moses heard the voice of God; the extended reference to the time when Jacob wrestled with the mysterious stranger "until the breaking of the day," when he won the stranger's blessing, and knew at

8. By 1650 Vaughan's earthly Church of England had in fact vanished: Vaughan's twin-brother Thomas, the parish priest of Vaughan's own local church, was evicted from his post in 1650, and the post remained vacant for nearly eight years. See F. E. Hutchinson, *Henry Vaughan: A Life and Interpretation* (Oxford, Clarendon Press, 1947), pp. 109–13.

last that he had "seen God face to face" (Genesis 32:24–30); and the shorter allusion to the familiar scene of Jacob's vision, after which "Jacob rose up early in the morning, and took the stone that he had put for his pillows, and set it up for a pillar, and poured oil upon the top of it" (Genesis 28:18).

The Bible, Nature, and the Self thus come together in a living harmony, as in Vaughan's "Religion" (a poem that, typically, seems to take its rise from Herbert's poem "Decay") :

> My God, when I walke in those groves,
> And leaves thy spirit doth still fan,
> I see in each shade that there growes
> An Angell talking with a man.
>
> Under a *Juniper,* some house,
> Or the coole *Mirtles* canopie,
> Others beneath an *Oakes* greene boughs,
> Or at some *fountaines* bubling Eye;
>
> Here *Jacob* dreames, and wrestles; there
> *Elias* by a Raven is fed,
> Another time by th' Angell, where
> He brings him water with his bread;
>
> In *Abr'hams* Tent the winged guests
> (O how familiar then was heaven!)
> Eate, drinke, discourse, sit downe, and rest
> Untill the Coole, and shady *Even* . . .

One must read several stanzas before it becomes clear that the "leaves" here are essentially the leaves of the Bible,[9] where the self can learn to live intimately with God; but at the same time the vivid apprehension of natural life here may suggest that nature itself is still inspired by the divine presence.

The fact that Vaughan so often, in his best poems, seeks out these individual ways of communion with God does not

9. For the trees of the second stanza see 1 Kings 19:4–8 (Elijah under the juniper tree); Zechariah 1:8–11 ("the man that stood among the myrtle trees"); Judges 6:11 ("And there came an angel of the Lord, and sat under an oak which was in Ophrah").

mean that he chooses to neglect or ignore traditional devotions to the Eucharist. On the contrary, he is acutely aware of the importance of the eucharistic allusions in Herbert's *Temple,* for he makes frequent efforts to follow Herbert's central mode of mental communion. But he does not often succeed, as we may see in four sizable poems in the 1650 volume that are devoted to eucharistic celebration. His poem "The Passion" is an extended effort to meditate upon the traditional themes, but the poem is wooden, labored, and forced in its effect. One may perhaps trace a cause of this failure to the fact that Vaughan does not visualize the Passion "as if he were present," in the ancient tradition of such meditations; instead, he puts the whole occasion in the past. He does not memorialize the Passion as a present reality. In another poem, "Dressing," he performs a preparation for "Thy mysticall *Communion,*" but the poem is so worried by contemporary doctrinal quarrels that it ends with a bitter attack on Puritan views, and not with any devotional presence. Another poem, entitled "The Holy Communion," begins by echoing the first two lines of George Herbert's eucharistic poem, "The Banquet": "Welcome sweet, and sacred feast; welcome life!" but Vaughan's poem immediately veers away from the feast to ponder the action of grace within the self, and the operation of God's creative power over the entire universe.

Vaughan's one and only success in this kind of poetic celebration comes significantly in his poem "The Sap," where he approaches the Eucharist indirectly, through a tale told to himself by his inmost self:

> Come sapless Blossom, creep not stil on Earth
> > Forgetting thy first birth;
> 'Tis not from dust, or if so, why dost thou
> > Thus cal and thirst for dew?
> It tends not thither, if it doth, why then
> > This growth and stretch for heav'n? . . .
> Who plac'd thee here, did something then Infuse
> > Which now can tel thee news.

There is beyond the Stars an hil of myrrh
　　From which some drops fal here,
On it the Prince of *Salem* sits, who deals
　　To thee thy secret meals . . .
Yet liv'd he here sometimes, and bore for thee
　　A world of miserie . . .
But going hence, and knowing wel what woes
　　Might his friends discompose,
To shew what strange love he had to our good
　　He gave his sacred bloud
By wil our sap, and Cordial; now in this
　　Lies such a heav'n of bliss,
That, who but truly tasts it, no decay
　　Can touch him any way . . .

The whole poem, as several readers have pointed out,[10] bears
some resemblance to Herbert's poem "Peace," but the contrasts
are more significant. In Herbert's poem the seeker after peace
comes upon a "rev'rend good old man" who tells him the story
of "a Prince of old" who "At Salem dwelt"—alluding to Christ
under the figure of Melchizedek, who "brought forth bread and
wine" (Genesis 14:18; Hebrews 7). Herbert's poem presents
an allegory of the apostolic succession: the "good old man"
offers the bread of life derived from the "twelve stalks of
wheat" that sprang out of Christ's grave:

> Take of this grain, which in my garden grows,
> 　　And grows for you;
> Make bread of it: and that repose
> 　　And peace, which ev'ry where
> With so much earnestnesse you do pursue,
> 　　Is onely there.

But Vaughan does not end his poem with such an echo of the
ecclesiastical ritual; instead he closes with what appears to be
yet another tribute to the poems of George Herbert, as he seems
to echo here at least four of Herbert's eucharistic poems.[11]

10. See *Works of Vaughan,* ed. Martin, 2d ed., p. 744.
11. See Herbert, "The H. Communion," two poems under one title; the

<blockquote>
Then humbly take
This balm for souls that ake,
And one who drank it thus, assures that you
Shal find a Joy so true,
Such perfect Ease, and such a lively sense
Of grace against all sins,
That you'l Confess the Comfort such, as even
Brings to, and comes from Heaven.
</blockquote>

But this comfort remains, in Vaughan's poetry, a promise and a hope: his central channels of communion lie elsewhere, channels with a long and venerable history.[12]

2. The Augustinian Quest

Perhaps the discussion of Vaughan's characteristic triad, the Bible, Nature, and the Self, has already suggested the three "books" cultivated by the medieval Augustinians, and especially by St. Bonaventure: the Book of Scripture, the Book of Nature, and the Book of the Soul.[1] The three books are, essentially, one: the revelation given in the Bible shows man how to read, first nature, and then his own soul. That is to say, in

---

first deals with the action of grace against sins; the second celebrates the "ease" with which the soul now communicates with heaven: "Thou hast restor'd us to this ease / By this thy heav'nly bloud." See also "The Invitation," esp. st. 4, dealing with "joy"; and "The Banquet," celebrating the "sweet and sacred cheer" of the Communion, and its power of raising the soul to "the skie."

12. The literary consequences of modifications in eucharistic doctrine form the subject of Malcolm Ross's controversial study, *Poetry and Dogma: The Transfiguration of Eucharistic Symbols in Seventeenth Century English Poetry* (New Brunswick, N.J., Rutgers University Press, 1954). Ross's work deserves attention for the light it throws upon the central issues; but many readers will disagree with his conclusions.

1. See G. H. Tavard, *Transiency and Permanence: The Nature of Theology According to St. Bonaventure* (Franciscan Institute, St. Bonaventure, N.Y., 1954), chs. 2–4.

Augustinian terms: man, enlightened by Biblical revelation, can grasp the Vestiges, the "traces," of God in external nature; and from this knowledge he can then turn inward to find the Image of God within himself.[2] It is an Image defaced by sin, but with its essential powers restored by the sacrifice of Christ. Man is not simply fallen: he is fallen and redeemed. It is man's responsibility, with the omnipresent help of grace, to clear and renew this Image, until it may become a true Similitude. But the renewal can never be wholly accomplished in this life: thus, as in "Regeneration," the poems that relate Vaughan's journey of the mind toward God end with a cry for help, a prayer for some momentary glimpse of perfection, as in his "Vanity of Spirit," where he performs a journey like that in Bonaventure's *Itinerarium*,[3] first searching through all Nature, and then finding at last within himself

> A peece of much antiquity,
> With Hyerogliphicks quite dismembred,
> And broken letters scarce remembred.
> I tooke them up, and (much Joy'd,) went about
> T' unite those peeces, hoping to find out
> The mystery; but this neer done,
> That little light I had was gone:
> It griev'd me much. At last, said I,
> *Since in these veyls my Ecclips'd Eye*
> *May not approach thee, (for at night*
> *Who can have commerce with the light?)*
> *I'le disapparell, and to buy*
> *But one half glaunce, most gladly dye.*

In this effort to piece together broken letters scarce remembered, by the aid of an interior light, Vaughan displays the essential action of that kind of meditation which may be termed Augustinian. Its finest explanation is still the one most easily available: it lies in the great climactic section of Augustine's *Confessions,* the chapters of the tenth book (6–27) where he

2. See Gilson, *Philosophy of Saint Augustine*, pp. 210–24.
3. See below, pp. 55–57.

marvels at and meditates upon the power of Memory. If we read and reread these chapters, we may come to feel them acting more and more as a commentary upon the poems of *Silex Scintillans,* 1650; and we may come to understand more clearly the ways in which Vaughan's finest poetry draws its strength from the great central tradition of Platonic Christianity.

The process of Augustinian meditation begins, as Vaughan's volume of 1650 begins, with an effort to apprehend the meaning of an experience of sudden illumination: *percussisti cor meum verbo tuo, et amavi te*—"Thou hast strucken my heart with thy word, and therupon I loved thee. . . . What now do I love, whenas I love thee?"

> not the beauty of any *corporall thing,* not the order of times; not the brightnesse of the *light,* which to behold, is so gladsome to our eyes: not the pleasant *melodies* of songs of all kinds; not the fragrant smell of flowers, and oyntments, and spices: not *Manna* and honey, nor any *fayre limbs* that are so acceptable to fleshly embracements.
>
> I love none of these things, whenas I love my God: and yet I love a certaine kinde of *light,* and a kind of *voyce,* and a kinde of *fragrancy,* and a kinde of *meat,* and a kind of *embracement.* Whenas I love my God; who is both the *light,* and the voyce, and the sweet *smell,* and the *meate,* and the *embracement* of my inner man: where that *light* shineth unto my soule, which no place can receive; that *voyce* soundeth, which time deprives me not of; and that fragrancy *smelleth,* which no wind scatters . . .
>
> This is it which I love, when as I love my God.[4]

Here is the spiritual landscape of the redeemed soul, described by Vaughan in his "Regeneration," glimpsed throughout his

4. *Confessions,* 10.6. Quotations from this work in English are in this section taken from the translation by William Watts (London, 1631); the contemporary version here seems especially helpful in bringing out affinities with Vaughan. In other portions of this book, where literal accuracy in the translation seems indispensable, I have used the corrected version of Watts's translation in the Loeb Library edition of the *Confessions,* from which the Latin quotations have been taken.

volume in the many fresh images from nature that he uses to relate the experience, and summed up once again near the close of the volume, in the poem "Mount of Olives." This title represents a traditional symbol of the soul's retirement to prayer and meditation, here to recall, like Augustine, a moment which gave his life its meaning:

> When first I saw true beauty, and thy Joys
> Active as light, and calm without all noise
> Shin'd on my soul, I felt through all my powr's
> Such a rich air of sweets, as Evening showrs
> Fand by a gentle gale Convey and breath
> On some parch'd bank, crown'd with a flowrie wreath;
> Odors, and Myrrh, and balm in one rich floud
> O'r-ran my heart, and spirited my bloud . . .
> I am so warm'd now by this glance on me,
> That, midst all storms I feel a Ray of thee;
> So have I known some beauteous *Paisage* rise
> In suddain flowres and arbours to my Eies,
> And in the depth and dead of winter bring
> To my Cold thoughts a lively sense of spring.

With the memory of such an experience within him, the Augustinian seeker turns to question external nature, as in the *Confessions:*

> I askt the *Earth,* and that answered me, *I am not it;* and whatsoever are in it, made the same confession. I asked the *Sea* and the *deepes,* and the *creeping things,* and they answered me, *We are not thy God, seeke above us.* . . . I asked the heavens, the Sunne and Moone, and Starres, Nor (say they) are wee the *God* whom thou seekest. [10.6]

All creatures give for Augustine the same answer: "they cryed out with a loud voyce, *He made us*" (10.6). It is the questioning of nature that runs throughout Vaughan's poetry, where "Each *tree, herb, flowre* / Are shadows of his *wisedome,* and his Pow'r."[5] Thus in "The Tempest" Vaughan prays that man "would hear / The world read to him!" and declares:

5. See "Rules and Lessons," lines 85–96.

20

all the vast expence
In the Creation shed, and slav'd to sence
Makes up but lectures for his eie, and ear.

(lectures in the old medieval sense, readings of the book, with commentary and elucidation:)

Sure, mighty love foreseeing the discent
Of this poor Creature, by a gracious art
Hid in these low things snares to gain his heart,
And layd surprizes in each Element.

All things here shew him heaven; *Waters* that fall
Chide, and fly up; *Mists* of corruptest fome
Quit their first beds & mount; trees, herbs, flowres, all
Strive upwards stil, and point him the way home.

And the way home lies through an interior ascent, climbing upward and inward through the deepest regions of the human soul:

I beg'd here long, and gron'd to know
Who gave the Clouds so brave a bow,
Who bent the spheres, and circled in
Corruption with this glorious Ring,
What is his name, and how I might
Descry some part of his great light.
I summon'd nature: peirc'd through all her store,
Broke up some seales, which none had touch'd before,
Her wombe, her bosome, and her head
Where all her secrets lay a bed
I rifled quite, and having past
Through all the Creatures, came at last
To search my selfe, where I did find
Traces, and sounds of a strange kind.

("Vanity of Spirit")

So Augustine turns to search within himself and comes "into these fields and spacious palaces of my *Memory,* where the treasures of innumerable *formes* brought into it from these things that have beene perceived by the *sences,* be hoarded up."

21

And yet doe not the things themselves enter the *Memory;* onely the *Images* of the things perceived by the *Sences,* are ready there at hand, when ever the *Thoughts* will recall them. . . .

For there have I in a readinesse, the heaven, the earth, the sea, and what-ever I can thinke upon in them. . . . There also meete I with my *selfe,* I recall my *selfe,* what, where, or when I have done a thing; and how I was affected when I did it. There be all what ever I remember, eyther upon mine owne experience, or others credit. Out of the same store doe I my selfe compare these and these likelyhoods of things; eyther of such as I have made experience of, or of such as I have barely beleeved upon experience of some things that bee passed: and by these do I compare actions to *come,* their *events* and *hopes:* and upon all these againe doe I meditate, as if they were now present. . . .

Great is this force of *memory,* excessive great, O my *God:* a large and an infinite roomthynes [*penetrale:* inner room], who can plummet the bottome of it? yet is this a *faculty* of mine, and belongs unto my nature: nor can I my self comprehend all that I am.   [10.8]

Yet things even more wonderful lie beyond, as he probes ever and ever more deeply into the recesses of the memory. "Here also bee all these precepts of those *liberall Sciences* as yet unforgotten; coucht as it were further off in a more inward place" (10.9). These things could not have been conveyed within by the senses; how was it then that he came to accept these precepts as true?

unlesse because they were already in my memory; though so farre off yet, and crowded so farre backeward as it were into certaine secret caves, that had they not beene drawne out by the advice of some other person, I had never perchance beene able so much as to have thought of them?   [10.10]

Here the hint of the presence of something like innate ideas[6]

6. For Augustine's view of "innatism," as distinguished from the Pla-

in the deep caves of the soul leads directly to a long account of what might be called the dramatic action of Augustinian meditation. It is an action significantly different from the method of meditation later set forth by Ignatius Loyola and his followers; for that later method shows the effects of medieval scholasticism, with its powerful emphasis upon the analytic understanding, and upon the Thomist principle that human knowledge is derived from sensory experience. Ignatian meditation is thus a precise, tightly articulated method, moving from the images that comprise the composition of place into the threefold sequence of the powers of the soul, memory, understanding, and will, and from there into the affections and resolutions of the aroused will. But in Augustinian meditation there is no such precise method; there is, rather, an intuitive groping back into regions of the soul that lie beyond sensory memories. The three powers of the soul[7] are all used, but with an effect of simultaneous action, for with Augustine the aroused will is using the understanding to explore the memory, with the aim of apprehending more clearly and loving more fervently the ultimate source of the will's arousal.

> Wherfore we find, that to learne these things whose *Images* we *sucke* not *in* by our Sences, but perceive *within* by themselves, without Images, as they are; is nothing else, but by *meditating* to *gather together,* and by diligent *marking,* to take notice of those same *notions* which the *memory* did before contayne more scatteringly and confusedly ...   [10.11]

But these things are evasive and elusive; unless we engage

---

tonic view, see the judicious discussion by Gilson, *Philosophy of Saint Augustine*, pp. 75–76.

7. Memory, understanding, and will are not discussed as "the powers of the soul" in the *Confessions,* although something close to this triad is implied in one chapter of the final book (13.11), where Augustine discusses the triad: *esse, nosse, velle.* The full development of Augustine's exploration of the interior trinity of powers, the Image of the Trinity in man, is found in his *De Trinitate,* completed about twenty years after the *Confessions.* See the discussion of Traherne, below, pp. 81–83.

in a continual act of re-collection, "they become so drowned againe, and so give us the slip, as it were, backe into such remote and privy lodgings, that I must be put againe unto new paines of meditation, for recovery of them to their former perfection . . . they must be *rallied* and drawne together againe, that they may bee knowne; that is to say, they must as it were be *collected* and *gathered together* from their dispersions: whence the word *cogitation* is derived" (10.11).

The seventeenth-century translator has been frequently rendering the word *cogitare* by the word *meditate,* thus providing his own account of Augustinian meditation: to draw together these things scattered in the memory. It would seem that poetry composed under the impulse of this kind of meditation would differ considerably in its structure from any poetry written under the impulse of the Ignatian mode of meditation—such as Donne's Holy Sonnets. The poetry of Augustinian meditation would perhaps tend to display an order akin to that which Pascal saw in the writings of Augustine: "Cet ordre consiste principalement à la digression sur chaque point qu'on rapporte à la fin, pour la montrer toujours."[8] That *Pensée* may at least

---

8. *Pensées,* ed. Léon Brunschvicg (5th edn., Paris, Hachette, 1909), no. 283.

   L'ordre. Contre l'objection que l' Écriture n'a pas d'ordre.—Le coeur a son ordre; l'esprit a le sien, qui est par principe et démonstration, le coeur en a un autre. On ne prouve pas qu'on doit être aimé, en exposant d'ordre les causes de l'amour: cela serait ridicule.

   Jésus-Christ, saint Paul ont l'ordre de la charité, non de l'esprit; car ils voulaient échauffer, non instruire. Saint Augustin de même. Cet ordre consiste principalement à la digression sur chaque point qu'on rapporte à la fin, pour la montrer toujours.

   This analogy was suggested by the citation of this *Pensée* in an essay by Jacques Maritain, "St. Augustine and St. Thomas Aquinas," in *A Monument to Saint Augustine* (London, Sheed and Ward, 1930). See also Gilson, *Philosophy of Saint Augustine,* pp. 235–37, where Gilson discusses the implications of this *Pensée* and concludes: "Digression is Augustinism's natural method. The natural order of an Augustinian doctrine is to branch out around one center, and this is precisely the order of charity."

suggest the poetry of Vaughan, where the order often consists chiefly in what appear to be digressions, but are really exploratory sallies or *excursus* in the manner indicated by the following passage of the *Confessions:*

> Great is this power of Memory; a thing, O my God, to bee amazed at, a very profound and infinite multiplicity: and this thing is the minde, and this thing am I. . . . Behold, in those innumerable fields, and dennes, and caves of my memory, innumerably full of innumerable kinds of things, brought in, first, eyther by the *Images,* as all *bodies* are: secondly, or by the *presence* of the *things* themselves, as the *Arts* are: thirdly, or by certaine *notions* or *impressions,* as the *Affections* of the mind are . . . Thorow all these doe I runne and tumble [*discurro et volito*]; *myning* into them on this side, and on that side, so farre as ever I am able, but can finde no bottome. So great is the force of memory, so great is the force of this life of man, even whilest hee is mortall.   [10.17]

Thus in many of Vaughan's best poems, as in "Regeneration," the characteristic movement is a "mining" of associations, a roving search over a certain field of imagery, a sinking inward upon the mind's resources, until all the evocative ramifications of the memory have been explored; and then the poem ends rather abruptly, with a cry for divine help, or some generalizing moral conclusion. The movement is seen at its best in "Corruption," where the mind lingers over the memories of the "early days" of Genesis:

> Sure, It was so. Man in those early days
>   Was not all stone, and Earth,
> He shin'd a little, and by those weak Rays
>   Had some glimpse of his birth.
> He saw Heaven o'r his head, and knew from whence
>   He came (condemned,) hither,
> And, as first Love draws strongest, so from hence
>   His mind sure progress'd thither.

Under the impulse of this love, Vaughan's mind progresses backward to recover the memory of Paradise:

> He sigh'd for *Eden,* and would often say
> *Ah! what bright days were those?*
> Nor was Heav'n cold unto him; for each day
> The vally, or the Mountain
> Afforded visits, and still *Paradise* lay
> In some green shade, or fountain.
> Angels lay *Leiger* here; Each Bush, and Cel,
> Each Oke, and high-way knew them,
> Walk but the fields, or sit down at some *wel,*
> And he was sure to view them.

Deep within all such associations lies that essential memory toward which Augustine's digressive and "tumbling" meditations have been subtly and inevitably leading: the memory of a "happy life," a "blessed life," *beata vita.*

Is not an happy life the thing which all desire; and is there any man that some way or other desires it not? But where gate they the knowledge of it, that they are so desirous of it? where did they ever see it, that they are now so enamored of it? Truely we have it, but which way, I know not . . .

How they come to know it, I cannot tell: and therefore have they it by, I know not, what secret notice; concerning which, in much doubt I am, whether it bee in the memory or no: which if it bee, then should wee sometimes have beene blessed heretofore. [*quia, si ibi est, iam beati fuimus aliquando; utrum singillatim omnes, an in illo homine, qui primus peccavit . . . non quaero nunc; sed quaero, utrum in memoria sit beata vita.*]

But whether every man should have beene so happy as severally considered in himself, or as in the loynes of that man who first sinned . . . I now inquire not: but this I demaund, whether this blessed life bee in the memory, or no? [10.20]

It must be so, he concludes, for it is known to people in different languages, under different names: "And this could not bee, unlesse the thing it selfe expressed by this name, were still reserved in their memory." But what, precisely, is this thing?

> there is a ioy which is not granted unto the ungodly; but unto those onely which love thee for thine owne sake; whose ioy thy selfe art. And this is the blessed life, *to reioyce unto thee, concerning thee, and for thy sake:* this is the happy life, and there is no other. [10.22]

> *a happy life is a ioying in the truth:* For this is a ioying in thee, who art the truth, O God my light, the health of my countenance, and my God. This is the blessed life that all desire . . . Where therefore gaynd they the knowledge of this happy life, but even there, where they learned the truth also? . . . which yet they would not love, were there not some notice of it remayning in their memory. . . . For there is a dimme glimmering of light yet un-put-out, in men: let them walke, let them walke, that the darknesse overtake them not. [10.23]

It is the central image of *Silex Scintillans:*[9] the flash, the spark, the glance, the beam, the ray, the glimmering of light that comes from the memory of an ancient birthright of blessedness—*utrum singillatim omnes, an in illo homine, qui primus peccavit:* whether it be a memory of each man's individual life, or whether it be a memory of Adam's original happy life—that memory remains, yet un-put-out in men. The image is notable in the poem "Silence, and stealth of dayes," where this Augustinian motif is used in recalling the memory of a loved one who has died (evidently Vaughan's brother):

> As he that in some Caves thick damp
> > Lockt from the light,
> Fixeth a solitary lamp,
> > To brave the night

9. For a group of suggestive passages in which Augustine refers to his intuition of God under the symbolism of a flash of light, see John Burnaby, *Amor Dei: A Study of the Religion of St. Augustine* (London, Hodder and Stoughton, 1938), p. 33.

And walking from his Sun, when past
That glim'ring Ray
Cuts through the heavy mists in haste
Back to his day,
So o'r fled minutes I retreat
Unto that hour
Which shew'd thee last, but did defeat
Thy light, and pow'r,
I search, and rack my soul to see
Those beams again . . .

The "Sun" here is the "solitary lamp" within the cave of the speaker's soul: the memory of his loved one is the light within that serves as an interior sun. Sometimes, carried toward the things of the outer world, the speaker tends to walk away from that "glim'ring Ray," but, remembering that he has forgotten, he walks, he walks, in Augustine's way, back toward the memory of light. The beams of this loved one's soul, he comes to realize, now shine in heaven, and he cannot track them there; yet something bright remains within, as he concludes:

Yet I have one *Pearle* by whose light
All things I see,
And in the heart of Earth, and night
Find Heaven, and thee.

It is the indestructible Image of God, apprehending the presence of God in the memory: "Sure I am, that in it thou dwellest: even for this reason, that I have preserved the memory of thee, since the time that I first learnt thee: and for that I finde thee in my memory, whensoever I call thee to remembrance" (*Confessions*, 10.25).

So the memory of that inner presence runs throughout Vaughan's volume of 1650, as Vaughan struggles backward on his ancient journey of return toward the memory of blessedness. Sometimes the journey backward takes the form of "The Retreate" toward the days of the individual's childhood:

28

Happy those early dayes! when I
Shin'd in my Angell-infancy.
Before I understood this place
Appointed for my second race,
Or taught my soul to fancy ought
But a white, Celestiall thought,
When yet I had not walkt above
A mile, or two, from my first love,
And looking back (at that short space,)
Could see a glimpse of his bright-face;
When on some *gilded Cloud,* or *flowre*
My gazing soul would dwell an houre,
And in those weaker glories spy
Some shadows of eternity . . .
O how I long to travell back
And tread again that ancient track!
That I might once more reach that plaine,
Where first I left my glorious traine,
From whence th' Inlightned spirit sees
That shady City of Palme trees;
But (ah!) my soul with too much stay
Is drunk, and staggers in the way.
Some men a forward motion love,
But I by backward steps would move,
And when this dust falls to the urn
In that state I came return.

The poem presents the essence of the *Phaedo,* as qualified and developed by Christian Platonism. Indeed, the *Phaedo* gives the closing image of the drunken man, in an important passage that suggests the kernel of this poem:

And were we not saying long ago [asks Socrates] that the soul when using the body as an instrument of perception, that is to say, when using the sense of sight or hearing or some other sense . . . were we not saying that the soul too is then dragged by the body into the region of the changeable, and wanders and is confused; the world spins round her, and she is like a drunkard, when she touches change? . . .

But when returning into herself she reflects, then she passes into the other world, the region of purity, and eternity, and immortality, and unchangeableness, which are her kindred . . .[10]

In Vaughan, as in Augustine's *Confessions,* there is of course only the most guarded and glancing use of the Platonic doctrine of reminiscence: any hint of the soul's pre-existence is used by Vaughan as a metaphor of innocence; and the whole poem is toward the close clearly transmuted into orthodox Christianity. The poet superimposes upon the Platonic suggestions the concept of the "Inlightned spirit" which catches a vision of the promised land, as did Moses when he "went up from the plains of Moab unto the mountain of Nebo . . . And the Lord shewed him all the land of Gilead . . . and all the land of Judah, unto the utmost sea, And the south, and the plain of the valley of Jericho, the city of palm trees . . . " (Deuteronomy 34:1–3).

So the "early days" of the individual's childhood become one with the "early days" of the human race, as related in the Old Testament; and both together form powerful symbols of the memory of a happy life that lives, however glimmeringly, within the soul that has, through regeneration, come into yet a third state of childhood: the state of the "children of God" set forth in the eighth chapter of Romans.

Such is the paradise within, compounded of the Bible, of Nature, and of the Self, which lies at the heart of Vaughan's *Silex Scintillans,* 1650: a vision that results from the constant effort to remember the beauty of the sudden illumination described in his opening Latin confession. That Latin poem and its emblem of the Flashing Flint, with its image of the man within, are once more brought to mind by the well-known passage that concludes Augustine's sequence of meditations on the force of memory:

10. *The Dialogues of Plato,* trans. B. Jowett (3d ed. 5 vols. Oxford University Press, 1892), *2,* 222.

Too late beganne I to love thee, O thou beauty both so ancient and so fresh, yea too too late came I to love thee. For behold, thou wert *within* mee, and I *out* of my selfe, where I made search for thee; deformed I, wooing these beautifull pieces of thy workmanship. . . . Thou *calledst,* and criedst unto mee, yea thou even brakest open my *deafenesse.* Thou discoveredst thy beames, and *shynedst* out unto mee, and didst chase away my blindnesse. Thou didst most *fragrantly blow* upon me, and I drew in my *breath* and panted after thee. I *tasted* thee, and now doe *hunger* and *thirst after thee.* Thou didst *touch* mee, and I even *burne* againe to enioy thy peace.   [10.27]

II

THOMAS TRAHERNE
Confessions of Paradise

Q. *What was Paradise?*

A. Paradise was the Similitude and Presence of God in the whole Creation. The Creation was a Garden: All the Creatures were Divine Flowers in this Garden, animated with a Divine Life, cloth'd with a Divine Beauty, breathing a Divine Sweetness. Every one did bear the Figure of, and answer to a Glory in the Face of God: The Face of God was as a Sun, shining with all its Glories upon these Flowers, distilling its own Influence upon them, attracting their Sweetnesses to itself; descending into them, drawing them up into itself. Thus was the Divine Similitude, and the Divine Presence in the Creation, the Earthly Paradise; In the midst of Man stood this Paradise; In the midst of this Paradise Man walk'd.

—Peter Sterry, "A Catechism"

1. The Forms of Truth and Good

IT IS MORE than a remarkable coincidence that the two greatest representations of Paradise in English literature should have been composed within the same quarter-century, perhaps within the same decade; and it is an emblematic fact that the writers of these visions both died in the same year, 1674. Traherne died at the age of 37, with his meditations of Paradise unpublished; Milton died at the age of 66, with his major poem of Paradise published in 1667, only about three years before Traherne appears to have begun the writing of his masterpiece, the prose *Centuries*. The younger man writes with all the exuberant optimism of the young Milton; while the older man conveys his vision within the dark enlacements prompted by his own bitter experience of the world's ways. Yet in their central imaginations Traherne and Milton share the Augustinian vision of a Paradise within, the vision that Vaughan also sought, and the vision that the Cambridge Platonists were seeking during this same era, in the way beautifully set forth by the Platonist Peter Sterry, Cromwell's chaplain, and Milton's colleague in the work of the Commonwealth:

> as Paradise, so the *pure Image* of God in the Soul, seems to some not to be *lost* or destroyed, but *hid* beneath the ruines of the fall. Thus *Knowledge* springing in the Soul, seems to be a *remembrance,* the Life of all good, an awakening by

EPIGRAPH: from the posthumous collection of Peter Sterry's works published under the title: *The Appearance of God to Man in the Gospel* [etc.] (London, 1710), pp. 463–64. See Vivian de Sola Pinto, *Peter Sterry, Platonist and Puritan, 1613–1672: A Biographical and Critical Study with passages selected from his Writings* (Cambridge University Press, 1934), p. 161.

reason of the primitive Image of pure Nature raising it self by degrees, and sparkling through the *Rubbish,* the confusions of the present state. Thus also hath the Soul in her self the *measure* of all Truth and Good in this pure Image, which hidden in the Center of the Soul, containeth all Forms of Truth and Good in it self.[1]

Paradise, then, may be regained by uncovering and developing these inner forms of truth and good, which the Platonist John Smith called "the *Truths of Natural inscription":* "those *Eternal Rules of Truth and Goodness* which are the Foundation of all Religion, and which God at the first Creation folded up in the Soul of man." "God hath stamp'd a Copy of his own Archetypal Loveliness upon the Soul, that man by reflecting into himself might behold there the glory of God, *intra se videre Deum,* see within his Soul all those Ideas of Truth which concern the Nature and Essence of God, by reason of its own resemblance of God; and so beget within himself the most free and generous motions of Love to God. Reason in man being *Lumen de Lumine,* a Light flowing from the Fountain and Father of Lights." It is of course true, Smith adds, that "those Principles of Divine truth which were first engraven upon mans Heart with the finger of God are now, as the Characters of some ancient Monuments, less clear and legible then at first." Nevertheless, through the revelation of the Bible and by the action of grace within the soul, we find "the way of our return to God" before us: a way that man may travel under the guidance and urging of "an inward living principle of virtue and activity." "And therefore *Plato* seems sometimes to reprove the ruder sort of men in his times for their contrivance of Pictures and Images to put themselves in mind of the . . . Angelicall Beings, and exhorts them to look into their own Souls, which are the fairest Images not onely of the Lower divine Natures, but of the Deity it self; God having so copied forth himself into the whole life and energy of man's Soul, as that the lovely

1. Peter Sterry, *A Discourse of the Freedom of the Will* (London, 1675), p. 99.

Characters of Divinity may be most easily seen and read of all men within themselves."[2]

Thus, with the collapse of ancient institutions in the middle of the seventeenth century, many of the finest minds in England sought a way toward God without the help of the old ecclesiastical establishment, and in that search the whole tradition of Platonic thought enjoyed a powerful revival.[3] Traherne, coming to maturity in the 1650s, felt the full and vital impact of that revival, as other students of Traherne have ably demonstrated[4]—and as Traherne himself suggests at the culmination of his Fourth Century, where he devotes three and a half meditations (4.74–77) to a long translation from Pico della Mirandola's famous treatise, the *Oratio de Dignitate Hominis,* that strange flower of the Platonic Renaissance in Italy.

The passage from Pico contains the essence of Traherne's meditative vision, for it is taken from the opening portion in which Pico tells[5] how "The Supreme Architect and our Everlasting father, having made the World," the heavenly spirits,

2. John Smith, *Select Discourses* (London, 1660), pp. 382, 383, 394, 123–24. Smith died in 1652; this posthumous volume was edited by John Worthington.

3. Ernst Cassirer's classic study, *The Platonic Renaissance in England,* trans. James P. Pettegrove (Austin, University of Texas Press, 1953), is highly valuable in placing the Cambridge Platonists in relation to European thought, although Cassirer tends to neglect the Platonic aspects of Augustinianism. See also the recent study by Aharon Lichtenstein, *Henry More: The Rational Theology of a Cambridge Platonist* (Cambridge, Mass., Harvard University Press, 1962), which contains a comprehensive bibliography of the subject. For an account of the many unconventional currents of thought at work in England in this era see Jackson I. Cope, *Joseph Glanvill, Anglican Apologist,* Washington University Studies (St. Louis, 1956).

4. See Gladys I. Wade, *Thomas Traherne* (Princeton University Press, 1944), ch. 20; and Robert Ellrodt, *Les Poètes Métaphysiques Anglais* (2 parts, Paris, Librarie José Corti, 1960), Pt. I, Vol. 2, pp. 263–79.

5. See the translation of Pico's *Oratio* by Elizabeth L. Forbes, in *The Renaissance Philosophy of Man,* ed. Cassirer, Kristeller, and Randall (University of Chicago Press, 1948), pp. 223–54. Traherne is translating from sections 1–4.

and "all Kind of Herds of Living Creatures," yet found his work incomplete. "He desired som one, that might Weigh and reason, lov the Beauty, and admire the Vastness of so Great a Work. All things therfore being, (as Moses and Tymaeus Witness) already finished, at last he thought of Creating Man." (*Moses and Timaeus:* the way of the Christian Platonist could not be more succinctly put.) And therefore, says Pico, God "took Man, the Image of all his Work, and placing him in the Middle of the World, spake thus unto him" in a passage that constitutes the whole of Traherne's Meditation 76 in the Fourth Century:

> O Adam, we hav given Thee neither a certain seat, nor a Private face, nor a Peculiar office, that whatsoever seat or face or office thou dost desire, thou mayst Enjoy. All other things hav a Nature bounded within certain Laws, Thou only art loos from all, and according to thy own Counsel in the hand of which I hav put Thee, mayst chuse and prescribe what Nature thou wilt to thy self. I hav placed Thee in the Middle of the World, that from thence thou mayst behold on every side more commodiously evry thing in the whole World. We hav made Thee neither heavenly nor Earthly Neither Mortal nor Immortal, that being the Honored Former and Framer of thy self, thou mayst shape thy self into what Nature thy self pleaseth.[6]

Traherne adds that of course Pico here "permitteth his fancy to wander a little Wantonly after the maner of a Poet: but most deep and serious things are secretly hidden under his free and luxuriant Language" (4.78). Those deep and serious things form the center of Traherne's thought, which lies in his belief

6. Margoliouth's transcription, quoted throughout this study, (*Thomas Traherne, Centuries, Poems, and Thanksgivings,* ed. H. M. Margoliouth, 2 vols. Oxford, Clarendon Press, 1958) preserves the irregularities of spelling, capitalization, and punctuation found in Traherne's manuscript; the effect may at first seem strange, but the irregularities gradually produce a significant impression related to the style and meaning of the work: the effect that one is watching and participating in the natural, intimate action of the meditative mind.

that the creative power bestowed on Adam still resides, though neglected, within man, and that it is man's duty, through the powers of his soul, to realize the restoration of the Paradise within made possible by the sacrifice of Christ. Traherne's "Infancy" is but another name for this inner Paradise, as we may see from many of his poems, such as "Eden" or "Innocence":

> That Prospect was the Gate of Heav'n, that Day
> The anchient Light of Eden did convey
> Into my Soul: I was an Adam there,
> A little Adam in a Sphere
>
> Of Joys! O there my Ravisht Sence
> Was entertained in Paradice,
> And had a Sight of Innocence.

Paradise, for Traherne, as for Peter Sterry, has always been essentially inward and spiritual: it has, from the beginning, consisted in "the Similitude and Presence of God in the whole Creation," and particularly in the soul of man. "In the midst of Man stood this Paradise," Sterry had declared: "In the midst of this Paradise Man walk'd."[7] Traherne's *Centuries* assert that this Paradise, this Similitude and Presence, still stand in the midst of man, and that therefore man still walks in the midst of a Paradise to be found in the whole Creation. But what is this Similitude, and how is this Presence to be apprehended? Traherne's answer is found in the style, the method of meditation, and the total progress of his *Centuries*.

2. The Universe of Wants

"I hav found," says Traherne at the outset of his meditations, "that Things unknown have a Secret Influence on the Soul: and like the Centre of the Earth unseen, violently Attract it. . . . So is there in us a World of Lov to somwhat, tho we know

7. See the epigraph for this study, above, p. 33.

not what in the World that should be. . . . Do you not feel yourself Drawn with the Expectation and Desire of som Great Thing?" (1.2).

We are drawn at once into an Augustinian universe of *desiderium* and *egestas:*[1] that world of divine wants and desires in which the soul longs for its Felicity, its Happiness. "Wants are the Bands and Cements between God and us. Had we not Wanted, we could never hav been Obliged. Wheras now we are infinitly Obliged, becaus we Want infinitly. From Eternity it was requisit that we should Want. We could never els have Enjoyed any Thing: Our own Wants are Treasures. And if Want be a Treasure, sure evry Thing is so. Wants are the Ligatures between God and us" (1.51). Thus the words "desire" and "want" become the key words of the First Century; twining and intertwining, in hundreds of repetitions, they delineate a universe based upon the principle discovered by Augustine in the last book of the *Confessions: pondus meum amor meus; eo feror, quocumque feror.* "My weight is my love: by that am I carried, whithersoever I be carried. We are inflamed by thy gift, and are carried upwards: we wax hot within, and we go on" (13.9). So Traherne, near the middle of the First Century, echoes this powerful Augustinian metaphor as he speaks of the Cross: "If Lov be the Weight of the Soul, and its Object the Centre. All Eys and Hearts may convert and turn unto this Object: cleave unto this Centre, and by it enter into Rest" (1.59).

The search after the knowledge of this mystery is represented by both Traherne and Augustine in the form of autobiographical reminiscence, in which the writer explores his memory for signs of the working of grace within his personal experience. Traherne's Third Century presents such a reminiscence, based upon the central view that the "Memory and Mind are a strange Region of celestial Light, and a Wonderfull place as well as a

1. Cf. Burnaby, *Amor Dei,* pp. 92–100. Augustine's early treatise, the *De Beata Vita* (ch. 4), contains a long discussion on the *wants* of man, his *egestas.*

large and sublime one," in which the "Ways of God" may be revealed to our meditation: "What is contained in the Souls of Men being as visible to us as the very Heavens" (3.89). Within this Augustinian view of the memory, Traherne presents his own individual account of a life spent under the impulse of the belief "that Felicity is a Glorious tho an unknown Thing."

> And certainly it was the infinit Wisdom of God, that did implant by Instinct so strong a Desire of felicity in the Soul, that we might be excited to labor after it, tho we know it not, the very force wherwith we covet it supplying the place of Understanding. That there is a Felicity we all know by the Desires after, that there is a most Glorious felicity we know by the Strength and vehemence of those Desires: And that nothing but Felicity is worthy of our Labor, becaus all other things are the Means only which conduce unto it.   [3.56]

And then he adds a point that finds a parallel in the seventh book of Augustine's *Confessions:* "I was very much animated by the Desires of Philosophers, which I saw in Heathen Books aspiring after it. But the misery is *It was unknown*" (3.56).

The *Confessions,* however, like the *Centuries,* are only in part comprised of autobiographical reminiscence: both works represent "confession" in the threefold sense discerned by Courcelle:[2] confession of sin, confession of praise, and confession of faith: confession as acknowledgment, avowal, and declaration. Both works are ultimately theocentric, not egocentric: the exploration of the personal memory exists only for the sake of affirming faith and praising God for all his many benefits of grace and creation. Above all, these works are confessions of praise, in the manner suggested by Augustine him-

2. Pierre Courcelle, *Recherches sur les Confessions de Saint Augustin* (Paris, Boccard, 1950), pp. 13–29. Cf. *Confessions,* ed. Pierre de Labriolle (4th ed. 2 vols. Paris, 1947), *1,* xi–xii, where the title is thus interpreted: "c'est surtout dans le sens d'une exaltation de la grâce divine qu'il convient de l'entendre. . . . Les *Confessions* sont une longue prière de gratitude et d'amour."

self in his *Retractations:* "My *Confessions,* in thirteen books, praise the righteous and good God as they speak either of my evil or good, and they are meant to excite men's minds and affections toward him."[3]

Thus Augustine opens his *Confessions* with the words: "Great art thou, O Lord, and greatly to be praised: great is thy power, and thy wisdom is infinite. [Psalms 147:5] And man, who being a part of what thou hast created, is desirous to praise thee; this man, bearing about his own mortality with him, carrying about him a testimony of his own sin . . . yet this man, this part of what thou hast created, is desirous to praise thee." Similarly Traherne, toward the end of the Third Century, sums up the aim of his own reminiscences: "Are not Praises the very End for which the World was created? . . . Praises are the Breathings of interior Lov, the Marks and Symptoms of an Happy Life, Overflowing Gratitud, returning Benefits, an Oblation of the Soul, and the Heart ascending upon the Wings of Divine Affection to the Throne of GOD" (3.82).

"An Happy Life"—the phrase is bound to recall Augustine's *beata vita,* just as Traherne's continual repetitions of the words "happiness," "felicity," and "blessedness" suggest a set of variations upon the single complex conception expressed by Augustine in the word *beatitudo.* Such variations are inevitable, for no single word in English can comprehend the full meaning of Augustine's *beatitudo,* as fully set forth in the nineteenth book of the *City of God:*[4] it includes "happiness" in the sense of general well-being and joyfulness; it includes "felicity" in the sense of "intense happiness," "chief delight"; it includes the specifically religious and Christian implications of "blessedness" and "beatitude." The word implies a state of mind that escapes all definition and can only be found in its action, in its demon-

3. Augustine, *Retractations,* 2.6; *Confessions,* trans. Albert C. Outler, Library of Christian Classics, 7 (London, SCM Press, Philadelphia, Westminster Press, 1955), 24.

4. See the study of the 19th book by R. H. Barrow, *Introduction to St. Augustine: The City of God* (London, Faber, 1950).

stration that the state of mind exists. It remains, as Traherne says, "the Mystery of Felicity."

3. The Technique of Repetition

In exploring this central mystery Traherne everywhere displays a pervasive Augustinian affinity in the form and literary method of the *Centuries,* both in total movement and in the detailed working-out of each individual meditation. For Traherne's book develops in a way very close to that found in Augustine's *Confessions* and in his *De Trinitate:* through the concatenation of repeated words and phrases, repeated always in a slightly different context, with a gradual increment of meaning, as the mind explores the central issues represented by these repeated words and phrases. As Margoliouth has said (*1,* 235), "Traherne does not ramble though he may digress." Or, as Traherne himself says at one point, "This Digression steals me a little further" (4.7). It is again the method so well described by Pascal,[1] in which the apparent digression serves rather to explore some possibility, while the repeated words and phrases constantly serve to keep the end in view.

Nevertheless, it is a troublesome way of writing, and was thought so, with regard to Augustine, even in the seventeenth century: Sir Tobie Matthew found it necessary to defend the repetitive style of the *Confessions* near the beginning of the long polemical Preface to his translation of 1620:

> Others there are, who play the *Critikes* upon this Booke; be-
> cause the Saint, sometimes, doth repeate the same thinges and
> words more then once; and so falleth, as they say, into the
> errour of *Tautology.* I pitty them, and I will pray for them;
> that they may read such books as this, with a mind which
> may rather become ingenuous, and noble *Christians,* then
> wofull, and illiberall Grammarians. Though indeed, I know
> not, but that they may deserve rather scorne and pitty; who

1. See the study of Vaughan above, pp. 24–25.

have not so much civility, and complement (as I may say)
of spirit, as to give a Saints pen leave to play; and passe the
entertaynment of a minute or two, upon the same wordes
(which yet nevertheles, in their very repetition, have a par-
ticuler tendernes, and grace to which the capacity of those
men can not arive) when at the selfe same tyme, either the
understanding part of his soule, is wrastling for the discovery
of some hidden *Truth;* or els the will is ingulfed, upon the
adoring, and loving of the supreme Good; of all which he
would yet be sure to give them a good account, if they could
but have patience, till the discourse, or Chapter were at an end.

Beneath his polemics, it may be that Sir Tobie, near the end
of his defense, shows the way toward a critical justification of
this literary technique, so marked in Augustine,[2] and even more
prominent in Traherne's *Centuries,* where it becomes the central characteristic of style.

What is the meaning of this technique, so deliberately,
relentlessly pursued by Traherne? It is true, though it is not
enough, to say that these repetitions gradually develop a unity
in the work, through the constant interlacing of thematic words
and phrases: for such elaborate repetitions may well produce
tedium, and indeed mental fatigue is perhaps at first the most
notable effect of any effort to read Traherne's *Centuries* steadily
for any considerable length of time. Yet the work cannot be
dismissed as one that shows only the unity of a clump or a
cluster, with a few brilliant meditations reaching out toward
the anthologies, chiefly those famous meditations of the Third
Century, where Traherne presents his memories of "Infancy."
The *Centuries,* although we may sometimes lay them aside in
weariness or bewilderment, leave behind a tantalizing sense of
some determined purpose underlying and created through those
massive repetitions.

A clue may be found by exploring the enigmatic, paradoxical

2. One can illustrate the technique to some extent in literal translations
from Augustine, but the technique is more prominent and more precise
in the Latin.

promise with which Traherne has begun his meditations, telling the friend who has given him this empty notebook that he will "fill it with those Truths you Love, without Knowing them." The mysterious nature of this opening promise is indeed appropriate in a work to which the author never gave a title; even the form of "centuries" is not apparent at the outset, for the manuscript begins without any heading for what we now call "The First Century."[3] The book, in every way, opens with the symbolism of an unknown space: "An Empty Book is like an Infants Soul, in which any Thing may be Written. It is Capable of all Things, but containeth Nothing. I hav a Mind to fill this with Profitable Wonders" (1.1).

> Do not Wonder that I Promise to fill it, with those Truths you love, but know not: For tho it be a Maxime in the Scholes, That there is no Lov of a thing unknown; yet I hav found, that Things unknown have a Secret Influence on the Soul: and like the Centre of the Earth unseen, violently Attract it. We lov we know not what: and therfore evry Thing allures us. As Iron at a Distance is drawn by the Loadstone, there being some Invisible Communications between them: So is there in us a World of Lov to somwhat, tho we know not what in the World that should be. There are Invisible Ways of Conveyance by which some Great Thing doth touch our Souls, and by which we tend to it. Do you not feel yourself Drawn with the Expectation and Desire of som Great Thing? [1.2]

The paradoxical argument strongly recalls the opening portion of the tenth book of Augustine's *De Trinitate*,[4] where he ponders the ways in which the soul knows, and yet does not know, the truth it seeks. Augustine's exploration of the problem opens with the assertion that "it is quite impossible to love anything which is entirely unknown." Consider, for instance, Augustine says, the case of a person who comes upon an un-

---

3. Cf. Margoliouth, *1*, x–xi, 235.

4. The following quotations from *De Trinitate* are given in the translation (and identified by the section and page numbers) of the *Later Works*, trans. Burnaby.

familiar word such as *temetum,* and at once desires to know the meaning of that word. What does a person love who seeks such knowledge?

> we are asking what it is that he loves in the object of his study, which obviously he does not yet know; and the reason for this love is a puzzle to us because we are assured that only things known can be loved. The only possible explanation is that in the universe of reason he knows and contemplates the beauty of that learning which embraces the knowledge of all signs or signals, and the usefulness of the technique which gives human society the power of inter-communication ... The beauty and the usefulness of this ideal is what the soul perceives, knows, and loves; and to enquire about what is unknown in significant sounds is to seek by study for the fuller realization of that ideal in oneself.

Thus a man beholds an ideal "in the light of truth" and that inner vision "may so inspire the studies of learners that it becomes the centre of their activity, and towards it is aimed all their labour in pursuit of a possession by which they may realize in practice what they have recognized in idea." In this "eager and ardent" love for learning "the enquirer appears to be loving a thing unknown to him." "But it is not so," Augustine concludes: "For what touches his soul is the ideal which he knows and meditates," and it is this ideal "that kindles in him the zeal for study, in which he will seek for what he does not know, but contemplate and love the known ideal to which it appertains" (10.1–2; pp. 73–75).

In this Platonic view of the mind's activity lies, I believe, the clue to the iterative manner of Augustine and Traherne, as we may see in one striking passage of the *De Trinitate,* where the technique of repetition is very close to that of Traherne. The opening sentence of the passage in itself represents the essential mode of tentative exploration, the varied efforts of approach, the pursuit of ever-new beginnings, that constitute the basic attitudes of both these seekers after Truth:

Try once again, and consider the matter this way. Nothing draws your love but what is good. Good is earth with its lofty mountains, its gentle hills, its level plains. Good is the beauteous and fertile land, good the well-built house with its symmetry, its spaciousness and light. Good are the bodies of living things, good is the temperate and wholesome air, good is the pleasant and healthful food, good is health itself free from pain and weariness. Good is the human face with its regular features, its cheerful expression, its lively colouring; good is the heart of a friend whose comradeship is sweet and whose love is loyal; good is a righteous man, good is wealth for the things it can enable us to do, good is the sky with its sun, moon, and stars, good are the angels of holy obedience; good is the speech that instructs the hearer winningly and counsels him appropriately, good is the poem of musical rhythm and profound thought. But enough! This is good and that is good: take away "this" and "that," and look if you can upon Good itself: then you will see God, good not by the possession of any other good thing, but the goodness of every good. For among all these good things, those I have named and any others you may see or conceive, we could not pronounce with a true judgment any one better than another, were there not imprinted on our mind the idea of Good itself, as the standard by which we should either approve or prefer. So our love must rise to God, not as we love this or that good thing, but as the Good itself. The soul must needs seek that Good over which it will not range superior as judge but to which it will cleave in love. And what is that Good but God? —not the good soul, the good angel, the good heavens, but the good Good! [8.4; pp. 41–42]

Here, in miniature, is the full method of Augustinian meditation. The mind in "cogitation" draws together, re-collects, the fragmentary hints of truth scattered about in the things that are made,[5] and in this way moves toward an apprehension of

5. *Invisibilia enim ipsius a creatura mundi per ea quae facta sunt intellecta conspiciuntur* (Romans 1:20). As Burnaby points out (*Amor Dei*, p. 33), when Augustine uses this text, as he frequently does in the *Confessions* (e.g. 7.10, 7.17, 10.6), one must remember that among the "things

the essential Idea that lives within the eternal mind of God. Very rarely, Augustine suggests, in the highest mystical state one may catch a glimpse of the Idea itself; but for the most part all we can hope to see is the reflection of the Divine Idea within our own minds, as in a mirror.[6] Thus by cogitating, assembling, various transitory examples of the good, the mind in meditation draws toward an inward understanding of the good.

A technique of repetition is essential to this mode of exploration, for in the vast "abyss" of memory repetition is a sign that one is on the trace of truth. Repetition is a mode of assuring the seeker that he is on his way, and is not merely wandering blindly through the chaos from which all form arises. Repetitions are, we might say, stepping stones that rise above the heaving mass of unformed matter in the mind. By repetition the mind gradually brings forward into the light of the Divine Idea that knowledge which lies, unformed, within the mind's unconscious and subconscious depths:

> All such knowledge in the mind of man, whether acquired through the mind itself, or through his bodily senses, or by the testimony of others, is preserved in the store-chamber of memory; and from it is begotten a true word, when we speak what we know. But this word exists before any sound, before any imagining of a sound. For in that state the word has the closest likeness to the thing known, of which it is offspring and image; from the vision which is knowledge arises a vision which is thought, a word of no language, a true word born of a true thing, having nothing of its own but all from that knowledge of which it is born. [*De Trinitate,* 15.22; p. 151]

The mind discovers such an unspoken word through a process of mental exploration which Augustine then describes in a passage that gives a dramatic account of the essential prose style of both Augustine and Traherne:

---

that are made," "the chief for Augustine is the human soul itself."
6. Gilson, *Philosophy of Saint Augustine,* p. 94.

But what *is* this potential word that claims the name of word? What is this thing capable of form but still unformed, but a process in our mind, darting hither and thither with a kind of movement of passage, as we turn our thought from one object to another in the course of discovery or presentation? It becomes a true word, only when what I have called this darting movement of passage comes upon what we know and takes form from it, receiving its likeness at every point; so that the mode of thought correspond to the mode of knowledge, and its object be spoken in the heart without voice, uttered or imagined, such as must belong to a particular language.   [*De Trinitate,* 15.25; pp. 155–56]

Such, I think, is the effect of continuous reading in the *Confessions* or in the *Centuries,* for these writings proceed through a "darting movement of passage," working through short segments of thought that often seem, in themselves, inchoate, obscure, aimlessly wandering; and yet, after a series of such darting, exploratory movements, the process finds its form in a perfect meditation, "fully made, fully apparent, fully found" —in the phrase of Wallace Stevens (a writer who himself works through a meditative mode of repetition). These perfect meditations, moments where the searching mind reposes in the temporary contemplation of completed form, may be seen in such moments as Augustine's meditation on the Good, quoted above, or in those frequent meditations of Traherne which open with a found truth, given in the form of aphorism or metaphor, or both together; then move on to explore that truth with a further darting movement, developing its implications by abstract analysis and by concrete example; and then conclude with a forward thrust that lifts the opening truth into a higher dimension:

As Pictures are made Curious by Lights and Shades, which without Shades, could not be: so is Felicitie composed of Wants and Supplies, without which Mixture there could be no Felicity. Were there no Needs, Wants would be Wanting themselvs: And Supplies Superfluous. Want being the Parent of Celestial Treasure. It is very Strange; Want itself is a Treasure in Heaven: And so Great an one, that without it there could be no Treasure. GOD did infinitly for us, when He made us to Want like GODS, that like GODS we might be satisfied. The Heathen DIETIES wanted nothing, and were therfore unhappy; For they had no Being. But the LORD GOD of Israel the Living and True GOD, was from all Eternity, and from all Eternity Wanted like a GOD. He Wanted the Communication of His Divine Essence, and Persons to Enjoy it. He Wanted Worlds, He wanted Spectators, He wanted Joys, He wanted Treasures. He wanted, yet he wanted not, for he had them.   [1.41]

The meditation displays the kind of suspended action that Augustine describes in yet another of his many efforts to describe the mind's movement in the quest for truth: "the striving which appears in the search proceeds from the seeker, remaining in a kind of suspense, and only coming to rest in the desired end, when the object sought is found and coupled to the seeker" (*De Trinitate,* 9.18; p. 70).

But that which is found may soon be lost: no one is more thoroughly aware of the evanescence of human certitudes than Augustine, as on that occasion related in the seventh book of the *Confessions,* where he tells how, after his reading of the Platonists, he ascended to a glimpse of the Truth above his own mind: "thus by a flash of the twinkling eyesight it [the intellect] came so far as that which is. And now came I to have a sight of those invisible things of thee, which are understood by those things which are made. But I was not able to fix mine eye long upon them: but my infirmity being beaten back again, I was turned to my wonted fancies; carrying along with me no more but a liking of those new thoughts in my memory, and an appetite, as it were, to the meat I had smelt" [*nisi amantem memoriam et quasi olefacta desiderantem*] (7.17). Thus the mind, having caught the flash of truth, lives a life that mixes memory and desire, striving always to renew the glimpse. And this is true from beginning to end of Augustine's career: even at the very close of his magnificent explication of the Trinity, he cries out to his own soul: "But to perceive this plainly and clearly, thou art not able to keep thine eye fixed firmly: I know thou art not able. I speak truth to myself, I know what exceeds my power" (*De Trinitate,* 15.50; p. 179).

Here, then, is another cause for the insistent technique of repetition: to revive the knowledge once found; to restore, by a continual effort of meditation, those truths that have been restored in the mind a hundred or a thousand times before. As Traherne says, in the closing exhortations of his Fourth Century:

> Having once studied these Principles you are Eternaly to Practise them. You are to warm your self at these fires, and to hav recours to them evry Day. When you think not of these Things you are in the Dark. And if you would walk in the Light of them, you must frequently Meditat. These Principles are like Seed in the Ground, they must continualy be visited with Heavenly Influences, or els your Life will be a Barren feild. Perhaps they might be cast into Better frame, and more Curiously Exprest; but if well Cultivated they will be as fruitfull, as if every Husk were a Golden Rinde. [4.94]

The repetitive, digressive, darting movement in both writers, then, is due to a shared view of the mind's action, a view set forth in Books 10 and 11 of the *Confessions,* after the completion of Augustine's autobiographical memories. These books present, perhaps even more richly than the *De Trinitate,* the extent of Augustine's belief in the spontaneous and indestructible creativity of the human mind, restored by grace through the sacrifice of Christ.

Book 10, as we have seen in the previous study of Vaughan, devotes its first half to exploring the immense power of the memory; but the latter half of this same book turns to deal with the ravages of sin still present in the speaker, and with the ways in which he at the present time of his life attempts to deal with concupiscence. Thus the whole of Book 10, with its two contrasting halves, suggests the constant struggle of man to rise from darkness into the light of truth—and the constant danger of falling away from the light into darkness.

Book 11 continues the exploration of the mind by discussing its relation to time. Augustine proceeds to show how the mind can in some measure transcend the oppressive transience of time, and act as an image of God's timeless mind, in which all things have their simultaneous existence. The problem is here explored by meditating upon the first verse of Genesis, and particularly upon the meaning of the words *in principio,* which Augustine takes to indicate not simply a beginning but the basic principle, the *principium,* of all being: *In hoc principio fecisti, deus, caelum et terram, in verbo tuo, in filio tuo, in virtute tua, in sapientia tua, in veritate tua, miro modo dicens et miro modo faciens.*

> In this Beginning, O God, hast thou made heaven and earth, namely, in thy Word, in thy Son, in thy Power, in thy Wisdom, in thy Truth; after a wonderful manner speaking, and after a wonderful manner making. Who is able to comprehend it? Who can declare it? What is that which shines through me, and strikes upon my heart without hurting it? And I shudder and kindle: shudder, in as much as I am unlike it; kindle, in as much as I am like it. 'Tis Wisdom, Wisdom's self which thus shines into me; even breaking through my cloudiness: which yet again overshadows me fainting from it, under the gross fog and heavy load of mine own punishment. . . . How wonderful are thy works, O Lord, in wisdom hast thou made them all; and this Wisdom is that Beginning; and in that Beginning hast thou made heaven and earth.
> [11.9]

Clearly that *principium* which made heaven and earth is also working within the mind of man, enabling the mind to act as a mirror of eternity, within the action of its own limited words. How this is done we see in chapter 28, where all the threads of thought in Book 11 are brought together in an account of the basic process that has produced the literary style and meditative method of the *Confessions:*

But how comes that future, which as yet is not, to be diminished or wasted away? Or how comes that past, which now is no longer, to be increased? Unless in the mind which acteth all this, there be three things done. For it expects, it marks attentively, it remembers; that so the thing which it expecteth, through that which attentively it marketh, passes into that which it remembereth. Who therefore can deny, that things to come are not as yet? Yet already there is in the mind an expectation of things to come. And who can deny past things to be now no longer? But yet is there still in the mind a memory of things past. And who can deny that the present time hath no space, because it passeth away in a moment? But yet our attentive marking of it continues so that that which shall be present proceedeth to become absent.

sed tamen perdurat attentio, per quam pergat abesse quod aderit: nevertheless, the act of attentive thought endures, through which the future becomes the past. That is to say, in its abiding attention, the mind becomes a focal point of light where all times exist in the present. As Augustine has earlier suggested:

Clear now it is and plain, that neither things to come, nor things past, are. Nor do we properly say, there be three times, past, present, and to come; but perchance it might be properly said, there be three times: a present time of past things; a present time of present things; and a present time of future things. For indeed three such as these in our souls there be; and otherwhere do I not see them. The present time of past things is our memory; the present time of present things is our sight; the present time of future things our expectation.

[11.20]

Something of this sort, I think, is represented in the continuous interrelationship of the meditations in Traherne's *Centuries*. Each meditation exists in its own present, and yet it holds the seed of future meditations, and it remembers the meditations past. Each meditation "looks forward, it considers, it remembers, so that the reality to which it looks forward passes through what it considers into what it remembers."[7] The only stability lies in the present cognition of truth that exists in the mind's reflection of the eternal light, by which the mind creates, or discovers, its own true inner word.

Through the action of such creative power, man, according to Traherne, may come to find his present life "far better" than the life of unfallen Adam. For now "the very Miseries and sins and offences that are in it, are the Materials of his Joy and Triumph and Glory." In man's original state, "to Enjoy Beauties, and be Gratefull for Benefits was all the Art that was required to Felicity, but now a Man must like a GOD, bring Light out of Darkness, and Order out of Confusion." And this, he adds, "we are taught to do by His Wisdom, that Ruleth in the midst of Storms and Tempests" (4.21).

4. Bonaventure's Journey

Thus the *Centuries* may be seen as Augustinian, in theme, in style, in method of meditation. But in saying this, I do not mean to imply that Traherne drew his chief inspiration directly from Augustine. Traherne was a deeply learned man: he was fully aware of the ramifications of Augustinian thought down through the ages; and at the same time he knew thoroughly the Platonic and Neoplatonic writings that influenced Augustine himself. He knew directly the writings of "Hermes Trismegistus," whom Augustine cites in the *City of God;*[1] he knew the writings of Pico; and he must have known the writings of his own contemporaries, the Cambridge Platonists. One can say no more than this: the principles of Augustine seem to have formed the nucleus around which all the literature of

7. *Confessions,* 11.28; in the translation by John K. Ryan (New York, Image Books, 1960), p. 301.

1. Book 8, chs. 23–26. For Traherne's knowledge of "Hermes" see Ellrodt, *Les Poètes métaphysiques,* Pt. I, Vol. 2, pp. 267–75.

Platonism, pagan and Christian, gathered to help Traherne create his own original exploration of the mind.

Can the principles of Augustine also be used to explore the full extent and progress of the *Centuries,* and to measure the degree of its success in achieving the action of an organic work? A modern synthesis of the principles of Augustinian mysticism might be used in this way, particularly the important studies of Butler or Cayré.[2] But for the *Centuries* it seems better to turn to an influential older synthesis, available to Traherne: the *Itinerarium Mentis in Deum* composed by Augustine's great medieval follower, Bonaventure. The treatise is brief, and it lies ready at hand in an excellent modern translation by George Boas.[3] Used with caution, the *Itinerarium* can throw considerable light upon the progress of the *Centuries.*

Bonaventure's journey of the mind is approached with careful preparation, as he explains in his brief Prologue. "For one is not disposed to contemplation which leads to mental elevation unless one be with Daniel a man of desires." These desires

2. Cuthbert Butler, *Western Mysticism* (2d ed. London, Constable, 1926); Fulbert Cayré, *La Contemplation Augustinienne* (2d ed. Bruges, Desclée de Brouwer, 1954). In the following discussion I am indebted to both these studies, as well as to Gilson's study of Augustine cited earlier, and to Gilson's masterpiece, *The Philosophy of St. Bonaventure,* trans. by Illtyd Trethowan and F. J. Sheed (New York, Sheed and Ward, 1938). I should like also to acknowledge a general indebtedness to the standard study of Eugène Portalié, *A Guide to the Thought of Saint Augustine,* trans. Ralph J. Bastian (from Portalié's article in the *Dictionnaire de Théologie Catholique),* with an Introduction by Vernon J. Bourke (London, Burns and Oates, 1960); and to the valuable study by John J. O'Meara, *The Young Augustine* (London, Longmans, 1954).

3. *The Mind's Road to God,* trans. George Boas, Library of Liberal Arts, 32 (New York, 1953); copyright (c), 1953, by the Liberal Arts Press, Inc.; all quotations reprinted by permission of the Liberal Arts Press Division of the Bobbs-Merrill Company, Inc.; all page-references are made to this translation. The original is in the standard Quaracchi edition of Bonaventure's *Opera* (10 vols. 1882–1902), 5, 295–316. The Quaracchi text is also available, with a French translation, in the admirable annotated edition by Henry Duméry (Paris, Librarie Philosophique J. Vrin, 1960).

must first be enkindled by "the cry of prayer through Christ crucified," since the way upward lies "only through the most burning love of the Crucified." "Bestir yourself then," in such preparatory prayer, "before you raise your eyes to the rays of wisdom shining in that mirror"—the "mirror of the mind" (pp. 4–5).

The journey proper then proceeds by three main stages, each subdivided into two aspects, according to "the symbol of the six-winged Seraph" (p. 4) upon which Bonaventure's central design is based. The first stage (the first pair of wings) consists in finding God by his traces in the external world; the second consists in finding God within the self, through discovering his image in man; and the third consists in contemplation of the essential attributes of God and the Trinity. Thus, says Bonaventure, we contemplate God "outside through His traces, inside through His image, and above us through His light, which has signed upon our minds the light of eternal Truth" (p. 34). One should stress the fact that all these operations are intellectual, rational, performed by the active intelligence of man. Thus Bonaventure's use of the term "contemplation" is not at all limited to the "prayer of quiet" or the "prayer of union" which modern writers often indicate when they speak of the "state of contemplation." In Bonaventure's usage, the terms "meditation" and "contemplation" are not firmly distinguishable, although it is clear that Bonaventure regards "meditation" as a lower stage of mental activity leading into "contemplation."[4] In Traherne the two terms are used as completely interchangeable: his treatise begins and ends by urging constant "meditation." The important point is that all three stages of the journey lie within the intellectual powers of man.

Upon this threefold structure Bonaventure has imposed another structure, revealed in his presentation of the journey in seven chapters. Each of the three stages is subdivided in a

4. See *Itinerarium*, 1.8; p. 10. For the close relation of the terms see Cayré's discussion of "la méditation contemplative" (*La Contemplation Augustinienne*, pp. 214–19).

way that does not quite accord with the symbolism of the three tiers of "wings," for the subdivision creates "six successive stages of illumination" by which one is "led in the most orderly fashion to the repose of contemplation" (p. 9). In this manner Bonaventure combines his favorite threefold symbolism with the sevenfold division of the soul's ascent set forth in Augustine's early treatise, the *De Quantitate Animae* (ch. 33). The seventh stage, the final state of "repose," in which "all intellectual operations should be abandoned" (p. 44), is highly important for understanding Traherne's conclusion, since this final state lies beyond the divisions of Bonaventure's basic threefold arrangement. Traherne's *Centuries* seem to accord in general with the Bonaventurean journey as thus divided:

Preparation: The First Century (*Itinerarium,* Prologue).

The Threefold Way:

    I. Through the Creatures of the external world: The Second Century (*Itinerarium,* chs. 1 and 2).

    II. Through the Image of God in the "Mind and Memory": The Third Century (*Itinerarium,* chs. 3 and 4).

    III. Through the Principles of Being and Good "signed upon our minds": The Fourth Century (*Itinerarium,* chs. 5 and 6).

Repose: in which "all intellectual operations should be abandoned": The Fifth Century, which consists of only ten meditations, followed by the number "11" at the beginning of the 49 blank leaves that end the manuscript volume (*Itinerarium,* ch. 7).

The following account of the progress of the *Centuries* will in general follow this chart, making allowance everywhere for the workings of Traherne's digressive and repetitive originality. The aim is not to show that Traherne was directly following the *Itinerarium,* but only to use the treatise as a guide in tracing the course of Traherne's Augustinian journey.

5. Preparation: The First Century

Traherne's First Century is in every way a "Preparation" of the kind advised in the seventeenth-century handbooks of meditation: it sets forth the topics and images to be considered; it "premeditates" the materials and foresees the desired end; it cultivates the presence of God and invokes the assistance of God in the performance of the meditative action. Meanwhile, Traherne makes it plain that he has in mind the writing of a treatise of instruction, an introduction to the devout life. The friend who has given him this empty notebook is a woman, as his prefatory quatrain makes clear; and the nature of the person directly addressed is highly important to the tone and manner of Traherne's devout instructions: "And since Love made you put it into my Hands I will fill it with those Truths you Love, without Knowing them: and with those Things which, if it be Possible, shall shew my Lov; To you, in Communicating most *Enriching Truths;* to Truth, in Exalting Her Beauties in such a Soul" (1.1). There is something of the *douceur* with which François de Sales addressed his devout friend, Madame de Chantal, in Traherne's opening addresses to his friend, Susanna Hopton: "As a Deep Friendship meditats and intends the Deepest Designes for the Advancement of its Objects, so doth it shew it self in Chusing the Sweetest and most Delightfull Methods, wherby not to Weary, but to Pleas the Person, it desireth to advance." "Even so God, Designing to shew his Lov in exalting you hath chosen the Ways of Eas and Repose, by which you should ascend" (1.4). "What is more Easy and Sweet then Meditation? yet in this hath God commended his Lov, that by Meditation it is Enjoyed" (1.8).

At the same time, Traherne's First Century is specifically a preparation of the kind advised by Bonaventure: it exhorts the reader to kindle the proper desires, and then evokes those desires through fervent meditation on the Cross and cries of prayer to the Crucified Christ. But Traherne's approach to the

Cross is significantly different from the direct and easy way assumed by Bonaventure in his brief Prologue. Too much has happened, theologically and ecclesiastically, for Traherne to enter into mental communion of this kind with the ease of a Herbert or a Crashaw or a François de Sales. His approach, though ultimately successful, is curiously indirect and remarkably difficult. He seems to tell us why in his fifth meditation, when he implies that meditation on the Passion has somehow been displaced from its primary position in the devotional life:

> The fellowship of the Mystery that hath been hid in God, since the Creation is not only the Contemplation of his Lov in the Work of Redemption: Tho that is Wonderfull: But the End, for which we are Redeemed: A Communion with Him in all His Glory. for which caus, S Peter saith The God of all Grace, hath called us unto His Eternal Glory by Jesus Christ. His Eternal Glory by the Methods of His Divine Wisdom being made ours: and our Fruition of it, the End for which our Savior suffered. [1.5]

That is to say, meditation on the "End," on the "fruition," the enjoyment, of "His Eternal Glory" has come to share at least an equal place with meditation on the Cross. Thus, in Traherne's preparatory Century, the Cross is never mentioned until Meditation 54: the first half of the preparation is completely given over to enkindling the love of God through meditation on his gifts to man in the Creation. The first thing to realize—and the last—is given in the phrase from Romans 4:13 that Traherne introduces in his third meditation and repeats persistently throughout the *Centuries:* man is "Heir of the World."

> Evry thing is ours that serves us in its Place. The Sun servs us as much as is Possible, and more then we could imagine. The Clouds and Stars Minister unto us, the World surrounds us with Beauty, the Air refresheth us the Sea revives the Earth and us. The Earth it self is Better then Gold becaus it produceth fruits and flowers. And therfore in the Beginning, was it made Manifest to be mine, becaus Adam alone was made to Enjoy it. [1.14]

With that last sentence Traherne introduces the primary symbol of his *Centuries:* Adam in Paradise becomes the symbol of all the possibilities still resident within redeemed mankind: "That all the World is yours, your very Senses and the Inclinations of your Mind declare. . . . The Powers of your Soul confirm it" (1.16). Our world includes "the Heavens and the Heavens of Heavens, and the Angels and the Celestial Powers," along with "all those infinit and Eternal Treasures that are to abide for ever, after the Day of Judgment." These are "all evry where, and at once to be Enjoyed," through the "Endless Powers of your Soul," by which the "Omnipresence and Eternity of God are your Fellows and Companions." And thus the world becomes for man "a very Paradice; and the Gate of Heaven" (1.18, 19, 20).

Now in a splendid series of seven tightly related meditations (25–31), Traherne exhorts his reader to a proper enjoyment of this gift, through variations on the theme: "You never Enjoy the World aright, till . . ." This motif is related to the theme of "infancy" announced at the close of Meditation 25: "I remember the Time, when the Dust of the Streets were as precious as Gold to my Infant Eys, and now they are more precious to the Ey of Reason." It is a foreshadowing of the Third Century, where the "Infant Ey" is like the eye of Adam before the Fall, while the "Ey of Reason" in redeemed mankind is found to have a far "more precious" vision, such as Traherne now spreads before us: "You never Enjoy the World aright, till you see how a Sand Exhibiteth the Wisdom and Power of God" (1.27). "Your Enjoyment of the World is never right, till evry Morning you awake in Heaven: see your self in your fathers Palace: and look upon the Skies and the Earth and the Air, as Celestial Joys" (1.28). "You never Enjoy the World aright, till the Sea it self floweth in your Veins, till you are Clothed with the Heavens, and Crowned with the Stars: and Perceiv your self to be the Sole Heir of the whole World: and more then so, becaus Men are in it who are evry one Sole Heirs, as well as you" (1.29). "Till you remember how lately you were made, and how wonderfull it was when you came into it: and more rejoyce in the Palace of your Glory, then if it had been made but to Day Morning" (1.30). Thus everyone, in potential, is now a renewed Adam, everyone is capable of finding this Paradise within.

But Traherne is no easy optimist: this sequence ends in Meditation 31, as these exhortations to realize Felicity are abruptly set off against "the Abominable Corruption of Men in Despising it." "The World is a Mirror of infinit Beauty, yet no Man sees it. It is a Temple of Majesty yet no Man regards it. It is a Region of Light and Peace, did not Men Disquiet it. It is the Paradise of God. It is more to Man since he is faln, then it was before." For the next five meditations (32–36) Traherne develops a bitter contrast between those who seek the "Riches of Darkness" and those who seek the "Riches of the Light." "The Riches of Darkness are those which Men hav made, during their Ignorance of God Almightie's Treasures. That lead us from the Lov of all, to Labor and Contention Discontentment and Vanity" (1.33). "That while Others liv in a Golgotha or Prison, we should be in Eden, is a very Great Mystery. And a Mercy it is that we should be Rejoycing in the Temple of Heaven, while they are Toyling and Lamenting in Hell, for the World is both a Paradice and a Prison to different Persons" (1.36).

This is a theme that Traherne picks up again in Meditations 47–50, after his disquisition on the "wants" of man and God. Hell and Heaven are here treated primarily as states of mind, in meditations that could serve as commentary upon certain scenes in *Paradise Lost:*

> To hav Blessings and to Prize them is to be in Heaven; To hav them, and not to Prize them, is to be in Hell, I would say upon Earth: To prize them and not to hav them, is to be in Hell. Which is Evident by the Effects. To Prize Blessings while we hav them is to Enjoy them, and the effect therof is Contentation Pleasure Thanksgiving Happiness. To Prize

them when they are gone Produceth Envy, Covetousness, Re-
pining, Ingratitud, Vexation, Miserie.   [1.47]

"No Miserie is Greater then that of Wanting in the Midst of
Enjoyments, Of Seeing and Desiring yet never Possessing"
(1.48). "But they that Prize not what they hav are Dead;
their sences are laid asleep, and when they com to Hell they
wake: And then they begin to feel their Misery" (1.49).

In Meditation 51 Traherne brings his consideration of
"wants" to a climax, and, in his characteristic way, not only
sums up a series, but modulates his meditations toward the
theme that dominates the last half of this preparatory Century:
the Love of God. "You are Created to be his Lov: and He is
yours" (1.52). Appropriately, in Meditation 53 we come
again to a name which has not been mentioned since its single
occurrence long ago, in Meditation 5: the name of Jesus
Christ. But we know why that name has been so long suspended: it is because Traherne has felt it necessary to grasp,
first, the glory of the end of man designed by God the Father,
Creator of Heaven and Earth.

Now the time has come to meditate upon the mystery of
redemption, and so, in Meditation 54, Traherne comes at last
to the Cross. But we note the care that Traherne takes to enfold
the Cross within the "all," repeating the word "all" fourteen
times within this single meditation: man lives in God's Omnipotence and Eternity:

He that is in all, and with all, can never be Desolat. All the
Joys and all the Treasures, all the Counsels and all the Per-
fections all the Angels and all the Saints of GOD are with
Him. All the Kingdoms of the World and the Glory of them
are continualy in his Ey: The Patriarchs Prophets and Apostles
are always before Him. The Counsels and the fathers, the
Bishops and the Doctors minister unto Him. All Temples are
Open before Him, The Melodie of all Quires reviveth Him,
the Learning of all Universities doth employ him, the Riches
of all Palaces Delight him, The Joys of Eden Ravish Him,

62

The Revelations of S. John Transport Him, The Creation and the Day of Judgment pleas Him, The Hosannas of the Church Militant, and the Hallelujahs of the Saints Triumphant fill Him, The Splendor of all Coronations entertain Him, The Joys of Heaven surround Him, And our Saviors Cross like the Centre of Eternity is in Him, It taketh up his Thoughts, and exerciseth all the Powers of his soul, with Wonder Admiration Joy and Thanksgiving. The Omnipotence of God is His Hous, and Eternity his Habitation. [1.54]

I have given the meditation entire, since it typically represents Traherne's repetitive technique: opening with an epigram, continuing with elaborate detail, and then concluding with an enriched restatement of the essential meaning of the opening epigram. Man lives to enjoy the infinite wonders of God's creative power, but he can no longer simply throw himself at the foot of the Cross, in his imagination, as the old devotional writers used to advise.

In Meditations 55–60 Traherne's approach to the Cross remains theoretical and distant. He explains that we should journey toward the Cross by "withdrawing our Thoughts from Wandering in the Streets of this World, to the Contemplation and Serious Meditation of his Bloody Sufferings." He explains that "Our Eys must be towards it, our Hearts set upon it, our Affections Drawn and our Thoughts and Minds united to it" (1.56). Above all, he insists that we must *see* the Cross—but as something *there,* not *here:* the Cross remains a theoretical point at the center of eternity: "There we might see all Nations Assembled with their Eys and Hearts upon it. There we may see Gods Goodness Wisdom and Power: yea his Mercy and Anger displayed. There we may see Mans Sin and infinit value" (1.59). The Cross is *there,* and the sufferings are in the past: "Was He not the Son of GOD and Heir of the Whole World? To this poor Bleeding Naked Man did all the Corn and Wine and Oyl, and Gold and Silver in the World minister in an Invisible Maner, even as he was exposed Lying and Dying upon the Cross" (1.60).

63

But suddenly, in the next four meditations (61–64) the perspective shifts and we are *here,* with the Cross placed in the midst of contemporary history: "This Man Bleeding here was Tutor to King Charles the Martyr" (1.61). And at once the speaker begins to utter, in the ancient, traditional way, his colloquies before the Cross: "O my joy! O my Sovereign Friend! O my Life, and my All! I beseech Thee let those Trickling Drops of Blood that run down Thy flesh drop upon me" (1.62). And in this mood he longs to perform an Ignatian application of the senses: "I Admire thy Lov unto me also. O that I could see it through all those Wounds! O that I could feel it in all those Stripes! O that I could hear it in all those Groans! O that I could Taste it beneath that Gall and Vinegre! O that I could smell the Savor of thy sweet Oyntments, even in this Golgotha or Place of a Skull" (1.63).

But it cannot yet be done. In Meditation 64 Traherne declares the difficulty of proceeding in this ancient way: the wounds of Christ, he declares, cannot in themselves arouse an adequate sense of God's Love. And in the very middle of this favorite theme of the Counter Reformation, Traherne abruptly turns away from the Cross to consider the Creation. To grasp the drama and significance of this powerful gesture one must read the whole meditation:

> These Wounds are in themselvs Orifices too small to let in my Sight, to the vast Comprehensions of thine Eternal Lov. These Wounds Engraven in thy Hands but Shady Impressions; unless I see the Glory of thy Soul, in which the fulness of the GODHEAD Dwelleth Bodily. These Bloody Characters are too Dim to let me read it, in its Lustre and Perfection. Till I see thy Person: and Know thy Ways! O Thou that Hangest upon this Cross before mine Eys, Whose face is Bleeding, and coverd over with Tears and filth and Blows! Angels Adore the GLORY of Thy GODHEAD in the Highest Heavens! Who in evry Thought, and in evry Work didst Glorious Things for me from Everlasting. What Could I O my Lord Desire more then such a World! Such Heavens and

such an Earth! Such Beasts and Fowls and fishes made for me. All these Do Homage unto me, and I hav Dominion over them from the Beginning! The Heavens and the Earth Minister unto me, as if no Man were Created but I alone. I willingly Acknowledg it to be thy Gift! Thy Bounty unto Me! How many thousand Ways do Men also minister unto me! O what Riches hast Thou prepared out of Nothing for me! All Creatures labor for my sake, and I am made to Enjoy all thy Creatures. O what Praises shall I return unto Thee, the Wisdom of the father, and the Brightness of the Glory of his Eternal Goodness! Who didst make all for me before thou didst redeem me.   [1.64]

Thus the old eucharistic devotions seem to fail, and Traherne returns to his primary mode of apprehending the Love of God: the vision of the self in Adam's Paradise: "Had I been alive in Adams steed, how should I hav Admired the Glory of the world!" But indeed he is alive in Adam's stead: this is the wonder of redemption, that man can still see Paradise about him: "It was Glorious while new: and is as new as it was Glorious" (1.65). Yet even this is not the major wonder, which lies within: "O my Soul, He hath made His Image. Sing O ye Angels, and Laud His Name ye Cherubims: Let all the Kingdoms of the Earth be Glad, and let all the Hosts of Heaven rejoyce. for He hath made His Image, the Likeness of himself, his own Similitude" (1.67). And the "Effect of Making Images" is that all creatures are bound together in God: "Here is Lov! Here is a Kingdom! Where all are Knit in infinit Unity" (1.74).

Now, with the realization that man has been redeemed to such a privilege, Traherne performs one of those sudden recoveries of an earlier motif by which all the meditations are bound together: nothing is ever started in the *Centuries* that does not somewhere, somehow, reappear with redoubled effect. So here, as he feels within himself the powers of Adam, he sees himself re-enacting the sin of Adam, and thus comes to the memory of how he has been redeemed:

Being to lead this Life within I was Placed in Paradice without with som Advantages which the Angels hav not. And being Designed to Immortality and an Endless Life, was to Abide with GOD from everlasting to everlasting in all His Ways. But I was Deceived by my Appetite, and fell into Sin. Ingratefully I despised Him that gav me my Being. I offended in an Apple against Him that gave me the whole World: But Thou O Savior art here upon the Cross suffering for my Sins. What shall I render unto Thee for so Great a Mercy!

[1.75]

The last ten meditations, we see, have been performed in the presence of the Cross: and the renewal of Adam's powers demonstrated and proclaimed in those meditations is itself the gift of God on the Cross, the gift that makes the world more glorious now than it was for Adam: "And now, O Lord, Heaven and Earth are infinitly more valuable then they were before. being all bought with thy Precious Blood" (1.76).

Thus the old devotions to the Cross have not failed: they have been absorbed into another mode of apprehension, in which the Cross becomes the ligature of all Creation, as Traherne now explains to his friend, in an intimate address—so intimate that it perhaps came to seem improper to Traherne, for the whole of this meditation (80) is crossed out in his manuscript:

What more Delightfull can be imagined, then to see a Savior at this Distance Dying on the Cross to Redeem a man from Hell, and to see one self the Beloved of GOD and all Kingdoms, yea the Admired of Ages, and the Heir of the whole World? Hath not His Blood united you and me, Cannot we see and Lov and Enjoy each other at 100 Miles Distance? In Him is the only Sweet and Divine Enjoyment. I Desire but an Amiable Soul in any Part of all Eternity, and can lov it unspeakably: And if lov it, Enjoy it.

It is this love, he adds, which binds together the community of "the Saints of all Ages" (1.81); even now, in these days, a few such saints may be found: "While the Wicked are like

Heaps of Rubbish, these few Jewels lie buried in the Ruins of Mankind: and must Diligently be Digd for" (1.82). This is a note not often struck in the *Centuries,* where the dominant temper is far from exclusive. But here and there, amid his meditations on the gifts available to every man, one is reminded by his passing allusions to the "few" that Traherne received his university education and his first ordination under the auspices of the Puritan regime.[1]

Assured of the Love of God shown in the original Creation and in the re-creation represented by the Cross, Traherne concludes his preparatory Century by entering fervently into the way of Bonaventure. At Meditation 86 he begins a series of powerful concluding prayers to the Crucified, stressing the antiquity of the manner by using the ancient vocative "Jesu," and by engaging at last in a series of vivid colloquies before the Cross:

> O Jesu, Thou King of Saints, whom all Adore . . . I Admire to see thy Crosse in evry Understanding, thy Passion in evry Memory, thy Crown of Thorns in evry Ey, and thy Bleeding, Naked Wounded Body in evry Soul. Thy Death liveth in evry Memory, thy Crucified Person is Enbalmed in evry Affection, thy pierced feet are Bathed in evry ones Tears, thy Blood all droppeth on evry soul: [1.86]

> Breath upon me, Inspire me, Quicken Me, Illuminat me, Enflame me, fill me with the Spirit of GOD; that I may overflow with Praises and Thanksgivings . . . fill me with the Riches of thy Glory, that Christ may Dwell in my Heart by faith, that I being rooted and Grounded in Lov may speak the Wonderfull Works of GOD.   [1.95]

1. Traherne was admitted to the rectory of Credenhill on December 30, 1657, with certification by Puritan clergymen from Hereford. As Miss Wade says (*Traherne,* pp. 62–63): "that these men should furnish Traherne with testimonials proves that he was at this time under no suspicion of secret use of the Book of Common Prayer, or of consorting with the 'malignant.' It seems in fact fairly plain that at this period Traherne must be regarded as a Puritan, and that he was ordained by the Puritan regula-

6. Traces of God: The Second Century

Near the close of the second chapter of the *Itinerarium*, Bonaventure sums up the first stage of the mind's threefold journey, and indicates the process of meditation that runs throughout Traherne's Second Century. This opening stage in the journey is performed in two steps, "by which we are led to seeing God in His traces"—*vestigia*, the footprints of God, by which, Bonaventure says,

> we can determine that all creatures of this sensible world lead the mind of the one contemplating and attaining wisdom to the eternal God; for they are shadows, echoes, and pictures, the traces, simulacra, and reflections of that First Principle most powerful, wisest, and best; of that light and plenitude; of that art productive, exemplifying, and ordering, given to us for looking upon God. They are signs divinely bestowed which, I say, are exemplars or rather exemplifications set before our yet untrained minds, limited to sensible things, so that through the sensibles which they see they may be carried forward to the intelligibles which they do not see, as if by signs to the signified. [p. 20]

The first step consists in "putting the whole sensible world before us as a mirror" and finding therein the traces of "the power, wisdom, and immense goodness of the Creator" (pp. 10–11). Power, wisdom, and goodness—that traditional triad, five times repeated in Bonaventure's opening chapter, is echoed in the first meditation of Traherne's Second Century: "The Services which the World doth you, are transcendent to all Imagination. . . . it Discovers the Being of GOD unto you, It opens His Nature, and shews you his Wisdom Goodness and Power . . . It enflameth you with the Lov of God, and is the Link of your Union and Communion with Him."

---

tions, and appointed to Credenhill as showing promise of also being 'godly, orthodox, and painful.' " He was re-ordained in the English Church on October 20, 1660. See the documents printed by Margoliouth, *1,* xxiv.

1

The Services wch ye World doth you, are transcendent to all Imagination. Did it only sustain yr Body & perform yr Life, & comfort yr Sences, yu were bound to value it as much as those services were worth: but it Discovers ye Being of GOD unto yu, It opens His Nature, & shews yu his Wisdom Goodness & Power, It magnifies His Lov unto yu, It serves Angels & Men for yu, It entertains yu with many Lovely & Glorious Objects, It feeds yu with Joys, & becomes a Theme, it furnishes yu wth perpetual praises & Thanksgivings, It enflameth yu wth ye Lov of God, & is ye Link of yr Union & Communion wth Him. It is ye Temple wherin yu are exalted to Glory & Honor, & ye visible Porch or Gate of Eternitie. A sure pledge of Eternal Joys, to all Gm yt walk before God & are perfect in it.

2

If yu desire Directions how to Enjoy it, place yr self in it alone, for it is as much yours, as if no one were created besides yr self. And consider all ye Services it doth unto you, even to yu alone. Prize those Services wth a Joy answerable to ye value of Gm, be Truly Thankfull, & as Gratefull for Gm, as their Merit deserves. And remember always how great soever the World is, it is ye Beginning of Gifts. The first Thing wch GOD bestows to every Infant, by ye very Right of His Nativity. Wch becaus Men are Blind they can not see & therfore they know not, & GOD is Liberal from ye first, Error proceed, & multiply their Mistaking all along. They know not yr selvs nor their own Glory, they understand not His Comandmts, they see not ye Sublimity of Righteous Actions, they know not ye Beauty of Truth, nor are acquainted wth ye Glory of the Holy Scriptures.

3

Till yu see ye ye World is yours, you cannot weigh ye Greatnes of Sin, nor ye misery of yr fall, nor prize yr Redeemers Lov. one would think these should be Motives sufficient to stir us up, to ye Contemplation of GODS Works, wherin all the Riches of His Kingdom will appear. for ye Greatnes of Sin proceedeth from ye Greatnes of His Lov whom we hav offended, from ye Greatnes of those Obligations wch were laid upon us, from ye great Blessednes & Glory of ye Estate wherin we were placed, none of wch can be seen, till Truth is seen, a great part of wch is, That ye World is ours. So yt indeed ye Knowledg of this is ye very real Light, wherin all Mysteries are Evidenced to us.

Autograph Manuscript of Traherne's *Centuries* (Bodleian MS. Eng. th. e. 50)

"If you desire Directions how to enjoy" the world, Traherne continues, "Place yourself in it as if no one were Created besides your self. And consider all the services it doth, even to you alone" (2.2). One must return by memory to Eden, become like the unfallen Adam in imagination, as Traherne finds the Bible urging in Revelation 2:5: *"Remember from whence thou art faln, and Repent":*

> Which intimates our Duty of Remembering our Happiness in the Estate of Innocence. For without this we can never Prize our Redeemers Lov: He that Knows not to what He is redeemed cannot Prize the Work of Redemption. The Means cannot there be valued, where the End is despised. Since therfore by the Second Adam, we are restored to that we lost in the first: unless we valu that we lost in the first, we cannot truly rejoyce in the second. But when we do, then all things receiv an infinit Esteem, and an Augmentation infinitly infinit, that follows after. Our Saviors Lov, His Incarnation, His Life and Death, His Resurrection, His Ascension into Heaven, His Intercession for us &c being then seen, and infinitly prized in a Glorious Light: as also our Deliverance from Hell, and our Reconciliation unto God. [2.5]

That passage, representing the central motive of Traherne's *Centuries,* may also be said to represent the essence of *Paradise Lost:* it may suggest why the vision of the lost paradise came to dominate the center of Milton's epic, why the Savior's Incarnation, Life, Death, Resurrection, and Ascension are found so briefly represented in the last book of *Paradise Lost,* and why Milton's full account of the Savior's mission on earth, in *Paradise Regain'd,* came to be published four years after the great vision of the first Paradise.

"How can I believ," asks Traherne, "that He gave His Son to die for me, who having Power to do otherwise gave me nothing but Rags and Cottages? But when I see once that He gave Heaven and Earth to me, and made me in His Image to Enjoy them in His Similitude, I can easily believ that He gave His Son also for me" (2.6). Consequently, he repeats, the first step in the mind's journey must be this: "Place yourself therfore in the midst of the World as if you were alone: and Meditat upon all the Services which it doth unto you" (2.7).

Thus he opens a series of five meditations on the services and beauties made possible by the earthly Sun, including the "Delightfull vicissitudes of Night and Day," "the Early Sweetness and Spring of the Morning the Perfume and Beauty in the cool of the Evening" (2.9). Considering such wonders as these, man may again become an inhabitant of Eden: "Why should you not render Thanks to God for them all? You are the Adam, or the Eve that Enjoy them" (2.12). Alone in Eden, "you were Lord over all: and bound to Admire His Eternal Lov who raised you out of Nothing into this Glorious World which He Created for you. To see infinit Goodness Wisdom and Power making the Heavens and the Earth the Seas, the Air the Sun and Stars! what Wonder, what Joy, what Glory, what Triumph, what Delight should this afford!" (2.13). And indeed, he adds, the world "is more yours then if you had been made alone," for now all mankind serves each man alone, in a marvellous unity:

> The world servs you, as in serving those Cattle which you feed upon, so in serving those Men, that Build and Plow, and Plant, and Govern for you. It servs you in those that Pray and Adore and Prais for you, that fill the World with Beauty and vertue; that are made to lov. and Honor, to Pleas and Advance you with all the Services that the Art of man can devise. So that you are alone in the World, tho there are Millions in it beside. You are alone to Enjoy and rejoyce in all, being the Adequat Object of His Eternal Lov, and the End of all.   [2.15]

Such are the "immediat Pleasures" that one may have by meditation on the world. But in addition to this "pleasure less," as Marvell might call it, the mind receives many "Sublime and Celestial Services" from the world: "It is a Glorious Mirror wherin you may see the verity of all Religion: Enjoy the Remainders of Paradice and Talk with the Dietie. Apply yourself

Vigorously to the Enjoyment of it. For in it you shall see the face of God: and by Enjoying it, be wholy Converted to Him" (2.17).

Thus far Traherne's meditations seem quite in accord with the initial step in Bonaventure's method, by which one contemplates God externally *through* the traces of God in the Creation. But now he seems to move on gradually into the second step, by which one contemplates God *in* these traces, by his "essence, potency, and presence." This is done by "the contemplation of God in all creatures which enter into our minds through the bodily senses" (p. 14). The whole "sensible world," Bonaventure explains, "enters our souls" by a threefold process of *apprehension, delight,* and *judgment,* which he describes in the technical terms of his own philosophy. There is no need to consider here the scholastic manner of Bonaventure's explanation, for Traherne is not working with these particular terms. The important points to note are that *delight* arises from apprehending, within our minds, the proportion and harmony of created things, and that *judgment* is made possible "by the immutable, illimitable, and endless reason."

If, then, all things of which we have more certain judgments are judged by this mode of reasoning, it is clear that this is the reason of all things and the infallible rule and light of truth, in which all things shine forth infallibly, indestructibly, indubitably, irrefragably, unquestionably, unchangeably, boundlessly, endlessly, indivisibly, and intellectually. And therefore those laws by which we make certain judgments concerning all sensible things which come into our consideration—since they [the laws] are infallible and indubitable rules of the apprehending intellect—are indelibly stored up in the memory as if always present, are irrefragable and unquestionable rules of the judging intellect.   [pp. 18–19]

This bold assertion of the presence of eternal light within the mind is true, he adds, "because, as Augustine says, no one judges these things except by these rules" (p. 19). Bonaventure is referring to the discussion of the mind's relation to "unchangeable truth" that occupies the second part of Augustine's early and highly neoplatonic treatise, the *De Libero Arbitrio*,[1] where Augustine establishes the freedom of the will by showing how the mind makes its judgments in "the light of wisdom" common to all men: "All these judgments we make according to those inward rules of truth, which we discern in common." "Just as the rules of numbers are true and unchangeable, and the science of numbers is unchangeably available for all who can learn it, and is common to them all, so the rules of wisdom are true and unchangeable."[2]

Bonaventure then concludes this discussion of the mind's inner judgment of the "traces" by appealing to two more treatises of the early Augustine, the *De Vera Religione* and the *De Musica*, for evidence of the ways in which the mind moves toward the Maker by its understanding of *number*. Bonaventure's summary here gives the essence of Augustine's view, especially as given in the latter part of the *De Vera Religione*:[3]

Since, therefore, all things are beautiful and in some way delightful, and beauty and delight do not exist apart from proportion, and proportion is primarily in number, it needs must be that all things are rhythmical [*numerosa*]. And for this reason number is the outstanding exemplar in the mind of the Maker, and in things it is the outstanding trace leading to wisdom. . . . It causes [God] to be known in all corporeal and sensible things while we apprehend the rhythmical, delight in rhythmical proportions, and through the laws of rhythmical proportions judge irrefragably.   [p. 20]

1. *De Libero Arbitrio*, 2.38, *Earlier Writings*, p. 159: "Externally it [Truth] suggests, internally it teaches. All who behold it, it changes for the better, and by none is it changed for the worse. No one judges it, and no one without it judges aright. Hence it is evident beyond a doubt that wisdom is better than our minds, for by it alone they are made individually wise, and are made judges, not of it, but by it of all other things whatever."
2. *De Libero Arbitrio*, 2.34, 29, *Earlier Writings*, pp. 156, 154.
3. See *De Vera Religione*, 79, *Earlier Writings*, pp. 266–67.

Thus in explaining the first stage of the mind's ascent, Bonaventure has opened with a brief and simple survey of the external creation, covering three pages (pp. 10–13), and has then moved on into a highly complex account of the way in which "the whole world can enter into the human soul," an account covering eight pages (pp. 14–21). Traherne's Second Century enacts, with almost the same proportions, the same movement of the mind from sensibles to intelligibles. In Meditation 22 Traherne brings to a climax his meditations on the external "World of Evidences," concluding with the same emphasis on *order* that marks the close of Bonaventure's first step. Then, in Meditations 23 and 24, Traherne announces the greater theme that dominates the remainder of this Century: the wonder of the way in which the other creatures may be comprehended within the mind of man:

> His Thoughts and Desires can run out to Everlasting. His Lov can extend to all Objects, His Understanding is an endless Light, and can infinitly be present in all Places, and see and Examine all Beings, survey the reasons, surmount the Greatness, exceed the Strength, contemplat the Beauty, Enjoy the Benefit, and reign over all it sees and Enjoys like the Eternal GODhead.

> The true exemplar of GODs infinity is that of your Understanding, which is a lively Patern and Idea of it. It excludeth Nothing, and containeth all Things. Being a Power that Permitteth all Objects to be, and is able to Enjoy them. . . . How Great doth God appear, in Wisely preparing such an Understanding to Enjoy his Creatures; such an Endles Invisible and Mysterious Receiver?

It is this power that receives the cry of the Creatures, as Augustine also heard it, leading man toward his "true real inward Happiness" (2.26), his knowledge of the Love of God: "They daily cry in a Living maner, with a silent, and yet most loud voice. We are all His Gifts: We are Tokens and Presents of His Lov" (2.28).

Thus Traherne moves toward the central portion of his Second Century, containing his highly Augustinian analysis of the trinitarian nature of Love, both in God, and in man.[4] The theme emerges in all its formal grandeur at the opening of Meditation 39: "GOD *by Loving Begot His Son.* For GOD is Lov. And by loving He begot His Lov." So begins the mode of interpretation that dominates the next thirty meditations; a trinity of Love is found at work throughout the universe:

> In all Lov there is a Lov begetting, a Lov begotten, and a Lov Proceeding. Which tho they are one in Essence, subsist Nevertheless in Three Several Maners. . . . The Lov from which it floweth, is the Fountain of Love. the Lov which streameth from it is the communication of Lov, or Lov communicated. and the Lov which resteth in the Object is the Lov which Streameth to it. So that in all Lov the Trinity is Clear. . . . Lov in the Bosom is the Parent of Lov, Lov in the Stream is the Effect of Lov, Lov seen, or Dwelling in the Object proceedeth from both. Yet are all three one and the self same Lov: tho three loves   [2.40]

> In all Lov there is some Producer, som Means, and som End: all these being Internal in the Thing it self. Lov Loving is the Producer, and that is the father; Lov produced is the Means, and that is the Son: for Lov is the Means by which a Lover loveth. The End of these Means is Lov: for it is Lov, by Loving: and that is the H. Ghost.   [2.46]

It is not at first easy to see exactly how this relates to meditation on the Creatures, but the implication gradually emerges, in Traherne's exploratory way. Traherne, as usual, has prepared for this long digression on the nature of Love, as far back as

4. See *De Trinitate,* Book 8, especially the conclusion: "Love is the activity of a lover, and it has a certain object. There, then, we have three things: the lover, that which is loved, and love. Love itself is nothing but a kind of life which couples together or seeks to couple some two entities, the lover and the loved. . . . What does any friend love in his friend but the soul? There too are the three: the lover, the loved, and love" (*Later Works,* pp. 54–55).

Meditation 21, where he alludes in a very general way to the Neoplatonic philosophers: "ancient Philosophers hav thought GOD to be the *Soul of the World.*" He at once accepts the principle as true, at least in metaphor, and proceeds to base Meditations 21-29 on the attributes of God that man may find manifested in the world, seen as the body of God:

> Since therfore this visible World is the Body of GOD, not his Natural Body, but which He hath assumed; let us see how Glorious His Wisdom is, in Manifesting Himself therby. It hath not only represented His infinity and Eternity which we thought impossible to be represented by a Body, but His Beauty also, His Wisdom, Goodness, Power, Life and Glory, His Righteousness, Lov, and Blessedness: all which as out of a plentifull Treasurie, may be taken and collected out of this World.   [2.21]

Thus all creation becomes a channel of Love's "streaming," a means, a nexus between the Love of God and the love of man. The Creatures show the Love of God streaming toward his object, each individual man, as promised in that verse from Romans (1:20) often cited by Vaughan, Augustine, Traherne, and Bonaventure: "as the Apostle saith, By Things that are seen the Invisible things of GOD are manifested, even His power and Godhead. becaus evry thing is a Demonstration of His Goodness and Power" (2.24). In turn, the Creatures provide a channel and occasion by which the love of man returns to its source in the Love of God. "By Loving a Soul does Propagat and beget it self," Traherne declares: "when it loveth, it gaineth Three Subsistences in it self by the Act of Loving. A Glorious Spirit that Abideth within: a Glorious Spirit that floweth in the Stream. A glorious Spirit that resideth in the Object" (2.56).

At the same time, these trinitarian views are constantly reminding the reader of that other bodily manifestation of God which has restored mankind to "Greater Beauty and Splendor then before," through "restoring the Soul to its Primitiv Beauty Health and Glory." "And thus we com again by the Works of

75

God to our Lord JESUS CHRIST" (2:30–31). That is to say, man's present power of realizing the Love of God through the creation serves as a constant reminder of the Love of God shown in the redemption; and thus the whole creation, bathed in a double memory of love, holds a greater glory than it ever held for unfallen Adam.

In the concluding portion of this digression on Love (Meditations 63–69), Traherne concentrates his attention upon considering the love of human beings for one another. This discussion takes on a subtle quality if we keep in mind the female friend to whom the whole book is addressed: these meditations become an oblique explanation of the quality of the writer's love for this particular friend, and of the quality that her love ought to bear toward him. It is impossible, he says, to love any creature too much: "That Violence wherwith som times a man doteth upon one Creature, is but a little spark of that lov, even towards all, which lurketh in His nature. We are made to lov: both to satisfy the Necessity of our Activ Nature, and to answer the Beauties in evry Creature. By Lov our souls are married and sodderd to the creatures: and it is our Duty like GOD to be united to them all. We must lov them infinitly but in God, and for God: and God in them: namely all His Excellencies Manifested in them" (2.66). "Suppose a Curious and fair Woman. Som have seen the Beauties of Heaven, in such a Person. It is a vain Thing to say they loved too much" (2.68). "The Sun and Stars Pleas me in Ministering to you. They Pleas me in ministering to a thousand others as well as you. And you pleas me becaus you can live and lov in the Image of GOD: not in a Blind and Bruitish maner, as Beasts do; by a meer Appetite and rude Propensitie, but with a Regulated well orderd Lov Upon Clear Causes, and with a Rational Affection, guided to Divine and Celestial Ends" (2.69).

With these thoughts, resembling Raphael's advice to Adam in *Paradise Lost,* Traherne's meditations on the nature of love reach their conclusion, and the last thirty meditations return to pick up the related theme that has never been lost, the theme of the immensity of man's understanding. For now the human understanding is seen to be working within the realm of love, and "Its Lov is a Dominion Greater then that which Adam had in Paradise" (2.70). Thus the abstract assertions of the mind's immense power found in Meditation 23 have been enriched by the intervening meditations on the trinity of love, and we can grasp now the full meaning of the act of meditation on the Creatures.

"An Act of the Understanding is the presence of the Soul," Traherne declares: "By an Act of the Understanding therfore be present now with all the Creatures among which you live: and hear them in their Beings and Operations Praising GOD in an Heavenly Maner. Som of them Vocaly, others in their Ministry, all of them Naturaly and Continualy" (2.76). Thus the whole universe, sustained by love, is brought within the "infinit Space" of the soul, for "GOD hath made it Easy to convert our Soul into a Thought containing Heaven and Earth" (2.87). By constant meditation a perpetual conversion of the Creatures into thought must be accomplished, for reasons that Traherne sums up in Meditation 90:

> The World within you is an offering returned. Which is infinitly more Acceptable to GOD Almighty, since it came from him, that it might return unto Him. Wherin the Mysterie is Great. For GOD hath made you able to Creat Worlds in your own mind, which are more Precious unto Him then those which He Created: And to Give and offer up the World unto Him, which is very Delightfull in flowing from Him, but much more in Returning to Him. Besides all which in its own Nature also a Thought of the World, or the World in a Thought is more Excellent then the World, becaus it is Spiritual and Nearer unto GOD.

In this way, with words that may remind us of the most famous stanza in Andrew Marvell's "The Garden," Traherne withdraws the mind toward its own interior "Happiness," and prepares the way toward a deeper "Felicity" by summing up

the full significance of his Second Century with a vision of
Adam fallen and redeemed:

> How Happy are you therfore, that you hav so Great a Lord,
> whose Lov rescued you from the Extremest Misery? Had you
> seen Adam turned into Hell, and going out of this fair Man-
> sion which the Lord had given him, into Everlasting Tor-
> ments, or Eternal Darkness: you would hav thought the
> World a Glorious Place, which was Created for him, and the
> Light of Eden would hav appeared in Greater Lustre then it
> did before: and his Lov by whom He was recovered the Great-
> est Jewel. It is a Heavenly thing to understand His Lov, and
> to see it well. Had Adam had no Esteem for the Place to
> which he was restored, he had not valued the Benefit of His
> Restitution. But now looking upon it with those Eys wher-
> with Noble Men look upon their Territories and Palaces,
> when they are going to Die, His Mercy who died for Him,
> that He after his Condemnation might return again into his
> Dear Enjoyments, maketh Him by whom they were purchased
> the Best and Greatest of all Enjoyments.   [2.95]

7. The Image of God: The Third Century

The meditations of the Second Century, in Bonaventure's
terms, "have led us to the point of entering into ourselves, that
is, into our minds in which the divine image shines" (p. 22).
Now, in the second stage of the threefold journey, the mind
moves beyond the traces of God in the other creatures, and
turns to discover "the resplendent image" of the Trinity within
itself, an image that Bonaventure, following Augustine, finds
in the three powers of the soul: memory, understanding (intelligence), and will. The search begins with *memory,* because the
mind could never "know itself unless it remembered itself"
(p. 22). For Bonaventure, as for his master Augustine, the
memory is a power of vast and infinite capacity, the reservoir
of all our knowledge: "The operation of memory is retention

and representation, not only of things present, corporeal, and temporal, but also of past and future things, simple and eternal." Memory "retains the eternal principles and the axioms of the sciences and retains them eternally"—not "as though it were perceiving them for the first time, but as if it were recognizing them as innate and familiar." Thus the memory "has the likeness of eternity whose indivisible present extends to all times." It has within itself certain "simple forms" which have not entered "through the doors of the senses." Above all, the memory "has an undying light present to itself in which it remembers unchangeable truths." "And thus, through the operations of the memory, it appears that the soul itself is the image of God and His likeness, so present to itself and having Him present that it receives Him in actuality and is susceptible of receiving Him in potency, and that it can also participate in Him" (pp. 22–23).

Traherne begins his Third Century by affirming, upon his own experience, that this ancient view of memory's power is true:

> Will you see the Infancy of this sublime and celestial Greatness? Those Pure and Virgin Apprehensions I had from the Womb, and that Divine Light wherewith I was born, are the Best unto this Day, wherin I can see the Universe. By the Gift of GOD they attended me into the World, and by his Special favor I remember them till now. Verily they seem the Greatest Gifts His Wisdom could bestow. . . . Certainly Adam in Paradice had not more sweet and Curious Apprehensions of the World, then I when I was a child.   [3.1]

Then follow the most splendid passages in Traherne's work, those memories of his early childhood, when "I saw all in the Peace of Eden; Heaven and Earth did sing my Creators Praises and could not make more Melody to Adam, then to me. All Time was Eternity, and a Perpetual Sabbath" (3.2). "Eternity was Manifest in the Light of the Day, and som thing infinit Behind evry thing appeared: which talked with my Expectation

79

and moved my Desire. The Citie seemed to stand in Eden, or to be Built in Heaven" (3.3).

After this superb opening Traherne provides, as his fourth meditation, a poem that he has made upon "those Pure and Virgin Apprehensions which I had in my Infancy." But the poem is stiffly didactic: it does not, like the preceding meditations in prose, grasp the memory of those glories. It simply comments abstractly upon the meaning of these memories:

> Those Thoughts His Goodness long before
> Prepard as Precious and Celestial Store:
> With Curious Art in me inlaid,
> That Childhood might it self alone be said
> My Tutor Teacher Guid to be,
> Instructed then even by the Dietie.

As in some of the poems of Vaughan, imaginative power here dies away into mere reflection, since the poem itself is not devoted to the very process of exploring the memory. Indeed, the full power of Traherne's symbolic use of Paradise and Infancy is not displayed within his poetry, which too often consists primarily in versified statement, assertion, or exclamation. The power of Traherne's mind seems hampered by the necessity of making ends meet in verse; his peculiar combination of visual imagery and subtle, repetitive analysis finds its best medium in the flexible form of the tightly-wrought prose paragraph. Still, the poem just quoted serves a purpose by making it plain that Traherne's "Childhood" is here a metaphor setting forth his belief that certain thoughts and principles have been "inlaid" within the mind from birth, and that "as I backward look again" this "Celestial Store" within the memory can be recovered.

True, Traherne says, the "first Light which shined in my Infancy in its Primitive and Innocent Clarity was totaly ecclypsed" for many years (3.7); but those things which he once knew "by Intuition" he has now "Collected again, by the Highest Reason" (3.2). If he has done so, others may do the same. Therefore, he says, "I will in the Light of my Soul shew you the Univers. . . . And by what Steps and Degrees I proceeded to that Enjoyment of all Eternity which now I possess I will likewise shew you. A Clear, and familiar Light it may prove unto you" (3.6).

The "Steps and Degrees" that he now represents in his own spiritual autobiography are essentially those of Bonaventure's whole *Itinerarium,* from the first traces of God in the creatures, to the state of ultimate "repose." At the same time, the Third Century bears a close resemblance to the process of self-exploration set forth in Bonaventure's account of the second stage in the threefold ascent (chapters 3 and 4). To see that resemblance, however, one must look beneath Bonaventure's abstract, scholastic analysis, with its intricate triadic groupings. It is clear that Traherne, as a man of the late seventeenth century, is highly impatient with what he here calls "the Placits and Doctrines of the Scholes" (3.20). His interest lies, as he says, in developing a view of the human mind which these older terms seem to him inadequate to express: the view that "infinit Worth shut up in the Limits of a Material Being, is the only way to a Real Infinity" (3.20). Consequently, in his Third Century, Traherne does not stress, as Bonaventure does, the Augustinian conception that the three powers of the soul represent a mirror of the higher Trinity. He nowhere speaks of *three* powers, although he constantly urges that souls must be "Awakened to a Discerning of their faculties, and Exercise of their Powers" (3.37).

Traherne's trinitarian views have been fully developed in the Second Century; with these views in the background, he now goes on to develop a view of the mind's infinite unity. In doing so he at first presents a conception of the memory that seems to resemble the undifferentiated *memoria* of Augustine's *Confessions;* but as the Century continues, the action of the mind there represented comes to bear a closer and closer resemblance to the unified action of a threefold power that constitutes the heart of Augustine's interpretation of the interior trinity in man. As our discussion of Vaughan has indicated, the three powers are for Augustine not separate faculties but aspects of one single entity:

> Now this triad of memory, understanding, and will, are not three lives, but one; nor three minds, but one. It follows that they are not three substances, but one substance. Memory, regarded as life, mind, or substance, is an absolute term: regarded as memory, it is relative. The same may be said of understanding and of will; for both terms can be used relatively. But life, mind, essence, are always things existing absolutely in themselves. Therefore the three activities named are one, inasmuch as they constitute one life, one mind, one essence. [*De Trinitate,* 10.18; p. 88]

Since the "powers," then, are "three activities" of one essence, no particular sequence can be discerned in their total action; when we speak of a "power," we are speaking relatively, directing attention to one aspect of the mind's whole and undifferentiated activity. All these aspects or activities are present whenever we talk of one aspect.

Thus in Traherne's Third Century we see the understanding in the process of exploring the memory, under the impulse of a deep desire, love, or will, until at last the whole soul bursts forth in the psalms of loving praise that dominate the last thirty meditations of this Century. It would be fair to say that the Century begins with memory, moves through a process of the analytic understanding, and concludes with the praises of the will; but at the same time every portion of the Century is alive with all three aspects, in accord with the central conception that Augustine thus describes:

> There is both understanding and love in that prime fount of memory, wherein we find ready and laid up the truth we can arrive at by the act of thought; for both of these we find there, present before we thought of them, when in the act of thought we discover our own understanding and love of any object. There is both memory and love in the understanding

which takes form in thought—the true word spoken inwardly
without any specific language, when we say what we know;
for our thought can only turn its observation upon anything
by remembering, and will only be concerned to do so by
loving. Love is that which takes the vision which has its
seat in memory, and the vision of thought which thence receives form, and joins them together as parent and offspring;
but in the same way unless it possessed the knowledge of purposive seeking, which involves memory and understanding,
it would be ignorant of its own proper object.

[*De Trinitate*, 15.41; p. 169]

This is of course the basic view that underlies Bonaventure's
discussion of the interior trinity: "From memory and intelligence is breathed forth love, which is the tie between the two.
These three—the generating mind, the word, and love—are in
the soul as memory, intelligence, and will, which are consub-
stantial, coequal, and coeval, mutually immanent" (p. 26);
but the scholastic nature of his analysis tends in places to
obscure this underlying reality.

In pursuing this Augustinian concept of "purposive seeking,"
Traherne here displays his greatest originality and indepen-
dence of mind, shaking off those bitter conceptions of man's
depravity that played so large a part in contemporary thought:
the doctrine that Augustine developed in his anti-Pelagian
writings, and which descended from him to find its place in
the ninth of the Thirty-Nine Articles of the English Church:

Original Sin standeth not in the following [i.e. the imitation]
of *Adam*, (as the *Pelagians* do vainly talk;) but it is the fault
and corruption of the Nature of every man, that naturally is
ingendered of the offspring of *Adam;* whereby man is very
far gone from original righteousness, and is of his own nature
inclined to evil, so that the flesh lusteth always contrary to
the spirit; and therefore in every person born into this world,
it deserveth God's wrath and damnation. And this infection
of nature doth remain, yea in them that are regenerated;
whereby the lust of the flesh . . . is not subject to the Law of

83

God. And although there is no condemnation for them that believe and are baptized, yet the Apostle doth confess, that concupiscence and lust hath of itself the nature of sin.

It is the view of man's plight summed up by Augustine in the fearsome chapter 22 of the last book of the *City of God,* where he shows how man is born in a state of "error and perverse affection": "For who does not know in what a mist of ignorance (as we see in infants) and with what a crew of vain desires (as we see in boys) all mankind enters this world . . . ?" That is why "little children" must be controlled by fear, by "rods, the strap, thongs, and suchlike": "what is the end of all these, but to abolish ignorance, and to bridle corruption, both of which we come wrapped into the world withal? What is our labour to remember things, our labour to learn, and our ignorance without this labour; our agility got by toil, and our dullness if we neglect it? Does it not all declare the promptness of our nature (in itself) unto all viciousness, and the care that must be had in reclaiming it?"[1]

Basing his belief upon his own experience, and supported by Augustine's doctrine of the interior light, Traherne's memories of his own childhood take up a deliberate stand against this view. The "eclipse" of his own "first Light" was caused, he declares, by the bad "Customs and maners of Men," and not by any compulsive inner depravity (3.7). On the contrary, Traherne's experience leads him to feel "how Docible our Nature is in natural Things, were it rightly entreated." He strongly believes that "our Misery proceedeth ten thousand times more from the outward Bondage of Opinion and Custom, then from any inward corruption or Depravation of Nature: And that it is not our Parents Loyns, so much as our Parents lives, that Enthrals and Blinds us." Of course he quickly adds that all our corruption is "Derived from Adam: inasmuch as all the Evil Examples and inclinations of the World arise from His Sin." Nevertheless, Traherne holds by the conviction

1. *City of God,* trans. Healey, 22.22.

gained from his own experience: "I speak it in the presence of GOD and of our Lord Jesus Christ, in my Pure Primitive Virgin Light, while my Apprehensions were natural, and unmixed, I can not remember, but that I was ten thousand times more prone to Good and Excellent Things, then evil. But I was quickly tainted and fell by others" (3.8).

Such a statement is deliberately bold, addressed to a world filled with Calvinist notions; it explicitly denies the common interpretation of the Augustinian doctrine of concupiscence: "it is not our Parents Loyns, so much as our Parents lives, that Enthrals and Blinds us." And yet, significantly, it is not far from the view expressed by Bonaventure at this stage of his treatise, for he, like Traherne, finds it "amazing," "when it is clear that God is so near to our minds, that there are so few who see the First Principle in themselves." But the reason, Bonaventure adds, is easy to find: "For the human mind, distracted by cares, does not enter into itself through memory; obscured by phantasms, it does not return into itself through intelligence; allured by concupiscence, it never returns to itself through the desire for inner sweetness and spiritual gladness" (p. 28). *Distracted, obscured, allured (distracta, obnubilata, illecta),* but not depraved: the full weight of the Augustinian doctrine of concupiscence is not allowed by Bonaventure to impede the potential of the mind. It could not be otherwise for one who has based his central view of the illumination of the human mind upon the view expressed in Augustine's early treatise, the *De Vera Religione,* which Bonaventure here cites by title and quotes in one of its most strikingly optimistic passages. Our knowledge of truth, says Bonaventure, "comes from the archetype in eternal art according to which things have an aptitude and a comportment toward one another by reason of the representation of that eternal art. As Augustine says in his *On True Religion,* 'The light of all who reason truly is kindled at that truth and strives to return to it'" (pp. 24–25). Bonaventure is here giving a free quotation from section 72 of this treatise, the conclusion of a passage in which Augustine declares that every man, through grace, is able to participate in the light of truth:

> What obstacle then remains to hinder the soul from recalling the primal beauty which it abandoned, when it can make an end of its vices? The Wisdom of God extends from end to end with might. By wisdom the great Artificer knit his works together with one glorious end in view. His goodness has no grudging envy against any beauty from the highest to the lowest, for none can have being except from him alone. So that no one is utterly cast away from the truth who has in him the slightest vestige of truth . . . Do not go abroad. Return within yourself. In the inward man dwells truth. If you find that you are by nature mutable, transcend yourself. But remember in doing so that you must also transcend yourself even as a reasoning soul. Make for the place where the light of reason is kindled. What does every good reasoner attain but truth?[2]

Indeed the whole treatise indicates the ways in which the earlier writings of Augustine provide a basis for the optimism displayed throughout Traherne's *Centuries*. The treatise begins by asserting that if Plato and his followers "could live their lives again to-day, they would see by whose authority measures are best taken for man's salvation, and, with the change of a few words and sentiments, they would become Christians, as many Platonists of recent times have done" (sec. 7). He then goes on to declare that the grace of God has made conversion to Christianity available to every man: "God in his ineffable mercy by a temporal dispensation has used the mutable creation, obedient however to his eternal laws, to remind the soul of its original and perfect nature, and so has come to the aid of individual men and indeed of the whole human race" (sec. 19). The optimistic point of view is summed up near the end with the words: "Let us therefore walk while we have the day, i.e., while we can use reason. Let us turn to God so that we may deserve to be illumined by his Word, the true light, and

2. *Earlier Writings,* p. 262.

that darkness may not take possession of us. Day is the presence of the 'light that lighteth every man coming into the world' (John 1:9), 'Every man,' says Scripture, meaning everyone who can use reason, and who, when he has fallen, can earnestly seek to rise" (sec. 79).[3]

This is the "Divine Light" by which, as Traherne remembers, he saw the world in his infancy, and it is still the light by which he now views the world with his "Highest Reason." In the view of Bonaventure, and of the early Augustine, the text of John 1:9 is universal in its application: Christ, the Word that was in the beginning, is "the true Light, which lighteth every man that cometh into the world"; *lux vera, quae illuminat omnem hominem venientem in hunc mundum.* There is nothing heretical or occult in Traherne's conviction that he came into the world with the illumination of the Divine Light.

That light illuminates even the "natural powers" that Bonaventure finds in the soul, as the title of his third chapter shows: "Of the Reflection of God in His Image Stamped upon our Natural Powers." The natural mind of man, uncommitted to Christian belief, contains within itself this breathing, generating force, which may be further developed, as Bonaventure says at the close of this chapter, by "the light of knowledge" found in "philosophy"—"either natural or rational or moral." The natural powers of man may be truly illuminated by the study of metaphysics, mathematics, and physics, grammar, logic, and rhetoric, and also by studies "monastic, economic, and political." For "all these sciences," Bonaventure insists, "have certain and infallible rules, like rays of light descending from the eternal law into our minds." And thus, he concludes, in a way very close to Traherne's belief that man's nature is highly "Docible in natural Things": "our minds, illumined and suffused by such great radiance, unless they be blind, can be led through themselves alone to the contemplation of that eternal light" (pp. 26–27).

It is this view of man's natural powers, restored by Christ,

3. Ibid., pp. 229, 235, 266.

that Traherne is presenting in the first half of his Third Century, which relates how the "Whispering Instinct of Nature" (3.16), based upon the glimmering memory of an "unknown Happiness" (3.15), led him to seek "with New and more vigorous Desires after that Bliss which Nature Whispered and Suggested to me" (3.22). This "natural" aspect of the soul's progress Traherne sums up in another didactic poem, "On News," which constitutes his Meditation 26:

> What Sacred Instinct did inspire
> My Soul in Childhood with a Hope so Strong?
> What Secret Force movd my Desire,
> To Expect my Joys beyond the Seas, so Yong?
> Felicity I knew
> Was out of View:
> And being here alone,
> I saw that Happiness was gone,
> From Me! for this,
> I Thirsted Absent Bliss . . .

In this spirit of expectation and desire he pursues his early studies and inquiries. First, in early childhood, by examining the world about him, he became convinced that he was made "to hold a Communion with the Secrets of Divine Providence in all the World: that a Remembrance of all the Joys I had from my Birth ought always to be with me" (3.23). Then, as he came to read the Bible, he came to understand "the Liveliness of interior presence, and that all Ages were for most Glorious Ends, Accessible to my Understanding, yea with it, yea within it" (3.24). Gradually, through long and ardent study of the Bible, he became satisfied with the manner in which that Book revealed the ways of God in all ages: "Thenceforth I thought the Light of Heaven was in this World: I saw it Possible, and very Probable, that I was infinitly Beloved of Almighty God, the Delights of Paradice were round about me, Heaven and Earth were open to me, all Riches were little Things, this one Pleasure being so Great that it exceeded all the Joys of Eden" (3.35).

To these studies were then added "the Taste and Tincture of another Education," at the University, where "I saw that Logick, Ethicks, Physicks, Metaphysicks, Geometry, Astronomy, Poesie, Medicine, Grammer, Musick, Rhetorick, all kind of Arts Trades and Mechanicismes that Adorned the World pertained to felicity." "At least," he adds, "there I saw those Things, which afterwards I knew to pertain unto it" (3.36). Actually, he admits, he did not learn at the university how these things pertained to felicity, for these things were, he says, studied only "as *Aliena*": "We Studied to inform our Knowledg, but Knew not for what End we so Studied" (3.37). Nevertheless it was all useful in "Clearing and preparing the Ey of the Enjoyer" (3.44), as we may see from his eloquent praise of his studies in "Humanity," that is, the "humanities":

> By Humanity we search into the Powers and Faculties of the Soul, enquire into the Excellencies of Humane Nature, consider its Wants, Survey its Inclinations Propensities and Desires. Ponder its Principles Proposals and Ends, Examine the Causes and fitness of all, the Worth of all, the Excellency of all. Wherby we com to know what Man is in this World, What his Soveraign End and Happiness, and what is the Best Means by which He may attain it. And by this we com to see what Wisdom is: Which namely is a Knowledg Exercised in finding out the Way to Perfect Happiness, by discerning Mans real Wants and Soveraign desires.   [3.42]

Thus "Humanity," as he sees it, leads into the study of "Divinity," that is, Theology, and finally—the order is significant of the tendency of seventeenth-century thought—to the study of "Natural Philosophy" and "Ethicks." The natural powers of man can do no more; in Meditation 45 the exploration of these powers ends with the warning that nothing will serve "to teach us the Infallibility of GODs Word or to shew us the Certainty of true Religion, without a Clear Sight into Truth it self that is into the Truth of Things."

So far, all has been tentative and preliminary: he has come so far as to see it "Possible, and very Probable, that I was infinitly Beloved of Almighty God" (3.35), but the certainty of faith still lies ahead: he has not yet committed himself to the full belief that leads toward Truth. This is the very point that Bonaventure makes as he opens his fourth chapter, explaining the second step in this middle stage of the threefold ascent: "Of the Reflection of God in His Image Reformed by the Gifts of Grace."

> Therefore, however much anyone is illuminated only by the light of nature and of acquired science, he cannot enter into himself that he may delight in the Lord in himself, unless Christ be his mediator, Who says, "I am the door. By me, if any man enter in, he shall be saved; and he shall go in, and go out, and shall find pastures" [John 10:9]. We do not, however, approach this door unless we believe in Him, hope in Him, and love Him. It is therefore necessary, if we wish to enter into the fruition of Truth, as into Paradise, that we enter through the faith, hope, and charity of the Mediator between God and man, Jesus Christ, Who is as the tree of life in the middle of Paradise. [pp. 28–29]

This further process of regeneration, in which "the image is repaired" by the "three theological virtues" (p. 29), is given its symbolical enactment by Traherne in a striking "parenthesis" that occurs near the middle of his Third Century, in Meditations 46–51. This interior action is thrown into sharp relief by being framed between the similar openings of Meditations 46 and 52:

> When I came into the Country, and being seated among silent Trees, had all my Time in mine own Hands, I resolved to Spend it all, whatever it cost me, in Search of Happiness, and to Satiat that burning Thirst which Nature had Enkindled, in me from my Youth. [3.46]

> When I came into the Country, and saw that I had all time in my own hands, having devoted it wholy to the study of Felicitie, I knew not where to begin or End; nor what Objects to chuse, upon which most Profitably I might fix my Contemplation. [3.52]

The experience enclosed within those two openings is, as Bonaventure says, one "which no one knoweth but he that receiveth it" (Rev. 2:17). "For it occurs in affective experience rather than in rational consideration" (p. 29). To convey that experience Traherne relies primarily upon three poems that constitute Meditations 47, 49, and 50. These consist mainly of conventional exclamations and pronouncements; but their versified form serves to emphasize the importance of the action there represented. It is the action of grace received through faith in Christ, leading to the renewal of inward vision, as Traherne suggests in Meditation 50, a Herbertian poem entitled "The Recovery":

> Sin! wilt Thou vanquish me!
> And shall I yeeld the victory?
> Shall all my Joys be Spoild,
> And Pleasures soild
> By Thee!
> Shall I remain
> As one thats Slain
> And never more lift up the Head?
> Is not my Savior Dead!
> His Blood, thy Bane; my Balsam, Bliss, Joy, Wine;
> Shall Thee Destroy; Heal, Feed, make me Divine.

"I cannot meet with Sin, but it Kils me," Traherne declares in Meditation 51, "and tis only by Jesus Christ that I can Kill it, and Escape." Sin, he adds, "breeds a long Parenthesis in the fruition of our Joys. Do you not see my Friend, how it Disorders and Disturbs my Proceeding?" The symbolic nature of this poetical digression is here stressed, and the reader is prepared to watch a new beginning, in which the meditative mind is "Guided by an Implicit Faith in Gods Goodness: and therfore led to the Study of the most Obvious and Common Things" (3.53). Under that guidance, as Bonaventure says, all things take on a new glory: "when by faith he believes in Christ . . . he recovers spiritual hearing and vision: hearing to receive the lessons of Christ, vision to look upon the splendor of His light"

(p. 29). In this way Traherne now considers the external universe and all the works and ways of God: "I believed that there were unspeakable Mysteries contained in them . . . These therfore I resolved to Study, and no other. But to my unspeakable Wonder, they brought me to all the Things in Heaven and in Earth, in Time and Eternity, Possible and Impossible, Great and Little, Common and Scarce, and Discovered them all to be infinit Treasures" (3.54).

All things are now seen as infinite treasures, because through faith he has come to find the place of everything "in Eternity, and in Gods Esteem." "Evry thing in its Place is Admirable Deep and Glorious: out of its Place like a Wandering Bird, is Desolat and Good for Nothing. How therfore it relateth to God and all Creatures must be seen before it can be Enjoyed" (3.55). Most important, he has now found the right way of enjoyment by "remembering that we were made in Gods Image" (3.58). "The Image of God implanted in us, guided me to the maner wherin we were to Enjoy. for since we were made in the similitud of God, we were made to Enjoy after his Similitude. Now to Enjoy the Treasures of God in the Similitud of God, is the most perfect Blessedness God could Devise" (3.59).

Upon this discovery, he says, "I was infinitly satisfied in God, and knew there was a Dietie, becaus I was satisfied" (3.59). The exact nature of this experience of "satisfaction" remains unexpressed and, apparently, inexpressible: all we know is that Traherne has received a brilliant glimpse of the essential image toward which all these meditations have been leading, and that as a result of that glimpse he has found himself "seated in a Throne of Repose and Perfect Rest" (3.60). For he now understands the immense powers of the image that lies within himself:

> The Image of God is the most Perfect Creature. . . . Able to see all Eternity with all its Objects, and as a Mirror to Contain all it seeth: Able to Lov all it contains, and as a Sun to shine upon its loves. Able by Shining to communicat it self in

Beams of Affection, and to Illustrat all it Illuminats with
Beauty and Glory: Able to be Wise Holy Glorious Blessed
in it self as God is, being adorned inwardly with the same
kind of Beauty, and outwardly Superior to all Creatures.

[3.61]

Thus the intuitive, Eden-like vision of his infancy has been
"Collected again, by the Highest Reason," illuminated by a
faith that leads to hope and charity: "Evry Thing being
Sublimely Rich and Great and Glorious. Evry Spire of Grass
is the Work of His Hand: And I in a World where evry Thing
is mine" (3.62). He has found the inward Paradise: the Similitude and Presence of God in the whole Creation.

This experience of renewal was so powerful, so miraculous,
that at first it seemed to him absolutely unique: "I was so
Ignorant that I did not think any Man in the World had had
such thoughts before. . . . but as I read the Bible I was here
and there Surprized with such Thoughts and found by Degrees
that these Things had been written of before, not only in the
Scriptures but in many of the fathers and that this was the Way
of Communion with God in all Saints, as I saw Clearly in the
Person of David." Under this new inspiration, "Me thoughts a
New Light Darted in into all his Psalmes, and finaly spread
abroad over the whole Bible" (3.66).

Again, the progress of the soul is in close accord with the
advice of Bonaventure, who notes that for "this grade of contemplation there is especially and outstandingly added as a
support the consideration of Holy Scripture divinely issued, as
philosophy was added to the preceding. For Holy Scripture is
principally concerned with the works of reparation" (p. 31).
Thus Traherne, reading the Bible in this "New Light," is
brought into the "very Heart" of God's Kingdom, and, like
Henry Vaughan, grasps the meaning of those "early days"
revealed in the Old Testament, as he shows in the climactic
Meditation 67:

There I saw Moses blessing the Lord for the Precious Things

93

of Heaven, for the Dew and for the Deep that coucheth beneath: . . . There I saw Jacob, with Awfull Apprehensions Admiring the Glory of the World, when awaking out of His Dream he said, How dreadfull is this Place? This is none other then the Hous of GOD, and the Gate of Heaven. There I saw GOD leading forth Abraham, and shewing him the Stars of Heaven; and all the Countries round about him, and saying All these will I give Thee, and thy Seed after thee. There I saw Adam in Paradice, surrounded with the Beauty of Heaven and Earth, void of all Earthly Comforts to wit such as were devised, Gorgeous Apparel, Palaces, Gold and Silver, Coaches, Musical Instruments &c, And entertained only with Celestial Joys. The sun and moon and stars, Beasts and fowles and fishes, Trees and fruits and flowers, with the other Naked and simple Delights of Nature. By which I evidently saw, that the Way to becom Rich and Blessed, was not by heaping Accidental and Devised Riches to make ourselvs great in the vulgar maner, but to approach more near, and to see more Clearly with the Ey of our understanding, the Beauties and Glories of the whole world: and to hav communion with the Diety in the Riches of GOD and Nature.

That meditation, along with the abstract summation of his discoveries in Meditation 68, marks the conclusion of his autobiographical memories, and demonstrates by its Adamic imagery the way in which his mind has journeyed backward and inward to reach the state of "childhood" set as his goal in Meditation 5. There he had presented his aim in these words: "Our Saviors Meaning, when He said, He must be Born again and becom a little Child that will enter into the Kingdom of Heaven: is Deeper far then is generaly believed." That verse from John (3:3), he says, indicates a need to achieve "the Peace and Purity of all our Soul." And this purity is also "a Deeper Thing then is commonly apprehended." For it means that "all our Thoughts must be Infant-like and Clear: the Powers of our Soul free from the Leven of this World, and disentangled from mens conceits and customs." To return to childhood in this sense, then, means that "Ambitions, Trades,

Luxuries, inordinat Affections, Casual and Accidental Riches invented since the fall would be gone, and only those Things appear, which did to Adam in Paradise, in the same Light, and in the same Colors. GOD in His Works, Glory in the Light, Lov in our Parents, Men, our selvs, and the Face of Heaven. Evry Man naturaly seeing those Things, to the Enjoyment of which He is Naturaly Born" (3.5). Thus, from beginning to end, his autobiography is founded upon the central symbol of the unfallen Adam, who knew by intuition the enjoyment of Felicity that Traherne has now recovered by Reason.

The remainder of the Third Century is a grand finale of praise and thanksgiving, performed by returning to the Biblical figure mentioned in Meditation 66: David the Psalmist. This final movement opens with a long poem in praise of David, constituting Meditation 69; but again the poem is a piece of labored didacticism, where the virtues of David are merely asserted. Meditation 70 provides a much better opening for the final sequence by attaching it firmly to the mode of reminiscence in which the topic of the Psalms had earlier been broached:

> you cannot imagine how unspeakably I was delighted, to see so Glorious a Person, so Great a Prince, so Divine a Sage, that was a Man after Gods own Heart by the testimony of God Himself, rejoycing in the same things, meditating on the same and Praising GOD for the same. For by this I perceived we were led by one Spirit: and that following the clew of Nature into this Labyrinth I was brought into the midst of Celestial Joys: and that to be retired from Earthly Cares and fears and Distractions that we might in sweet and heavenly Peace contemplat all the Works of GOD, was to live in Heaven and the only way to becom what David was a Man after Gods own Heart. [3.70]

In Meditations 71–94 Traherne proceeds to compose what might be called a duet of praise, with lavish quotations from the Psalms providing the melody, while Traherne's commentary brings in the second voice. He ranges through the book of Psalms, pointing out in sequence those passages that best display the Psalmist's ways of finding God in all his works. For the most part he follows the King James version, but with frequent adaptation, sometimes influenced by the phrasing of the Prayer Book version.[4] Traherne has brought the Psalms into the center of his own mind and memory, with the result that his own voice is sometimes almost inseparably interfused with the voice of the Psalmist, as we may see from the conclusion of Meditation 76, where the last sentence represents Traherne's commentary upon the preceding passage from Psalm 36:

> How Excellent is Thy Loving Kindness O God! therfore the Children of Men put their Trust under the Shadow of thy Wings. They shall be abundantly satisfied with the fatness of thy Hous; and Thou shalt make them Drink of the River of thy Pleasures. For with Thee is the fountain of Life. In thy Light we shall see Light. The Judgments of God, and his Loving Kindness, His Mercy and faithfulness, are the fatness of his Hous, and his Righteousness being seen in the Light of Glory is the Torrent of Pleasure at His right hand for evermore.

In this manner Traherne gradually creates a double symbol of the ways in which the Image of God may be restored by "Joyfull Meditation," for his summary of the meaning of the Psalms will apply both to "David" and to Traherne's own hopes:

> His Soul recovered its Pristine Liberty and saw thorow the Mud Walls of flesh and Blood. Being alive, he was in the Spirit all his Days, while his Body therfore was inclosed in this World his Soul was in the Temple of Eternity . . . Kingdoms and Ages did surround him, as clearly as the Hills and Mountains: and therfore the Kingdom of God was ever round about Him.   [3.95]

---

4. Cf. Margoliouth's notes to this portion of the *Centuries*.

8. *Divine Principles: The Fourth Century*

The key to Traherne's Fourth Century is contained in its opening sentence: "Having spoken so much concerning his Enterance and Progress in Felicity, I will in this Centurie speak of the Principles with which your friend endued Himself to enjoy it!" The word "principles" is repeated approximately fifty times in the course of the Century, often with clustered repetitions that give it a strong thematic emphasis: "I speak not His Practices but His Principles. I should too much Prais your friend did I speak his Practices, but it is no shame for any man to declare his Principles, tho they are the most Glorious in the world. Rather they are to be Shamed that have no Glorious Principles: or that are ashamed of them. This he desired me to tell you becaus of Modesty" (4.30).

The manner of the writing and the thematic word both point in the same direction: in this Century Traherne is attempting to move beyond the limitations of personal experience and to grasp the essential principles of a life lived in the presence of God, with the Image of God restored as fully as possible within this life. Consequently, he here attempts to project an ideal image of his best possible self, and he speaks of that projected self as though it were another person: "This he desired me to tell you becaus of Modesty." "He from whom I received these things . . ." (4.20). "He from whom I derived these things . . ." (4.66). The dominant mode of the writing is thus in the third person, as contrasted with the intimate autobiography of the Third Century—and yet the personal "I" is always breaking through to make it clear that the "friend" and the "He" are ideal projections of the man who has revealed himself in the previous Century:

It was your friends Delight to Meditat the Principles of Upright Nature: and to see how things stood in Paradice before they were Muddied and Blended and Confounded. for

97

now they are lost and buried in Ruines. Nothing appearing but fragments, that are worthless shreds and Parcels of them. To see the Intire Piece ravisheth the Angels. It was his Desire to recover them and to Exhibit them again to the Eys of Men.

[4.54]

They are the very principles that Traherne remembers from his infancy: "Abov all things he desired to see those Principles which a Stranger in this World would covet to behold upon his first appearance." For these are the principles by which men today may learn "to liv Blessedly." "He found them very Easy, and infinitly Noble . . . We hav named them, and they are such as these, A Man should Know the Blessings he enjoyeth. A Man should prize the Blessings which he Knoweth. A Man should be Thankfull for the Benefits which he prizeth. A Man should rejoyce in that for which He is Thankfull" (4.54).

Margoliouth (1, 281–84) discerns twenty-five such principles distributed throughout the Fourth Century, but all these may be summed up in the one paramount principle which breaks through in the splendidly personal terms of Meditation 61:

> Since Lov will thrust in it self as the Greatest of all Principles, let us at last willingly allow it Room. I was once a Stranger to it, now I am familiar with it as a Daily acquaintance. Tis the only Heir and Benefactor of the World. It seems it will break in evry where, as that without which the World could not be Enjoyed. Nay as that without which it would not be Worthy to be Enjoyed. for it was Beautified by Lov, and commandeth the Lov of a Donor to us. Lov is a Phaenix that will revive in its own Ashes, inherit Death, and smell sweetly in the Grave.

Thus the ultimate wisdom found by the "Divine Philosopher" lies in the discovery of Love. The true Philosopher, Traherne says, is he who "having seen the Secrets, and the Secret Beauties of the Highest reason, orders his Conversation, and lives by Rule: tho in this Age, it be held never so strange that He should do so. Only He is Divine becaus he does this upon Noble Principles, Becaus GOD is, becaus Heaven is, becaus Jesus Christ hath Redeemd him, and becaus he Lovs Him" (4.8). Since Love lies at the center of the universe, "those Principles that relate to Communication are more Excellent" than those that relate to "Enjoyment" in a solitary way (4.18). But indeed "Communication" is itself a higher form of Enjoyment: "He generaly held, that Whosoever would enjoy the Happiness of Paradice must put on the Charity of Paradice" (4.22). All happiness, he says, lies in that diffusion of Love found in the operation of the Trinity: "God and he are to becom one Spirit, that is one in Will, and one in desire. Christ must liv within him. He must be filled with the H. Ghost which is the God of Lov" (4.28).

Through participation in this Principle of Love man comes to participate in "the Superlative Bounty of GOD," in the endless, infinite emanation of his "Goodness" (4.46). For Love "is an interminable Sphere, which as som say of the Sun, is infinities infinita, in the Extention of its Beams, being equaly vigorous in all Places, equaly near to all Objects, Equaly Acceptable to all Persons, and equaly abundant in all its Overflowings" (4.66). He is speaking here of "Naked and Divested Lov in its true Perfection," that "Lov in the Abstract" which, he says, "is a Soul exerted" (4.70).

> Its Greatness is Spiritual, like the Dieties. It filleth the World, and exceeds what it filleth. It is present with all Objects, and Tasts all Excellencies, and meeteth the Infinitness of GOD in evry Thing. So that in Length it is infinit as well as in Bredth, being equaly vigorous at the utmost Bound to which it can extend as here, and as wholy there as here and wholy evry where. Thence also it can see into further Spaces, Things present and Things to come Hight and Depth being open before it, and all things in Heaven Eternity and Time equaly near. [4.66]

Participating in this power, man comes to know the oneness, the unity, "the Simplicity of God" (4.65). What Pico said in his account of human dignity is true: "that Man by retiring from all Externals and withdrawing into Him self, in the centre of his own Unity becometh most like unto GOD" (4.81). For the soul participates in the Love of God both as a mirror and as a fountain: it both reflects the beams of love, and sends forth those beams from a source deep within the self (4.84–85). "All this Goodness is so like Gods, that Nothing can be more" (4.85).

By "frequent Meditation" on these principles, Traherne concludes, one at last becomes "familiar with them" (4.96) and comes to grasp the "Infinit Extent of the Understanding and Affection of the Soul," which can reach out to comprehend those infinite "Wonderfull Things" that Traherne sums up in the abstraction of the perfect number, ten:

> 1. A manifestation of GODs infinit Lov. 2. The Possession of infinit Treasures. 3. a Return of infinit Thanksgivings. 4. A Fulnes of Joy which nothing can exceed. 5. an infinit Beauty and Greatness in the Soul. 6. An infinit Beauty in GODs Kingdom. 7. an Infinit Union between GOD and the soul, (as well in Extent, as fervor.) 8. An Exact fitness between the Powers of the Soul and its Objects . . . 9. An Infinit Glory in the Communion of Saints . . . 10. A Perfect Indwelling of the Soul in GOD, and GOD in the Soul.   [4.100]

Thus Traherne, in his Fourth Century, has carried through the process of intellection represented in the third stage of Bonaventure's journey, and set forth in chapters 5 and 6 of the *Itinerarium*. The whole effort of this final stage is to carry the mind as far as reason can be carried—moving ever closer to ultimate Truth by a process of refinement through abstraction. This is possible, says Bonaventure, "through His light, which has signed upon our minds the light of eternal Truth, since the mind itself is immediately formed by Truth itself" (p. 34). Therefore the mind is able to seek God by inquiring into the "essential attributes" of God and into the "properties" of the Trinity. These things may be summed up, says Bonaventure, in two "names": Being and Good *(esse* and *bonum)*. In chapter 5 he explains how man may fix the mind's gaze upon "purest Being itself": "Being primary, eternal, most simple, most actual, most perfect, and one to the highest degree" (p. 36).

Having grasped these attributes of Being, the mind moves on to grasp the meaning of Good, which lies in the "self-diffusive" power of the Trinity, its power of "communicability":

> If then you can look with the mind's eye upon the purity of goodness, which is the pure actualization of the principle of Charity, pouring forth free and due love, and both mingled together, which is the fullest diffusion according to nature and will—the diffusion as Word, in which all things are expressed, and as Gift, in which all other gifts are given—you may see by the highest communicability of the Good that a Trinity of Father and Son and Holy Spirit is necessary. [p. 40]

In the consideration of this "principle of Charity," summed up in the Incarnation of the Son, Bonaventure finds "the perfection of the mind's illumination" (p. 42).

9. Repose: The Fifth Century

Nothing more remains "save the day of rest," the state of mystical repose, which Bonaventure describes in the seventh and last chapter of his *Itinerarium:* "Of Mental and Mystical Elevation, in which Repose is Given to the Intellect when the Affections Pass Entirely into God through Elevation." "In this passage, if it is perfect," says Bonaventure, "all intellectual operations should be abandoned, and the whole height of our affection should be transferred and transformed into God" (p. 44).

So, in the ten meditations of the Fifth Century, Traherne suggests, with an ultimate refinement of abstraction, how the soul of man finds its proper home in the Infinity, Eternity, and

Omnipresence of God:[1] "there is a Space also wherin all Moments are infinitly Exhibited, and the Everlasting Duration of infinit Space is another Region and Room of Joys" (5.6). "But the infinit immovable Duration is Eternitie, the Place and Duration of all Things even of Infinit Space it self: the Cause and End, the Author and Beautifier, the Life and Perfection of all" (5.7). "The Essence of God therfore being all Light and Knowledg, Lov and Goodness, Care and Providence, felicity and Glory, a Pure and simple Act; it is present in its Operations, and by those Acts which it eternaly exerteth, is wholly Busied in all Parts and places of his Dominion, perfecting and compleating our Bliss and Happiness" (5.10). After those closing words, the solitary numeral, 11, stands at the head of a blank page in the manuscript, followed by 49 blank leaves.

"In spite of this numerical heading for another section," Margoliouth has said (*1, 297*), "and in spite of Traherne's obvious idea of writing 'The fifth Centurie' I cannot but look on V. 10 as a triumphant and perfect conclusion. How could Traherne have gone beyond it? The *Centuries* are not unfinished." Another way of summing up this sense of completion would be to say that the conclusion lies in the eloquent silence of those blank pages, suggesting the "darkness of instructive silence" described by "Dionysius the Areopagite" in a quotation given by Bonaventure near the close of his seventh chapter: a darkness and silence "in which all is aglow, pouring out upon the invisible intellects the splendors of invisible goodness." Seen from this point of view, that solitary numeral, 11, seems to reach out toward the silence of mystical repose.

1. For Traherne's conception of the Infinite, see the important article by Rosalie L. Colie, *Huntington Library Quarterly, 21* (1957), 69–82.

III

PARADISE LOST
The Journey of the Mind

It was your friends Delight to Meditat the Principles of Upright Nature: and to see how things stood in Paradice before they were Muddied and Blended and Confounded. for now they are lost and buried in Ruines. Nothing appearing but fragments, that are worthless shreds and Parcels of them. To see the Intire Piece ravisheth the Angels. It was his Desire to recover them and to Exhibit them again to the Eys of Men.

—Traherne, *Centuries,* 4.54

Hear the voice of the Bard!
Who Present, Past, & Future, sees;
Whose ears have heard
The Holy Word
That walk'd among the ancient trees ...

—Blake, *Songs of Experience*

1. The Voice of the Bard

TRAHERNE'S "Eye of Reason" and the inward, irradiated vision of the bard in *Paradise Lost* are both devoted to recovering the same essential image of "Peace and Purity." "Which Purity," says Traherne in the *Centuries,* "is a Deeper Thing then is commonly apprehended," for it consists in a state of mind in which "Ambitions, Trades, Luxuries, inordinat Affections, Casual and Accidental Riches invented since the fall would be gone, and only those Things appear, which did to Adam in Paradice, in the same Light, and in the same Colors. GOD in His Works, Glory in the Light, Lov in our Parents, Men, our selvs, and the Face of Heaven. Evry Man naturaly seeing those Things, to the Enjoyment of which He is Naturaly Born" (3.5). Such a renewal of human vision is the central theme of *Paradise Lost;* the title does not suggest simply regret and nostalgia for what is lost: it suggests that what has been lost may also be found, that man, as Augustine had said, "has the power to remember"[1] the presence and the bounty of God.

In this theme of recovery we may find one reason why the voice of the bard, the presence of the poet, looms so large in Milton's poem, exercising what Frank Kermode has called "the epic poet's privilege of intervening in his own voice."[2] That voice is of course most obvious in the great prologues that open Books 1, 3, 7, and 9, prologues carefully spaced so that we never lose sight of this human composer, who tells us of his hopes and aims, and of his blindness, and of how he sings

1. See above, Preface, note 11.
2. See his important essay, "Adam Unparadised," in *The Living Milton,* ed. Frank Kermode (New York, Macmillan, 1961), p. 106.

<blockquote>
unchang'd
To hoarce or mute, though fall'n on evil dayes,
On evil dayes though fall'n, and evil tongues;
. In darkness, and with dangers compast round,
And solitude; yet not alone . . .   [7.24–28]
</blockquote>

He tells us too his views on the proper "Subject for Heroic Song," and how this subject "Pleas'd me long choosing, and beginning late," and how he fears that the "cold Climat" of his land or his own advanced years may "damp" the writing of his song (9.25–47).

These personal touches are no mere self-indulgence: they have a function—to remind us, intimately, that this poem is an action of thoughts within a central, controlling intelligence that moves with inward eyes toward a recovery of Paradise. Thus at the outset of Book 3 the bard emerges at the center of the action, Satan's human antagonist, as he takes us out of Hell and Chaos into the creative Light and for a time dominates the poem by the intimate repetition of his personal "I," "my," "me," given in a tone utterly different from that of Satan's ego-centered "I":

<blockquote>
Hail holy light, ofspring of Heav'n first-born,
Or of th' Eternal Coeternal beam
May I express thee unblam'd? . . .
Thee I re-visit now with bolder wing,
Escap't the <i>Stygian</i> Pool, though long detain'd
In that obscure sojourn, while in my flight
Through utter and through middle darkness borne
With other notes then to th' <i>Orphean</i> Lyre
I sung of <i>Chaos</i> and <i>Eternal Night,</i>
Taught by the heav'nly Muse to venture down
The dark descent, and up to reascend,
Though hard and rare: thee I revisit safe,
And feel thy sovran vital Lamp; but thou
Revisit'st not these eyes, that rowle in vain
To find thy piercing ray, and find no dawn;
So thick a drop serene hath quencht thir Orbs,
Or dim suffusion veild.   [3.1–26]
</blockquote>

These are the words of a poet well aware of his hopes for a place in the great tradition of bard and prophet; but he speaks here not as a hierophant in his heavy ritual robes; these are rather the words of a suffering and highly individual man, conversing with himself in the presence of God:

> Then feed on thoughts, that voluntarie move
> Harmonious numbers; as the wakeful Bird
> Sings darkling, and in shadiest Covert hid
> Tunes her nocturnal Note. Thus with the Year
> Seasons return, but not to me returns
> Day, or the sweet approach of Ev'n or Morn,
> Or sight of vernal bloom, or Summers Rose,
> Or flocks, or herds, or human face divine;

(*divine* still, with all its present deterioration, since the interior light still gives it beauty:)

> So much the rather thou Celestial light
> Shine inward, and the mind through all her powers
> Irradiate, there plant eyes, all mist from thence
> Purge and disperse, that I may see and tell
> Of things invisible to mortal sight.   [3.37–55]

These prologues are only the most prominent places where this individual voice of the bard appears; they help to remind us that this voice is indeed everywhere in the poem, advising, exhorting, warning, praising, denouncing, lamenting, promising, judging, in all ways guiding us (or, as some have complained, attempting to manipulate us)[3] by his strong evaluative comments. Sometimes he speaks quietly, as when he wryly warns:

3. See, for example, A. J. A. Waldock, *Paradise Lost and Its Critics* (Cambridge University Press, 1947), pp. 77–83, where Waldock objects to the "long line of automatic snubs, of perfunctory jabs and growls," and the "running fire of belittling commentary," leveled by Milton against Satan and the fallen angels in the first two books. For a favorable view of Milton's constant use of evaluative adjectives, see Isabel Gamble MacCaffrey, *Paradise Lost as "Myth"* (Cambridge, Mass., Harvard University Press, 1959), pp. 102–07.

> Let none admire
> That riches grow in Hell; that soyle may best
> Deserve the pretious bane.   [1.690–92]

At other times more violently, as when he cries:

> O shame to men! Devil with Devil damn'd
> Firm concord holds, men onely disagree
> Of Creatures rational, though under hope
> Of heavenly Grace . . .   [2.496–99]

Or we find him setting forth vehemently his independent views on wedded love in Paradise,

> Whatever Hypocrites austerely talk
> Of puritie and place and innocence . . . [4.744–45]

Or, in more than one place, we find him participating spontaneously in the immediate action, to a point where he seems to ignore or forget the other actions and assertions of his poem.[4] Thus, at the beginning of Book 4:

> O for that warning voice, which he who saw
> Th' *Apocalyps,* heard cry in Heav'n aloud,
> Then when the Dragon, put to second rout,
> Came furious down to be reveng'd on men,
> *Wo to the inhabitants on Earth!* that now,
> While time was, our first Parents had bin warnd
> The coming of thir secret foe, and scap'd
> Haply so scap'd his mortal snare; for now
> *Satan,* now first inflam'd with rage, came down,
> The Tempter ere th' Accuser of man-kind,
> To wreck on innocent frail man his loss
> Of that first Battel, and his flight to Hell:

But Adam is to be warned at length by Raphael, and we have just been told by God himself that man is not frail: "I made

4. See the examples of "artistic opportunism" cited by John Peter, *A Critique of Paradise Lost* (New York, Columbia University Press, 1960), pp. 33–34.

him just and right, / Sufficient to have stood, though free to
fall" (3.98–99). And again, after the Fall, we hear the bard
emphatically declaring:

> what can scape the Eye
> Of God All-seeing, or deceave his Heart
> Omniscient, who in all things wise and just,
> Hinder'd not *Satan* to attempt the minde
> Of Man, with strength entire, and free Will arm'd,
> Complete to have discover'd and repulst
> Whatever wiles of Foe or seeming Friend.   [10.5–11]

Far from manipulating his readers, the bard himself seems
rather to be guided by the revelations of the action as he
explores the way toward Eden: in the terms of Mark Schorer,
technique is discovery:[5] in the act of creation the poet discovers
the true, developing nature of his own response. Thus in Book
3 his voice seems subtly to emerge at the close of the angelic
hymn in Heaven, praising the offer of the Son of God to sacrifice himself for mankind's good:

> O unexampl'd love,
> Love no where to be found less then Divine!
> Hail Son of God, Saviour of Men, thy Name
> Shall be the copious matter of my Song
> Henceforth, and never shall my Harp thy praise
> Forget, nor from thy Fathers praise disjoine.
>   [3.410–15]

Likewise, at the close of the great morning-psalm in Paradise,
the individual voice of the bard seems to join the voices of
Adam and Eve:

> Witness if I be silent, Morn or Eeven,
> To Hill, or Valley, Fountain, or fresh shade
> Made vocal by my Song, and taught his praise.
>   [5.202–04]

5. See Schorer's essay, "Technique as Discovery," *Hudson Review, 1*
(1948), 67–87.

Thus everywhere in the poem we hear this human, flexible, responsive voice of an individual living in a great tradition, interpreting the discoveries of his "unpremeditated Verse," and encouraging us to read the poem as the progress of an interior journey, toward the center of the soul.

2. *The Earthly City*

Consider the development of the first four books: from Satan and the fallen angels in Hell upward through Chaos toward the light of Heaven and then on toward the vision of Paradise on earth. Literally, as we follow Satan's voyage to earth, we may seem to perform a journey forward in time, moving from Hell to the new earth. Yet from another standpoint, we are performing a more significant journey backward in time, from the fallen world of the first two books toward the pristine, earlier world of Book 4: a journey backward toward the sort of purity that Traherne described when he spoke of putting aside those things so notable in Milton's Hell: "Ambitions, Trades, Luxuries, inordinat Affections, Casual and Accidental Riches invented since the fall"—putting these things aside in order to penetrate toward a vision of the world as it appeared "to Adam in Paradice, in the same Light, and in the same Colors."[1] And if it is a journey backward it is also a journey inward, from the fallen world of everyday toward that center of remembrance where, as Milton's colleague, Peter Sterry, said, the soul may experience "an awakening by reason of the primitive Image of pure Nature raising it self by degrees, and sparkling through the *Rubbish,* the confusions of the present state."[2]

This effect of a journey backward and inward is created largely by the imagistic action of the opening books, most notably in that immense roll call of evil that dominates the

1. *Centuries,* 3.5.
2. Sterry, *Discourse,* p. 99.

middle of the first book. Milton's device of calling the roll of fallen angels under the names of the later false gods has the effect of gradually dissolving our consciousness of Hell as any special place, and instead we find ourselves watching the operations of evil as it spreads itself out over the face of the earth:

> First *Moloch,* horrid King besmear'd with blood
> Of human sacrifice, and parents tears,
> Though for the noyse of Drums and Timbrels loud
> Their childrens cries unheard, that past through fire
> To his grim Idol. Him the *Ammonite*
> Worshipt in *Rabba* and her watry Plain,
> In *Argob* and in *Basan,* to the stream
> Of utmost *Arnon.* . . .
> Next *Chemos,* th' obscene dread of *Moabs* Sons,
> From *Aroer* to *Nebo,* and the wild
> Of Southmost *Abarim;* in *Hesebon*
> And *Horonaim, Seons* Realm, beyond
> The flowry Dale of *Sibma* clad with Vines,
> And *Eleale* to th' *Asphaltick* Pool.   [1.392–411]

Every name here has of course its concrete and evocative identity in the Old Testament, including even here some promise of redemption, for, as Merritt Hughes has noted, every name connotes "the defeat of some gentile deity by Jehovah."[3] Yet the names create their major effect without recognition of their specific biblical context: they locate the action in the world of watery plains and flowery dales and vines and slimy pools. What Milton gives, then, in this roll call is a summation of all human vice, depravity, and irreligion, enacted in the landscapes of the earth.

It is the world we know, the world conveyed with equal vividness through the working of Milton's epic similes, whose subtle interrelations with his theme and action have been successfully shown by many critical readings.[4] Thus in the great

3. See *Paradise Lost,* ed. Merritt Hughes (New York, Odyssey Press, 1935), p. 24.

4. See James Whaler, "The Miltonic Simile," *PMLA, 46* (1931), 1034–

cluster of comparisons (1.286–313) that comes just before the roll call of devils, the reference to the moon as a "spotty Globe" indicates a universe where decay has already set in; *"Vallombrosa"* adumbrates the valley of the shadow of death; *"Etrurian* shades" evoke some ghostly images of a civilization long dead; *"Orion* arm'd" suggests the retributive justice of God, whose power is immediately after this displayed by reference to the destruction of the Egyptian host in the Red Sea. These are the tentacles of association and implication by which the forces of evil are bound to earth; and these ties are essential in maintaining the unity of the poem. Yet, curiously, these ties, having performed their function, are not the matters that remain foremost in mind after the reading: what vividly remains is rather the sharp and sometimes tenuously relevant imagery of the actual world. Despite all that has been said about Milton's lack of "particularity," it is not some vague astronomer who views that moon resembling Satan's shield: it is the famous *"Tuscan* Artist," viewing the moon "from the top of *Fesole,* / Or in *Valdarno."* It is not simply some tall pine to which Satan's spear is compared: it is a pine "Hewn on *Norwegian* hills, to be the Mast / Of some great Ammiral." The fallen angels on the lake are not simply compared with fallen autumnal leaves, but with those particular leaves "that strow the Brooks / In *Vallombrosa,* where th' *Etrurian* shades / High overarch't imbowr." It is not Pharaoh and his Egyptian chivalry, but specifically, *"Busiris* and his *Memphian* Chivalrie." And the pursued Israelites are, specifically, the "Sojourners of *Goshen."* These particular details cling to the mind long after the basis for their introduction has been forgotten.

The ultimate effect of all these similes, then, is simple and sensuous: they serve, like the roll call, to settle us within a world we know, as in that famous simile of the Leviathan, to which the vague floating figure of Satan is compared:

> Him haply slumbring on the *Norway* foam
> The Pilot of some small night-founder'd Skiff,
> Deeming some Island, oft, as Sea-men tell,
> With fixed Anchor in his skaly rind
> Moors by his side under the Lee, while Night
> Invests the Sea, and wished Morn delayes:
> So stretcht out huge in length the Arch-fiend lay . . .
> [1.203–09]

In a manner characteristic of these similes, the mind has moved so far away from the initial, alleged basis of the comparison that the sudden return to the literal basis strikes the reader with surprise and even amusement; but the sleight-of-hand works, as the deceptive qualities of Satan are set to work within the world of men—a world that has its moments of peace and beauty, along with its turmoil and deformity.

Such an effect is perhaps even more obvious in the brilliant simile that appears in Book 2, just as the Satanic parliament is adjourning:

> Thus they thir doubtful consultations dark
> Ended rejoycing in thir matchless Chief:
> As when from mountain tops the dusky clouds
> Ascending, while the North wind sleeps, o'respread
> Heavn's chearful face, the lowring Element
> Scowls ore the dark'nd lantskip Snow, or showre;
> If chance the radiant Sun with farewell sweet
> Extend his ev'ning beam, the fields revive,
> The birds thir notes renew, and bleating herds
> Attest thir joy, that hill and valley rings. [2.486–95]

The action moves, suddenly, to the world we know; and thus the similes of the first two books come to include the varied landscapes of the earth, and all the world's activities. They include war and the literature of war, as when Satan stands before his hosts in pride and Milton compares this army with

the "Heroic Race . . . That fought at *Theb's* and *Ilium*" and
recalls everything that resounds

> In Fable or *Romance* of *Uthers* Son
> Begirt with *British* and *Armoric* Knights;
> And all who since, Baptiz'd or Infidel
> Jousted in *Aspramont* or *Montalban*,
> *Damasco*, or *Marocco*, or *Trebisond*,
> Or whom *Biserta* sent from *Afric* shore
> When *Charlemain* with all his Peerage fell
> By *Fontarabbia*.   [1.580–87]

They include the superstitions of the English peasant, with his
moonlight elves; the barbarian hordes that overran the Roman
Empire; and the great fleets that carry the world's trade:

> As when farr off at Sea a Fleet descri'd
> Hangs in the Clouds, by *Aequinoctial* Winds
> Close sailing from *Bengala*, or the Iles
> Of *Ternate* and *Tidore*, whence Merchants bring
> Thir spicie Drugs: they on the trading Flood
> Through the wide *Ethiopian* to the Cape
> Ply stemming nightly toward the Pole.   [2.636–42]

Those similes will penetrate even to the remotest regions of
India or China, however great the strain may be upon the
comparison's congruity: thus Limbo too must have its earthly
setting:

> As when a Vultur on *Imaus* bred,
> Whose snowie ridge the roving *Tartar* bounds,
> Dislodging from a Region scarce of prey
> To gorge the flesh of Lambs or yeanling Kids
> On Hills where Flocks are fed, flies toward the Springs
> Of *Ganges* or *Hydaspes*, *Indian* streams;
> But in his way lights on the barren plaines
> Of *Sericana*, where *Chineses* drive
> With Sails and Wind thir canie Waggons light:
> So on this windie Sea of Land, the Fiend
> Walk'd up and down alone bent on his prey . . .
>   [3.431–41]

The implications of the threat to Eden are indeed beautifully congruent—and yet the main vigor of the simile resides in those irrelevant Chineses and their Waggons; irrelevant to Satan's immediate situation, but highly important in extending the range of the poem's geography and the scope of its human ingenuities.

To all these comparisons one must of course add the impact of those huge symbolic scenes of worldly activity: the building of the renaissance or baroque palace of Pandemonium; the Council of Satan and his Peers, with all the familiar political maneuvers; and the arts and exploits displayed by the fallen angels after the Council adjourns: feats of "Olympian Games," music of harp and song, philosophic reasoning "Of Providence, Foreknowledge, Will, and Fate," expeditions of discovery "O're many a Frozen, many a Fierie Alpe."[5]

The range and the exactitude of all these images, whether in epic simile or in literary allusion or in metaphorical tableau, succeed in creating a double action for the first four books. Literally, the action moves from Hell, through Chaos in Book 2, to Heaven in Book 3, and then at last to earth in Book 4. But more deeply, more essentially, the action moves from the world we know toward the inward Light by which man is enabled to see a Paradise that lies within the center of the poem and within the center of the mind and memory. It is a brilliant poetical strategy. The eyes of the imagination, looking back over the first two books from the vantage point of Paradise, can see a thousand varied images of the world we know, imbedded in a "darkness visible," licked on all sides by flame, " 'Twixt upper, nether, and surrounding Fires." Thus the literal, initial impact of these opening books becomes subtly inverted. Literally, we may say, these images from the fallen world are used to describe Hell and the fallen angels, to give them body and actuality. But essentially this whole fiery setting in Hell

5. Cf. MacCaffrey, pp. 181–84; and the detailed study of Milton's Hell by J. B. Broadbent, *Some Graver Subject* (London, Chatto and Windus, 1960), pp. 80–124.

becomes a vast metaphor by which Milton interprets the actions of the world we know. It is from this world that Milton's bard performs a journey backward and inward, toward the Light, leaving behind that city of false love described by Augustine:

> And so the two cities have been fashioned by two loves, the earthly city by the love of self to the contempt of God, the heavenly city by the love of God to the contempt of self. In a word, the one glories in itself, the other in the Lord; the one looks for glory from men; to the other God, who is the witness of its good conscience, is its greatest glory. The one in its own glory lifts up its head; the other says to its God 'Thou art my glory and Thou art he who lifts up my head.' Lust for domination dominates the one, as is shown by its rulers and the nations which it subjugates; in the other rulers and ruled alike serve one another in love, rulers taking thought for their subjects and their subjects rendering obedience to their rulers. The one loves its own earthly strength in its potentates; the other says to its God 'I will love thee, O Lord, my strength.' Hence the wise men and philosophers of the one city lived by the standards of men; they either pursued the goods of their bodies or of their minds or the goods of both; or else, when they were able to know God, did not honour Him as God nor render thanks to Him; their speculations have come to nothing and their foolish hearts have been clouded over. They have said that they were wise (that is, they have exalted themselves in their own wisdom because they were dominated by pride) and so they have been made foolish. They have changed the glory of the incorruptible God into the likeness of the image of corruptible man or birds or beasts or reptiles (in praying to such images they either led the peoples or were led by them); and they have worshipped and served created things rather than the Creator who is blessed for ever.[6]

6. Augustine, *City of God,* 14.28; in the translation by R. H. Barrow, *Introduction to St. Augustine, The City of God* (London, Faber, 1950), pp. 36–38; Barrow's version here is more effective than that of John Healey, used elsewhere in this book.

3. *The Various Style*

Now, in the Paradise of Book 4, one may feel, more and more, how deceptive has been all that grand heroic show of human art and effort in the first two books. There will no doubt always be readers who feel as Hazlitt felt, that "Satan is the most heroic subject that ever was chosen for a poem," and that the first two books "are like two massy pillars of solid gold."[1] Surely these books are superb within their function, and yet, after a reading of Book 4, their quality is subject to some question. All this show of power, Milton seems to say, is only an effort to compensate for an enormous loss. That vast array of allusions to biblical and classical matters, those frequent clustered similes, the strange effect of foreign idiom, Greek, Latin, or Italianate, and all that curious neglect or defiance of normal English usage by which Milton gains something like the compression and onward flow of Vergil[2]—all these things show one way in which the poet can attempt to surpass the achievement of Homer and Vergil—to soar "Above th' *Aonian* Mount." All this epic imitation Milton certainly performs to admiration, but it is important to notice that this style of writing is gradually subdued, diminished, and in places almost refined away, as the mind moves backward and inward. The first sight of Paradise, as Satan views it with envy and dismay, presents a moderated, simpler style, in keeping with this different scene:

> So on he fares, and to the border comes
> Of *Eden,* where delicious Paradise,
> Now nearer, Crowns with her enclosure green,
> As with a rural mound the champain head

1. William Hazlitt, "Lectures on the English Poets," *Collected Works,* ed. A. R. Waller and Arnold Glover (12 vols. London, Dent, 1902–04), 5, 63.

2. Cf. F. T. Prince, *The Italian Element in Milton's Verse* (Oxford, Clarendon Press, 1954), pp. 108–30; and Davis P. Harding, *The Club of Hercules* (Urbana, University of Illinois Press, 1962), chapter 6.

Of a steep wilderness, whose hairie sides
With thicket overgrown, grottesque and wilde,
Access deni'd; and over head up grew
Insuperable highth of loftiest shade,
Cedar, and Pine, and Firr, and branching Palm,
A Silvan Scene, and as the ranks ascend
Shade above shade, a woodie Theatre
Of stateliest view.   [4.131–42]

It is a moderated style, not utterly different from that of the
opening books, for epic continuity must be maintained, that
onward impulse so well described by C. S. Lewis.[3] Thus the
passage has strong traces of Latinate inversion, along with one
overt Vergilian reference, the "Silván Scene."[4] The passage
represents in little the manner of Milton's presentation of
Paradise: with a generous infiltration of epic similes and classical allusions, though widely spaced, and not so frequent by
half as in the opening book. And there remains a considerable
degree of that foreign idiom, and that uniquely suspended and
compressed syntax, or melting down of syntax. But the difference is nevertheless striking, and one may feel it strongly by
recalling the way in which Milton has presented Satan's first
view of Hell:

At once as far as Angels kenn he views
The dismal Situation waste and wilde,
A Dungeon horrible, on all sides round
As one great Furnace flam'd, yet from those flames
No light, but rather darkness visible
Serv'd only to discover sights of woe,
Regions of sorrow, doleful shades, where peace
And rest can never dwell, hope never comes
That comes to all; but torture without end
Still urges, and a fiery Deluge, fed
With ever-burning Sulphur unconsum'd: [1.59–69]

3. *A Preface to Paradise Lost* (London, Oxford University Press, 1942),
chapter 7.
4. *Aeneid*, 1.164.

It is a style that might fairly be called *tormented,* in its ambiguity and shifting of syntax, in its abrupt compression. One cannot say whether "kenn" is verb or noun, or whether "Angels" is a plural subject, or a possessive, either singular or plural. "Dungeon horrible" at first may seem to be in apposition to "dismal Situation," but the phrase then veers about to become, perhaps, the subject of the verb "flam'd"—or is "flam'd" perhaps a participle modifying "Furnace"? So it goes throughout the passage, a "melting down of the ordinary units of speech."[5] It is a manner well designed to convey the strenuous agonies of Hell—or Hell on earth—but it will not do for Paradise. Thus the style of Book 4 represents a development out of the highly wrought style of Book 1, which now, as one looks back, may seem deliberately overwrought, excessively elaborated, though quite in keeping with its subject, the pretensions of the fallen world. The "purer air" of Paradise demands a purer style moving out of the high epic manner toward something that at times comes close to a pastoral simplicity, though always enfolded within the epic mode:

> Under a tuft of shade that on a green
> Stood whispering soft, by a fresh Fountain side
> They sat them down, and after no more toil
> Of thir sweet Gardning labour then suffic'd
> To recommend coole *Zephyr,* and made ease
> More easie, wholsom thirst and appetite
> More grateful, to thir Supper Fruits they fell,
> Nectarine Fruits which the compliant boughes
> Yeilded them, side-long as they sat recline
> On the soft downie Bank damaskt with flours:
> The savourie pulp they chew, and in the rinde
> Still as they thirsted scoop the brimming stream . . .
>
> [4.325–36]

The relatively simpler style of Book 4 points toward a way of life that truly lies beyond the inspiration of the old heroic Muse. Here in Paradise the moderated style, profuse, but

5. Lewis, p. 46.

moving with a clear design, conveys the underlying order of idyllic life. Everywhere, within the wild, luxuriant growth of Paradise, lies the clear evidence of a basic plan, as in that orderly, conical hill which meets the view at first, or in the flexible manner of its watering:

> Southward through *Eden* went a River large,
> Nor chang'd his course, but through the shaggie hill
> Pass'd underneath ingulft, for God had thrown
> That Mountain as his Garden mould high rais'd
> Upon the rapid current, which through veins
> Of porous Earth with kindly thirst up drawn,
> Rose a fresh Fountain, and with many a rill
> Waterd the Garden; thence united fell
> Down the steep glade, and met the neather Flood,
> Which from his darksom passage now appeers . . .
> [4.223–32]

It has all been made by the Divine Architect, "Chos'n by the sovran Planter, when he fram'd / All things to mans delightful use": all organic, all alive, all a harmony, like the love song of Eve, which, for all its ceremonious iteration, achieves with simple, pastoral words a remarkable variety of cadence, ordering all nature in relation to her love for Adam:

> With thee conversing I forget all time,
> All seasons and thir change, all please alike.
> Sweet is the breath of morn, her rising sweet,
> With charm of earliest Birds; pleasant the Sun
> When first on this delightful Land he spreads
> His orient Beams, on herb, tree, fruit, and flour,
> Glistring with dew; fragrant the fertil earth
> After soft showers; and sweet the coming on
> Of grateful Eevning milde, then silent Night
> With this her solemn Bird and this fair Moon,
> And these the Gemms of Heav'n, her starrie train:
> But neither breath of Morn when she ascends
> With charm of earliest Birds, nor rising Sun

On this delightful land, nor herb, fruit, floure,
Glistring with dew, nor fragrance after showers,
Nor grateful Evening mild, nor silent Night
With this her solemn Bird, nor walk by Moon,
Or glittering Starr-light without thee is sweet.

[4.639–56]

An effect of ritual celebration certainly emerges here, as it does elsewhere, on specific, local occasions: notably in the morning hymn of Adam and Eve in Book 5. But these are timeless moments of a special intensity, "transformations of time"[6] that concentrate the ordered variety of Paradise within an incantatory mode of unusually high formality. Such "cantilations" (as Ezra Pound might call them) cannot be maintained for long: in the two lines that immediately follow Eve's love song, her sudden, unexpected question seems to threaten all this harmony:

But wherfore all night long shine these, for whom
This glorious sight, when sleep hath shut all eyes?

Thus Milton's variations in style continually escape our efforts at a simple definition. As his poem is not a forbidding Chinese Wall, so it is not a rite that we must join as attendants at the altar.[7] Milton's orisons, like those of Adam and Eve, are paid

In various style, for neither various style
Nor holy rapture wanted they to praise
Thir Maker, in fit strains pronounc't or sung
Unmeditated, such prompt eloquence
Flowd from thir lips, in Prose or numerous Verse . . .

[5.146–50]

6. See MacCaffrey, p. 77.

7. C. S. Lewis's defense of the style as "hierophantic" and "ritual" represents a polemical overstatement in an otherwise superb account. In discussing "The Style of Secondary Epic" (*Preface to Paradise Lost,* chapter 7), Lewis admirably describes the way in which, within the "appearance of an extremely carpentered structure," Milton includes the effect of a "plunge back into something more like the indivisible, flowing quality of immediate experience" (p. 46). But his subsequent emphasis upon ritual (chapter 8)

4. Chaos and Creation

The pastoral of Paradise, like all pastoral actions, cannot exist unthreatened. The beauty of the ideal, indeed, arises only within a constant pressure of corruption. Thus Satan is there, mouthing his threats, and troubling the sleep of Eve; Eve herself betrays some tendencies toward vanity and curiosity; the ominous myths are there—Proserpine, Narcissus, Pandora —creating a quiet pressure of the fallen against the ideal; and there are many other allusions and comparisons that maintain the presence of the fallen world: the "fishie fume" of Asmodeus; the "lewd Hirelings" of the Church; the desecration of love by "the bought smile / Of Harlots" or in "Court Amours / Mixt Dance, or wanton Mask, or Midnight Bal"; the "Smuttie graine" of gunpowder; the "careful Plowman doubting" lest his "hopeful sheaves / Prove chaff."[1] Thus Milton maintains a sense of continual struggle in this effort of the mind to remember the pristine ideal of what a man might be.

Within these threats the pastoral of Paradise nevertheless weaves its way toward more and more precise accounts of the Idea of Order that underlies the pristine universe. Again, Milton's poetical strategy is magnificent. He first allows this order

leads gradually to a slighting of the effect of spontaneity in the poem. Lewis indicates the extent of his overstatement when he says: "Thus far of Milton's style on the assumption that it is in fact as remote and artificial as is thought. No part of my defence depends on questioning that assumption, for I think it ought to be remote and artificial. But it would not be honest to suppress my conviction that the degree to which it possesses these qualities has been exaggerated." However this may be, he concludes, "I am defending Milton's style as a ritual style" (p. 59). Yet Milton's variations in style provide their own defense, ranging as they do from Eve's delicate love song down to the satirical language of Limbo ("the backside of the World") and the fearsome language of God, denouncing Sin and Death: "My Hell-hounds, to lick up the draff and filth / Which mans polluting Sin with taint hath shed / On what was pure, till cramm'd and gorg'd, nigh burst / With suckt and glutted offal . . ." (10.630–33).

1. Book 4, lines 168, 193, 765–68, 817, 983–85.

in variety to remain implicit, as the rich scenes in Paradise unfold their bounty, "pouring forth more sweet, / Wilde above rule or Art; enormous bliss" (5.296–97). That is to say, above ordinary human notions of rule or art. But just a little before these lines about the "Wilderness of sweets" we have heard the morning hymn of Adam and Eve (and the bard), celebrating the "Power Divine" that made "this universal Frame," with the "mystic Dance" of the planets and the Elements "that in quaternion run / Perpetual Circle, multiform." That hymn (5.153–208) presents the most explicit view thus far of the intricate relationship of all created things. And soon the angelic intelligence of Raphael provides the full, detailed, scientific account of these relationships (5.414–32, 469–90), summed up in the brilliant image of organic growth:

> So from the root
> Springs lighter the green stalk, from thence the leaves
> More aerie, last the bright consummate floure
> Spirits odorous breathes: flours and thir fruit
> Mans nourishment, by gradual scale sublim'd
> To vital Spirits aspire, to animal,
> To intellectual, give both life and sense,
> Fansie and understanding, whence the soule
> Reason receives, and reason is her being . . . [5.479–87]

But even here Milton has not penetrated to the deep center of his vision of Paradise. To prepare for that ultimate vision, Milton now introduces, in the latter half of Book 5 and throughout Book 6, a violent eruption of evil: his version of the War in Heaven. Milton's unsteady handling of this long episode is a measure of the difficult problem in poetic decorum that the movement of his poem here presents. After the rich and splendid view of Paradise, no heroic action of the old kind can ever again in this poem be allowed to assert the appeal that Satan and his fallen host have temporarily held in the opening books. The account of the War in Heaven, in returning to the heroic mode, must work in a diminished way, with touches of the old heroic ardor, but with a clear effect of futility, indicating beyond any doubt the ultimate emptiness of all these ancient postures. Thus the angels' metaphoric armor becomes so actual that they are trapped and crushed by its weight.

Arnold Stein may go too far in saying that the effect here is "almost a kind of epic farce,"[2] but there is truth in his view. The frequent stiffness and clumsiness of the writing (along with the ponderous efforts at witty irony) seem to result from a deliberate withholding of Milton's full poetic power, in an effort to attenuate and ridicule the heroic mode. It is a dangerous poetical strategy, especially when carried on at such length, and the results are far from being completely successful: the attenuation too often produces heaviness and awkwardness in the writing, tedium and embarrassment in the reader.

Yet the narration is successful enough to fulfill the major function of the episode: to create a symbolic action containing all the spiritual combats ever fought. It is essentially a threefold action, presenting (1) the original defeat of Satan and his crew in Heaven; (2) the later defeat of Satan by the Crucified Christ, as indicated by the way in which the combat here endures uncertainly for two days, until on the third morn the Son of God arises and comes forth to win his victory; and (3) the ultimate victory of good over evil at the final Day of Judgment. In other words, the episode represents the universal struggle between Chaos and Creation, whether in the outer universe, or in the angels, or in the mind and soul of man. Thus Satan's host is cast into Chaos and out of that same Chaos God creates the heaven and the earth.

From this standpoint the whole effect of these middle books becomes highly reminiscent of Augustine's meditations upon Chaos and Creation in the last two books of his *Confessions*. There, in meditating upon the second verse of Genesis, Augustine takes the words to refer to an act of creation that occurred

2. Stein, *Answerable Style* (Minneapolis, University of Minnesota Press, 1953), p. 22.

(causally) *before* the beginning of *days,* that is, before the
creation of formed creatures: *earth* thus refers to formless
matter, *informitas,* the *abyssus,* the deep, out of which the lower
heavens and all other forms of our own universe were created.
The second verse, in short, describes "Chaos," as Watts calls
it in the chapter headings of his translation of 1631: "The
Chaos was created out of nothing, and out of that, all things."[3]
In Augustine's view the second verse of Genesis indicates that

> all this whole was almost nothing, because hitherto it was
> altogether without form: but yet there was now something
> apt to be formed. For thou, Lord, madest the world of a matter
> without form; which being next to nothing, thou madest out
> of nothing: out of which thou mightest make those great
> works which we sons of men do wonder at.   [12.8]

Then, in one of those darting transitions that characterize
his mode of searching, Augustine transmutes this conception
of *informitas* into a symbol of the state of fallen man: the
formless matter comes to represent the state of chaos in which
mankind now exists unless it follows the call of the divine
light:

> O let truth, the light of my heart, and not mine own darkness,
> now speak unto me! I fell off into those material things, and
> became all be-darkened: but yet even thence, even thence
> came I to love thee. I went astray, and I remembered thee. I
> heard thy voice behind me calling to me to return; but scarcely
> could I discern it for the noise of the enemies of peace. And
> see here I return now, sweating and panting after thy foun-
> tain.   [12.10]

Thus the same divine power that brought form out of the
unformed deep is now continually engaged in offering form
to the disordered state of fallen man.

3. See the *Confessions,* 1631 ed., Book 12, chapter 8; also the headings
to chapters 4 and 5. The following quotations from the *Confessions* are
taken from the corrected version in the Loeb Library.

This point becomes completely clear in the final Book 13 of the *Confessions,* where Augustine meditates upon the whole account of the days of creation in Genesis and finds the account symbolical of the creative power that works within mankind, urging and enabling man to rise up out of the unformed darkness of sin:

> Yea, and our earth, before it received the form of doctrine, was invisible and unformed, and we were covered over with the darkness of ignorance, for thou hast chastised man for his iniquity, and thy judgments are a great deep. But because thy spirit moved upon the waters, thy mercy forsook not our misery, and thou saidst: Let there be light; repent ye, for the Kingdom of Heaven is at hand. Repent, Let there be light. And because our soul was troubled within us, we remembered thee . . . and so we were displeased at our own darkness, and we turned unto thee, And there was light. And behold, we having sometimes been darkness, are now light in the Lord.
>
> [13.12]

Against this threat of darkness and chaos, then, Milton's Book 7 sets forth the full power of the divine creativity, heralded by the *Gloria* which in the Gospel of Luke the heavenly host sang to shepherds watching in the field by night:

> Great triumph and rejoycing was in Heav'n
> When such was heard declar'd the Almightie's will;
> Glorie they sung to the most High, good will
> To future men, and in thir dwellings peace:
>
> [7.180–83]

5. *Creative Light*

Milton creates now a poetical meditation on Genesis by using the symmetry of the so-called Priestly account of Creation found in the first chapter of the Bible: six days, with eight acts of creation, two on the third day, and two on the sixth day. Upon this symmetrical frame, enforced by the liturgical repetitions of the first chapter of Genesis, Milton builds a vast celebration of the variety and bounty of the gifts arising out of this firm order. He brings in at a few appropriate points materials from the alternative account of Creation found in the second chapter of Genesis, but most of this he saves for Adam himself to tell in the eighth book. Thus Milton deftly solves the problem of the two different Biblical accounts, allowing the angelic intelligence of Raphael to relate the grand harmonious design implied in the opening chapter of Genesis, while giving to Adam the more limited, human, anthropomorphic view of the second chapter.

It is here, in Milton's treatment of the Creation, that one may find the best answer to those who contend that Milton's God is wicked, or that Milton's view of religion is too legalistic, intent on the justice and power of the Deity, to the sad exclusion of Faith, Hope, and Charity—especially Charity.[1] Here, too, one may find a remedy for that antipathy which T. S. Eliot expressed in his famous declaration, worthy of Samuel Johnson himself: "Either from the moralist's point of view, or from the theologian's point of view, or from the psychologist's point of view, or from that of the political philosopher, or judging by the ordinary standards of likeableness in human beings, Milton is unsatisfactory."[2]

It is true that Milton's God often speaks in a rasping, arbitrary way, and it is true that the terms Milton tends to apply directly to his Deity are such words as "Omnific," "Omniscient," "Almighty," "Omnipotent": "Immutable, Immortal, Infinite,

1. As in William Empson's witty tirade, *Milton's God* (London, Chatto and Windus, 1961), or in the remarks of Lord Davil Cecil, in *The Oxford Book of Christian Verse* (Oxford, Clarendon Press, 1940), p. xxi: "Milton . . . was not essentially a religious poet. He was a philosopher rather than a devotee. His imagination was lucid and concrete, unlit by heavenly gleams; theology to him was a superior branch of political science, the rule of reason and the moral law as exhibited in the working of the cosmos. Nor was his moral sensibility a Christian one. . . . He did not live by faith, scorned hope, and was indisposed to charity . . ."

2. See Eliot's famous "Note" of 1936, reprinted in *On Poetry and Poets* (London, Faber, 1957), p. 138.

Eternal King." And it is true that *Paradise Lost* does not deal centrally with the sacrificial aspects of God's Love: the events represented in Christmas and Easter play a subordinate role in this poem, as they do in the writings of Vaughan, Traherne, and Marvell. Nevertheless, Charity is not neglected, only otherwise represented, as Milton's placing of the *Gloria* may indicate. Like Traherne, Milton finds the Love of God best demonstrated in his universal creativity, in a bountiful emanation of goodness that wells forth everywhere in the universe,[3] as it did on that day of Genesis when God

> saw that it was good, and said, Let th' Earth
> Put forth the verdant Grass, Herb yeilding Seed,
> And Fruit Tree yeilding Fruit after her kind;
> Whose Seed is in her self upon the Earth.   [7.309–12]

Upon those simple Biblical pentameters Milton proceeds to create a meditative vision in which the height of the vegetation rises gradually toward a climax, and then disperses swiftly outward and downward on every side as far as eye can see:

> He scarce had said, when the bare Earth, till then
> Desert and bare, unsightly, unadorn'd,
> Brought forth the tender Grass, whose verdure clad
> Her Universal Face with pleasant green,
> Then Herbs of every leaf, that sudden flour'd
> Op'ning thir various colours, and made gay
> Her bosom smelling sweet: and these scarce blown,
> Forth flourish't thick the clustring Vine, forth crept
> The smelling Gourd, up stood the cornie Reed
> Embattell'd in her field: add the humble Shrub,
> And Bush with frizl'd hair implicit:

3. See the excellent study of Milton's treatment of Creation by W. B. C. Watkins, *An Anatomy of Milton's Verse* (Baton Rouge, Louisiana State University Press, 1955), pp. 42–86; also the perceptive commentary by M. M. Mahood, *Poetry and Humanism* (New Haven, Yale University Press, 1950), chapter 6, esp. pp. 201–03.

(whatever we may think of that last phrase, neither "ritual" nor "latinism" will rightly describe it)

> last
> Rose as in Dance the stately Trees, and spred
> Thir branches hung with copious Fruit: or gemm'd
> Thir Blossoms: with high Woods the Hills were crownd,
> With tufts the vallies & each fountain side,
> With borders long the Rivers.   [7.313–28]

Everywhere, on sea and land and in the air, the universe bursts forth with an incredible vitality and fertility, as when Milton, with a show of wit, chooses to take literally the Biblical phrase that says the animals were formed "out of the ground." Milton transmutes the phrase into a sudden drama of creative power:

> The grassie Clods now Calv'd, now half appeer'd
> The Tawnie Lion, pawing to get free
> His hinder parts, then springs as broke from Bonds,
> And Rampant shakes his Brinded main; the Ounce,
> The Libbard, and the Tyger, as the Moale
> Rising, the crumbl'd Earth above them threw
> In Hillocks;

(and of course the mole *is* rising thus, at the same time: the lines give both comparison and reality)

> the swift Stag from under ground
> Bore up his branching head: scarse from his mould
> *Behemoth* biggest born of Earth upheav'd
> His vastness: Fleec't the Flocks and bleating rose,
> As Plants: [7.463–73]

One wonders how there could ever have been any question of Milton's "visual imagination," or of his ability to use direct, colloquial phrasing in conjunction with his high style.

All this, then, is given to mankind, and more than this. Man, as Milton's poem presents him, not only enjoys, potentially, the use of this splendid creation; but, being made in the Image of God, he also participates in this very power of creation: man has within himself, though he may be old, blind, and surrounded by enemies, a creative power derived from the same source that created the first Paradise.

The bard has said this from the very outset of his poem, when, in his Invocation, he prayed to the Spirit to instruct him:

> Thou from the first
> Wast present, and with mighty wings outspread
> Dove-like satst brooding on the vast Abyss
> And mad'st it pregnant: What in me is dark
> Illumine, what is low raise and support . . . [1.19–23]

It is this creative power that Satan envies and denies, the power that Satan is ironically forced to hear described by the angel Uriel, at the close of Book 3:

> For wonderful indeed are all his works,
> Pleasant to know, and worthiest to be all
> Had in remembrance alwayes with delight;
> But what created mind can comprehend
> Thir number, or the wisdom infinite
> That brought them forth, but hid thir causes deep.
> I saw when at his Word the formless Mass,
> This worlds material mould, came to a heap:
> Confusion heard his voice, and wilde uproar
> Stood rul'd, stood vast infinitude confin'd;
> Till at his second bidding darkness fled,
> Light shon, and order from disorder sprung: [3.702–13]

It is this remembrance, recovered in the middle books of *Paradise Lost,* that spreads forth its wings to raise and support the world that falls forward into fragments and ruins in the last four books of the poem, as the race of mankind enters upon its long history of disorder. Milton's manifestation of creative power in his middle books shows how that Paradise may be regained, within, through meditation on what Traherne called "the Principles of Upright Nature."[4]

4. *Centuries,* 4.54.

Adam himself, in Book 8, provides the best demonstration of those principles: as he recalls his earliest remembrance, he creates a dramatic image of the Augustinian movement of the mind toward God, drawn by the intuitive knowledge of a happiness that lies beyond the bounds of man:

> Strait toward Heav'n my wondring Eyes I turnd,
> And gaz'd a while the ample Skie, till rais'd
> By quick instinctive motion up I sprung,
> As thitherward endevoring, and upright
> Stood on my feet; about me round I saw
> Hill, Dale, and shadie Woods, and sunnie Plaines,
> And liquid Lapse of murmuring Streams; by these,
> Creatures that livd, and movd, and walk'd, or flew,
> Birds on the branches warbling; all things smil'd,
> With fragrance and with joy my heart oreflow'd.[5]
>
> [8.257–66]

Now Adam proceeds to examine himself and his surroundings in exactly the mood of wonder and gratitude shown by Traherne in the poems that open his meditative sequence in the Dobell manuscript, the poems entitled "The Salutation," "Wonder," "Eden," "Innocence":

> These little Limmes,
> These Eys and Hands which here I find,
> These rosie Cheeks wherwith my Life begins,
> Where have ye been? Behind
> What Curtain were ye from me hid so long!
> Where was? in what Abyss, my speaking Tongue?
>
> *   *   *   *   *
>
> I that so long
> Was Nothing from Eternitie,
> Did little think such Joys as Ear or Tongue,

5. The last line seems to evoke a reminiscence of Book 1, line 788: "At once with joy and fear his heart rebounds"—the response of the fallen peasant to the dance of the "Faerie Elves"; and at the same time we note the total difference between this rising from the fragrant earth and Satan's rising from the burning lake.

To Celebrat or See:
Such Sounds to hear, such Hands to feel, such Feet,
Beneath the Skies, on such a Ground to meet.

*   *   *   *   *

From Dust I rise,
And out of Nothing now awake,
These Brighter Regions which salute mine Eys,
A Gift from GOD I take.
The Earth, the Seas, the Light, the Day, the Skies,
The Sun and Stars are mine; if those I prize.

*   *   *   *   *

Into this Eden so Divine and fair,
So Wide and Bright, I com his Son and Heir.[6]

My self I then perus'd, and Limb by Limb
Survey'd, and sometimes went, and sometimes ran
With supple joints, as lively vigour led:
But who I was, or where, or from what cause,
Knew not; to speak I tri'd, and forthwith spake,
My Tongue obey'd and readily could name
What e're I saw. Thou Sun, said I, faire Light,
And thou enlight'nd Earth, so fresh and gay,
Ye Hills and Dales, ye Rivers, Woods, and Plaines
And ye that live and move, fair Creatures, tell,
Tell, if ye saw, how came I thus, how here?
Not of my self; by some great Maker then,
In goodness and in power praeeminent;
Tell me, how may I know him, how adore,
From whom I have that thus I move and live,
And feel that I am happier then I know.   [8.267–82]

Adam's intuitive movement toward the love of God represents the fulfillment of the creative power manifested in the pre-ceding book: it is a movement in "This happie Light" toward the "Garden of bliss," the "Presence Divine," and "that celestial Colloquie sublime."[7]

6. The above lines are all taken from "The Salutation."
7. Book 8, lines 285, 299, 314, 455. In Milton's original ten-book ver-

6. Tragic Redemption

When Milton says, in the prologue of Book 9, that he must now change his notes to "Tragic," he speaks, as usual, quite exactly. Implications of the generic form of Greek tragedy underlie the action of Book 9, as the form of the first chapter of Genesis underlies the present Book 7. The voice of the epic bard, along with its usual functions, now undertakes something like a choric role, as that voice emerges to interpret and present a series of dramatic episodes in which the speakers re-enact the fall of man. One might distinguish eight such spoken episodes,[1] each carefully separated by the bardic narrative-chorus, although the bardic voice is also frequently present within these episodes, interpreting and narrating. At the same time, Satan's long soliloquy before this action (9.99–178) bears some affinity to the Euripidean prologue of the supernatural agent, such as the prologue of Aphrodite in the *Hippolytus,* or the prologue of Dionysus in *The Bacchae.* All these suggestions of dramatic

sion of 1667, the present Books 7 and 8 were appropriately one long book, the seventh, the book of God's bounty. This original seventh book received a special prominence by being considerably longer than any of the preceding books (235 lines longer than the longest of the earlier books, and about 380 lines longer than the two books immediately preceding). The Vergilian division of materials in 1674 has resulted in a slight loss of emphasis upon the thematic continuity that flows throughout the angel's account and Adam's own remembrance of Creation, concluding with the discussion of Love at the close of what is now Book 8. Indeed, Milton's ten-book division conveys the poem's essential structure more clearly than his twelve-book division: Book 7 is the book of Creation, Book 8 tells the story of the Fall, Book 9 shows the action of recovery through God's redemptive grace, and Book 10 provides an Epilogue, the story of mankind.

1. The episodes might be distinguished as follows: (1) the parting of Adam and Eve: 205–384; (2) Satan's soliloquy at sight of Eve: 473–93; (3) Satan and Eve: preliminary encounter: 532–631; (4) Satan and Eve before the Tree: Eve's Fall: 647–833; (5) Eve's return to Adam: Adam's Fall: 856–989; (6) Adam's invitation to lust: 1017–33; (7) Adam's discovery of shame: 1067–98; (8) the quarrel of Adam and Eve: 1134–86.

form are, of course, closely interwoven with the epic mode and should not be pressed too hard. Still the effect is there: the oldest of tragic events is being re-enacted in the oldest of tragic forms.

Meanwhile, within this dramatic form, the epic similes and pagan allusions, refined away in Books 7 and 8,[2] have returned in profusion; the purified style of the Creation now lapses, and the return to the world of fallen men is superbly foreshadowed in the famous simile describing Satan's view of Eve:

> As one who long in populous City pent,
> Where Houses thick and Sewers annoy the Aire,
> Forth issuing on a Summers Morn to breathe
> Among the pleasant Villages and Farmes
> Adjoynd, from each thing met conceaves delight,
> The smell of Grain, or tedded Grass, or Kine,
> Or Dairie, each rural sight, each rural sound;
> If chance with Nymphlike step fair Virgin pass,
> What pleasing seemd, for her now pleases more,
> She most, and in her looks summs all Delight.
> Such Pleasure took the Serpent to behold
> This Flourie Plat . . .   [9.445–56]

With beautiful decorum, the drama that thus begins in a setting of idyllic pastoral concludes with Milton's subtle and detailed description of the fig tree, not in the form of a simile, but in the form of a literal description of the world we know: a fallen pastoral, where a real herdsman in a particular setting seeks refuge from excessive heat within the shade of a barren, grotesque, monstrous tree:

> The Figtree, not that kind for Fruit renown'd,
> But such as at this day to *Indians* known
> In *Malabar* or *Decan* spreds her Armes
> Braunching so broad and long, that in the ground
> The bended Twigs take root, and Daughters grow

2. After the prologue to Book 7 has simultaneously evoked and dismissed the pagan myths by calling on the inspiration of Urania: "For thou art Heav'nlie, shee [the pagan muse] an empty dreame."

> About the Mother Tree, a Pillard shade
> High overarch't, and echoing Walks between;
> There oft the *Indian* Herdsman shunning heate
> Shelters in coole, and tends his pasturing Herds
> At Loopholes cut through thickest shade:
>
> [9.1101–10]

So, with allusions to the "*Amazonian* Targe" and to the wild American discovered by Columbus, and with the angry bickering of husband and wife, this tragic action ends in the curt comment of the bard:

> Thus they in mutual accusation spent
> The fruitless hours, but neither self-condemning,
> And of their vain contest appeer'd no end.

Yet the word "appeer'd" opens the way toward a further action, in Book 10: an action of reconciliation and recovery which derives from an overarching apprehension of the Creator's goodness revealed in Books 7 and 8. Tillyard's account of the function of Book 10 has admirably shown the way in which this reconciliation is effected, with elements of reprise and parody that make this book the nodal culmination of the many strands that have run throughout Milton's various poem.[3] Only one point needs to be added, from the special standpoint of the discussion here: the way in which the epic style of the first book here reappears in a stiffened, hardened form that suggests a subtle parody of the grandeur that one has admired in the poem's beginning. Inverting the structure of the whole poem, Book 10 presents the action of redemptive love at beginning and end, while the central portion re-enacts the fallen images and postures of the first two books. The first 228 lines of Book 10 are wholly successful in presenting God as "the mild Judge and Intercessor both." Then at line 229 the images of Sin and Death return, and along with them a cluster of similes and classical allusions, presented with a concentrated

3. E. M. W. Tillyard, "The Crisis of Paradise Lost," in *Studies in Milton* (New York, Macmillan, 1951).

latity of diction and syntax. Indeed the pun on the word "Pontifical" seems to carry the style over the edge into deliberate self-parody, and appropriately, since the whole passage, as Tillyard has said,[4] is a parody of the account of Creation in Book 7. Sin and Death are seen "Hovering upon the Waters"

> As when two Polar Winds blowing adverse
> Upon the *Cronian* Sea, together drive
> Mountains of Ice, that stop th' imagin'd way
> Beyond *Petsora* Eastward, to the rich
> *Cathaian* Coast. The aggregated Soyle
> Death with his Mace petrific, cold and dry,
> As with a Trident smote, and fix't as firm
> As *Delos* floating once; the rest his look
> Bound with *Gorgonian* rigor not to move,
> And with *Asphaltic* slime; broad as the Gate,
> Deep to the Roots of Hell the gather'd beach
> They fasten'd, and the Mole immense wraught on
> Over the foaming deep high Archt, a Bridge
> Of length prodigious joyning to the Wall
> Immoveable of this now fenceless world
> Forfeit to Death; from hence a passage broad,
> Smooth, easie, inoffensive down to Hell.
> So, if great things to small may be compar'd,
> *Xerxes,* the Libertie of *Greece* to yoke,
> From *Susa* his *Memnonian* Palace high
> Came to the Sea, and over *Hellespont*
> Bridging his way, *Europe* with *Asia* joyn'd,
> And scourg'd with many a stroak th' indignant waves.
> Now had they brought the work by wondrous Art
> Pontifical, a ridge of pendent Rock
> Over the vext Abyss, following the track
> Of *Satan* . . .   [10.289–315]

Then, as Satan returns to Pandemonium, his approach is heralded by a simile of desolation, appropriately lacking in the broad evocative power found in the similes of the opening books:

4. Ibid., p. 32.

As when the *Tartar* from his *Russian* Foe
By *Astracan* over the Snowie Plaines
Retires, or *Bactrian* Sophi from the hornes
Of *Turkish* Crescent, leaves all waste beyond
The Realme of *Aladule,* in his retreate
To *Tauris* or *Casbeen.* So these the late
Heav'n-banisht Host, left desert utmost Hell
Many a dark League . . .   [10.431–38]

So it is with the following allusions to the "blood of *Gorgon,*
or the Isle / *Ophiusa,*" to "Huge *Python*" and the "snakie locks
/ That curld *Megaera,*" or the reference to

how the Serpent, whom they calld
Ophion with *Eurynome,* the wide-
Encroaching *Eve* perhaps, had first the rule
Of high *Olympus,* thence by *Saturn* driv'n
And *Ops,* ere yet *Dictaean Jove* was born.
                                         [10.580–84]

The rich elaboration and implication of the opening books are
gone, and only the rind of that gorgeous style remains, as in
the epic roll call of winds with which Milton ends his long
reprise of the style of Book 1:

Boreas and *Caecias* and *Argestes* loud
And *Thrascias* rend the Woods and Seas upturn;
With adverse blast up-turns them from the South
Notus and *Afer* black with thundrous Clouds
From *Serraliona;* thwart of these as fierce
Forth rush the *Levant* and the *Ponent* Windes
Eurus and *Zephir* with thir lateral noise,
Sirocco, and *Libecchio.*   [10.699–706]

If one compares this list of highly limited allusiveness with
the grand roll call of devils in Book 1, a fair measure of the
diminution of the grand style will emerge. The effect here is
thoroughly functional, completely in accord with the whole
poem's movement. For in Books 1 and 2 the grand style, with
its dense array of imagery, was designed as the basis for a two-

137

fold action: to start a train of evil leading from the fallen angels to the fall of man in Book 9, and at the same time to start a redemptive action, leading from the world of fallen men backward and inward toward the Paradisal visions of the middle books. Hence arises the remarkable richness of the epic similes in the opening books,[5] which correlate with the evil in Hell and at the same time locate the essential action concretely and specifically in scenes from the world of men: scenes both of terror and of beauty, suggesting the struggle of chaos and creation:

> As when Heavens Fire
> Hath scath'd the Forrest Oaks, or Mountain Pines,
> With singed top their stately growth though bare
> Stands on the blasted Heath.   [1.612–15]

> from Morn
> To Noon he fell, from Noon to dewy Eve,
> A Summers day; and with the setting Sun
> Dropt from the Zenith like a falling Star,
> On *Lemnos* th' *Aegaean* Ile: [1.742–46]

The need for such allusiveness is now gone: the imagery of Paradise and of the new Creation has brought its redemptive connotations; and at the same time these idyllic images from pure nature have served to locate the action upon earth. Now, after the Fall, there is no poetic need to give the motives and qualities of humanity to Satan and his crew; for humanity is here, stretched out in agony upon the ground, as Satan once lay stretched out upon the burning lake. As John Peter has suggested in regard to Book 4,[6] the interest of the poem has shifted from Satan to Adam and Eve, and with that shift the power of the imagery applied to Satan has lost much of its earlier force. There is no problem of "degrading" Satan. He has from

---

5. See the article by Geoffrey Hartman cited earlier (*ELH*, 25, 1–12) for a fine interpretation of the presence of Creation in the similes of the opening book.

6. Peter, *Critique*, pp. 55–62.

the beginning represented the subtle, pervasive evil that leaks and seeps through all the vivid imagery of the first two books, culminating in the vicious allegory of Satan, Sin, and Death, the trinity of evil. The emergence of Satan into allegory, both in Book 2 and again in Book 10, is the key to his function throughout the poem: he has never possessed reality; what reality he has comes from the world of men. So now the symbol of Satan, having served its purposes, can be discarded by Milton with contempt. Adam lies before us, "in a troubl'd Sea of passion tost" (10.718).

As Adam's memory of his first upspringing has foretold, the redemptive action of God's goodness is now displayed in the interior action of Adam's renewed free will. Lying on his sea of passion, he explores the great central questions of the race: why was I born? what is death? why should all mankind be condemned for my sin? But his rigorous self-examination, utterly different from Satan's self-deception, leads to an emphasis on "mee" that shows the signs of a regenerated will:

> all my evasions vain
> And reasonings, though through Mazes, leads me still
> But to my own conviction: first and last
> On mee, mee onely, as the sourse and spring
> Of all corruption, all the blame lights due;
> So might the wrauth.   [10.829–34]

Thus the minds of Adam and Eve move toward their own difficult recovery of Paradise, a recovery that reaches its culmination in the purified and simple words of Eve, and in Adam's gentle, measured reply:

> both have sin'd, but thou
> Against God onely, I against God and thee,
> And to the place of judgement will return,
> There with my cries importune Heaven, that all
> The sentence from thy head remov'd may light
> On me, sole cause to thee of all this woe,
> Mee mee onely just object of his ire.   [10.930–36]

139

But rise, let us no more contend, nor blame
Each other, blam'd enough elsewhere, but strive
In offices of Love, how we may light'n
Each others burden in our share of woe;
Since this days Death denounc't, if ought I see,
Will prove no sudden, but a slow-pac't evill,
A long days dying to augment our paine,
And to our Seed (O hapless Seed!) deriv'd.

[10.958–65]

These scenes of reconciliation, well described by Tillyard and Summers,[7] bring to the poem a sense of fulfillment and completion. The ways of God toward men have been justified in the supple powers of recovery here displayed by Adam and Eve: their powers of sympathy and love are here shown to be enriched, as their powers of reasoning are strengthened by the need to overcome adversity and understand the nature of their change. The world is all before them now, the world of Milton's first two books, which Milton proceeds to unfold again, in his somber epilogue.

Thus Milton's poem comes to assume a form that might be described in visual terms as a picture with a dark border but a bright center. The opening books and the closing books present the dark border of the world we know, in flames, in ruins: but the center holds, for at the center the voice of the bard has performed a journey backward and inward to discover the springing center of creativity described by Peter Sterry:

> as Paradise, so the *pure Image* of God in the Soul, seems to some not to be *lost* or destroyed, but *hid* beneath the ruines of the fall. Thus *Knowledge* springing in the Soul, seems to be a *remembrance,* the Life of all good, an awakening by reason of the primitive Image of pure Nature raising it self by degrees, and sparkling through the *Rubbish,* the confusions of the present state.[8]

7. Tillyard, *Studies in Milton,* pp. 39–42; Joseph H. Summers, *The Muse's Method* (London, Chatto and Windus, 1962), pp. 176–85.
8. Sterry, *Discourse,* p. 99.

7. *Descent from Paradise: the Temperate Design*

The last two books of *Paradise Lost,* with their darkly pessimistic view of human history, have offended and disappointed many readers, who have felt here a failure of imagination, a failure of human sympathy, and a consequent falling-off in Milton's poetical powers. Has old age, as the poet feared, damped his "intended wing," or has the effort of pursuing his great enterprise at last exhausted his powers, or has the bitterness of personal defeat exacted its tirade against a thankless world? Rajan has well explained that the emphasis on man's depravity here is not merely personal, since this dark view of the world's plight was one that the age preferred.[1] And Madsen has very ably argued that "the last two books are not an intrusion in the epic design but rather an integral part of the poetic and intellectual structure," since they serve to create a "deadly parallel between fallen angel and fallen man, carrying us back to the first two books of the epic."[2] And Summers, very recently, has given a valuable account of the way in which the last two books have been designed to convey the process of redemption: "the gradual unfolding in history of the nature and victory of the Seed."[3]

These are all convincing arguments, and especially helpful to the present interpretation, which sees the poem as an image with a bright center, bordered with darkness. Yet as one returns

1. B. Rajan, *Paradise Lost & the Seventeenth Century Reader* (London, Chatto and Windus, 1947), pp. 78–92. Rajan makes it clear that he is not attempting to defend every aspect of these books, but to explain their central design: "It is not a plan which of itself is pessimistic, though Milton's agony contrives to make it so. He says many things which he does not have to say, and which he would have disdained to say when he wrote the 'Second Defence'" (p. 83).

2. William G. Madsen, "The Idea of Nature in Milton's Poetry," in a composite volume, *Three Studies in the Renaissance* (New Haven, Yale University Press, 1958), pp. 259–67.

3. Summers, *Muse's Method,* chapter 8.

to the poem, at every reading, the disappointment with the last two books returns. It is hard to say exactly how this happens, for there is surely no abrupt deterioration in the poetry. Book 11 indeed maintains a poetical power quite continuous with and worthy of the power displayed in Book 10, and at the very close of Book 12, as C. S. Lewis has said, there is indeed "a great recovery" (p. 125).

The trouble grows, half-realized, as we read: there is no saying exactly where it begins, but one has come to sense it acutely after reading on a hundred lines or so into Book 12. Then, looking back, one feels that the worry has been coming on throughout the last half of Book 11: a growing sense that something has gone out of control, that the poet has somehow gradually lost touch with the central conception of his poem, and that with this loss of touch, the poetry of Book 12 has begun to flag. The voice of the bard and seer has lost its vigor, and the writing has become, at its worst, the Biblical paraphrase of an almost ordinary versifier:

> I see him, but thou canst not, with what Faith
> He leaves his Gods, his Friends, and native Soile
> *Ur* of *Chaldaea,* passing now the Ford
> To *Haran,* after him a cumbrous Train
> Of Herds and Flocks, and numerous servitude;
> Not wandring poor, but trusting all his wealth
> With God, who call'd him, in a land unknown.
> *Canaan* he now attains, I see his Tents
> Pitcht about *Sechem,* and the neighbouring Plaine
> Of *Moreh;* there by promise he receaves
> Gift to his Progenie of all that Land;
> From *Hamath* Northward to the Desert South
> (Things by thir names I call, though yet unnam'd)
> From *Hermon* East to the great Western Sea,
> Mount *Hermon,* yonder Sea, each place behold
> In prospect, as I point them . . .   [12.128–43]

Yet Book 11 has opened well, with the Son's account of the first effects of "Prevenient Grace," renewing man's free will

and allowing him to choose the way of repentance in sighs
and prayers:

> Fruits of more pleasing savour from thy seed
> Sow'n with contrition in his heart, then those
> Which his own hand manuring all the Trees
> Of Paradise could have produc't, ere fall'n
> From innocence. Now therefore bend thine eare
> To supplication, heare his sighs though mute . . .
> Accept me, and in mee from these receave
> The smell of peace toward Mankinde, let him live
> Before thee reconcil'd, at least his days
> Numberd, though sad, till Death, his doom (which I
> To mitigate thus plead, not to reverse)
> To better life shall yeeld him, where with mee
> All my redeemd may dwell in joy and bliss,
> Made one with me as I with thee am one.   [11.26–44]

The Son's plea is accepted by the Father "without Cloud,
serene," and although the Father adds that the human pair can
no longer live in Paradise, his tone is equable, not harsh.
Death itself is beneficent, he says, since after a life "Tri'd in
sharp tribulation" Death allows the possibility of a happier
life "Wak't in the renovation of the just." In this tone of
mingled severity and pity, the Father sends down Michael to
announce the exile:

> Yet least they faint
> At the sad Sentence rigorously urg'd,
> For I behold them soft'nd and with tears
> Bewailing thir excess, all terror hide.
> If patiently thy bidding they obey,
> Dismiss them not disconsolate; reveale
> To *Adam* what shall come in future dayes,
> As I shall thee enlighten, intermix
> My Cov'nant in the Womans seed renewd;
> So send them forth, though sorrowing, yet in peace:
> [11.108–17]

All this is fully in accord with the complex reconciliation represented by Milton in Book 10.

Certainly the hopes of Adam and Eve need moderation. In the joy of their unexpected recovery they allow themselves too easy an optimism:

> while here we dwell,
> What can be toilsom in these pleasant Walkes?
> Here let us live, though in fall'n state, content.
>
> [11.178–80]

Such hopes are quickly dashed by the grim epic omens:

> The Bird of *Jove,* stoopt from his aerie tour,
> Two Birds of gayest plume before him drove:
> Down from a Hill the Beast that reigns in Woods,
> First Hunter then, pursu'd a gentle brace,
> Goodliest of all the Forrest, Hart and Hinde . . .
>
> [11.185–89]

The pitying admiration of the last line here is quite appropriate to the subtle manner in which Michael and his military angels are now presented:

> A glorious Apparition, had not doubt
> And carnal fear that day dimm'd *Adams* eye.
> Not that more glorious, when the Angels met
> *Jacob* in *Mahanaim,* where he saw
> The field Pavilion'd with his Guardians bright;
> Nor that which on the flaming Mount appeerd
> In *Dothan,* cover'd with a Camp of Fire,
> Against the *Syrian* King, who to surprize
> One man, Assassin-like had levied Warr,
> Warr unproclam'd.   [11.211–20]

These allusions to the beneficent presence of divine power, as experienced by Jacob and Elisha (Genesis 32:1–2; 2 Kings 6:17), foreshadow Michael's assurance of God's omnipresence, and thus serve proleptically to moderate the effect of horror with which Adam and Eve receive the word of their expulsion.

For the two fall from the excess of optimism into the excess of despair, Adam being "Heart-strook with chilling gripe of sorrow," while Eve utters her piercing lament for her flowers and her home—a last farewell to the pastoral of Paradise:

> O flours,
> That never will in other Climate grow,
> My early visitation, and my last
> At Eev'n, which I bred up with tender hand
> From the first op'ning bud, and gave ye Names,
> Who now shall reare ye to the Sun, or ranke
> Your Tribes, and water from th' ambrosial Fount?
> Thee lastly nuptial Bowre, by mee adornd
> With what to sight or smell was sweet; from thee
> How shall I part, and whither wander down
> Into a lower World, to this obscure
> And wilde, how shall we breath in other Aire
> Less pure, accustomed to immortal Fruits? [11.273–85]

The tone of the angel's reply to these laments is perfectly tempered: he is firm, but "milde," performing his mission "with regard benigne." The poem, it seems, is to end in a delicate poise, a balance of attitudes, where the sense of immense loss is subtly qualified by a sense of gain. Though the chief actors are condemned to death, they are to be reconciled with the universal scheme of things, and we are to sense a restoration of the world to order, though at heavy cost.

It is such an assurance of restoration that Michael now eloquently gives, in answer to Adam's crushed and hopeless lament for the expected loss of God's presence:

> This most afflicts me, that departing hence,
> As from his face I shall be hid, deprivd
> His blessed count'nance; here I could frequent,
> With worship, place by place where he voutsaf'd
> Presence Divine, and to my Sons relate;
> On this Mount he appeerd, under this Tree
> Stood visible, among these Pines his voice

I heard, here with him at this Fountain talk'd: . . .
In yonder nether World where shall I seek
His bright appearances, or footstep trace?   [11.315–29]

As with the earlier allusions to Jacob and Elisha, the phrasing
of Adam's lament itself implies the continued presence of God
with the sons of Adam: Moses and Elijah will hear the voice
of the Lord upon a Mount; the Lord or his angel will appear to
Gideon and Zechariah under an oak or myrtle tree, as in
Vaughan's "Religion"; and the woman of Samaria will speak
with Jesus as he sits by Jacob's well. Thus Michael assures
Adam, as the Augustinian tradition assured Vaughan and
Traherne, that the *vestigia,* the traces, the footsteps and footprints of God will be everywhere present:

> *Adam,* thou know'st Heav'n his, and all the Earth,
> Not this Rock onely; his Omnipresence fills
> Land, Sea, and Aire, and every kinde that lives,
> Fomented by his virtual power and warmd:
> All th' Earth he gave thee to possess and rule,
> No despicable gift; surmise not then
> His presence to these narrow bounds confin'd
> Of Paradise or *Eden:*   [11.335–42]

The power manifested in the original Creation will remain as
"virtual power," inward, essential, life-giving power, for Adam
and his sons, though they are now "brought down / To dwell
on eevn ground":

> Yet doubt not but in Vallie and in Plaine
> God is as here, and will be found alike
> Present, and of his presence many a signe
> Still following thee, still compassing thee round
> With goodness and paternal Love, his Face
> Express, and of his steps the track Divine.
> Which that thou mayst beleeve, and be confirmd,
> Ere thou from hence depart, know I am sent
> To shew thee what shall come in future dayes
> To thee and to thy Ofspring; good with bad

Expect to hear, supernal Grace contending
With sinfulness of Men; thereby to learn
True patience, and to temper joy with fear
And pious sorrow . . .   [11.349–62]

It is a clear and wholly successful statement of the desired poise and "temper": Michael is to play the role of Traherne's "Physician" in a world of "folly and Perversness," showing how the "Oyl of Pitty and the Balm of Lov" may remedy and heal "Blind Wretches."[4] The whole effect, then, according to Michael's promise, will be akin to that achieved in the great contemporary windows of University College, where the scene of Abraham's entertainment of his three heavenly guests (Genesis 18) is placed *between* the panel depicting the Expulsion from Eden and the two panels showing Adam and Eve, with Cain and Abel, in their fallen world of labor.[5] From the upper left-hand corner of the panel of Abraham, the sun of God's Grace casts its golden rays diagonally toward Adam and Eve, while the whole conception of the three panels shows a

4. *Centuries*, 4.20: "On every side we are environed with Enemies, surrounded with Reproaches encompassed with Wrongs, beseiged with offences, receiving evil for Good, being disturbed by fools, and invaded with Malice. This is the true Estate of this World. . . . Blind Wretches that Wound themselvs, offend me. I need therfore the Oyl of Pitty and the Balm of Lov to remedie and heal them. Did they see the Beauty of Holiness or the face of Happiness, they would not do so. To think the World therfore a General Bedlam, or Place of Madmen, and one self a Physician, is the most necessary Point of present Wisdom: an important Imagination, and the Way to Happiness."

5. See the illustrations, which reproduce the first two windows on the south side of the chapel; since the windows are placed closely together, the scene of Abraham functions as the fourth in this series of six panels. The windows are contemporary with *Paradise Lost* in a curiously parallel way. As the dating on the windows indicates, the glass was completed in 1641, but completion of the new chapel for which they were designed was delayed until 1666. The glass was evidently stored with care for a period of about 25 years, and thus escaped possible destruction during the period of the Civil Wars and the Commonwealth. See William Carr, *University College* (London, Robinson, 1902), 210–11.

subtle intermingling of evil and good, of pain and happiness. As Eve feels the pangs of childbirth in her side, her expression suggests simultaneously a grimace of pain and a smile of joy. And although Adam sits in sorrow in the third panel, the center of the middle panel represents a mingled outlook, in the fertile plowing and the folded flock and herd, suggesting the occupations of Cain and Abel. The serpent writhes on his belly at the bottom of the scene, but his head is very close to Eve's heel.

8. Visions of Evil

As Adam now ascends the hill to see the visions of the future, Milton skillfully brings in the means of redemption, through alluding to Christ's Temptation in the Wilderness and using an ambiguous syntax that for a time allows us to see the kingdoms of the world through the eyes of both the second Adam and the first:[1]

> Not higher that Hill nor wider looking round,
> Whereon for different cause the Tempter set
> Our second *Adam* in the Wilderness,
> To shew him all Earths Kingdomes and thir Glory.
> His Eye might there command wherever stood
> City of old or modern Fame, the Seat
> Of mightiest Empire, from the destind Walls
> Of *Cambalu,* seat of *Cathaian Can*
> And *Samarchand* by *Oxus, Temirs* Throne,
> To *Paquin* of *Sinaean* Kings, and thence
> To *Agra* and *Lahor* of great *Mogul*
> Down to the golden *Chersonese,* or where
> The *Persian* in *Ecbatan* sate . . .   [11.381–93]

And so for over twenty lines we have the gorgeous roll of names, with Milton manifesting all the power of his high style, recalling in one final burst of grandeur the epic panoply of the

1. Cf. Lerner, *Essays in Criticism, 4,* 307.

opening book. And all to excellent purpose here: for, as the allusion to the second Adam indicates, these are all "glories" of the fallen world, as they were in Book 1, though we were then certainly inclined to place their worth higher, despite their setting in the flames of Hell. The obvious excess of the grand roll of empires here carries the mind back through the whole poem to the building of Pandemonium and the roll call of fallen angels, and makes a deliberate judgment of those "heroic" scenes: "but to nobler sights / *Michael* from *Adams* eyes the Filme remov'd" (11.411–12).

Now we know at this point what those nobler sights are to be, for Michael has just told us: they are to be sights that will prove the constant presence of God in the world of men, his "goodness and paternal Love": "supernal Grace contending / With sinfulness of Men." One might perhaps expect that the matter of sinfulness had by now been sufficiently represented, after all the scenes of Hell, the War in Heaven, and the agony of Adam and Eve after the Fall; this has all been emblematic of man's history, and little more is needed, if Milton will trust to his earlier images and allegories.

Instead, Milton arranges an effect of deliberate shock. Here is the first of the "nobler sights":

> His eyes he op'nd, and beheld a field,
> Part arable and tilth, whereon were Sheaves
> New reapt, the other part sheep-walks and foulds;
> Ith' midst an Altar as the Land-mark stood
> Rustic, of grassie sord; thither anon
> A sweatie Reaper from his Tillage brought
> First Fruits, the green Eare, and the yellow Sheaf,
> Uncull'd, as came to hand; a Shepherd next
> More meek came with the Firstlings of his Flock
> Choicest and best; then sacrificing, laid
> The Inwards and thir Fat, with Incense strew'd,
> On the cleft Wood, and all due Rites perform'd.
> His Offring soon propitious Fire from Heav'n
> Consum'd with nimble glance, and grateful steame;

The others not, for his was not sincere;
Whereat hee inlie rag'd, and as they talk'd,
Smote him into the Midriff with a stone
That beat out life; he fell, and deadly pale
Groand out his Soul with gushing bloud effus'd.
Much at that sight was *Adam* in his heart
Dismai'd, and thus in haste to th' Angel cri'd.

    O Teacher, some great mischief hath befall'n
To that meek man, who well had sacrific'd;
Is Pietie thus and pure Devotion paid?

    T' whom *Michael* thus, hee also mov'd, repli'd.
These two are Brethren, *Adam,* and to come
Out of thy loyns; th' unjust the just hath slain,
For envie that his Brothers Offering found
From Heav'n acceptance; but the bloodie Fact
Will be aveng'd, and th' others Faith approv'd
Loose no reward, though here thou see him die,
Rowling in dust and gore. To which our Sire.

    Alas, both for the deed and for the cause!
But have I now seen Death? Is this the way
I must return to native dust? O sight
Of terrour, foul and ugly to behold,
Horrid to think, how horrible to feel!   [11.429-65]

The passage may suggest the basic cause of our dissatisfaction with the last two books: the effects of sin are presented at length with vivid and relentless horror, while the effects of "supernal Grace" are for the most part given in the form of brief and abstract statement. It is noteworthy here that Michael's brief consolation has no effect whatsoever on Adam's terror.

But Milton's plan seems clear: to put Adam through a series of fearful and destructive tableaux, saying the worst that can be said of the world—and then to promise the redemption of all this at the end of Book 11 by displaying the rainbow of God's covenant. Theologically, the design may be said to work; poetically, it is a disaster. For if the reader is expected to grasp the workings of grace against sin, they must somehow be given an adequate imagistic and dramatic presentation, to counter the powerful thrust of the scenes of sin. Milton has done exactly this in Book 10, in presenting the recovery of Adam and Eve. Here he fails to present any such organic vision, and instead allows a fissure to develop between the concrete representations of sin and the abstract assertions of Adam's "Teacher." This is particularly noticeable in the second of the noble sights now shown to Adam, the vision of the Lazar-house:

> wherein were laid
> Numbers of all diseas'd, all maladies
> Of gastly Spasm, or racking torture, qualmes
> Of heart-sick Agonie, all feavorous kinds,
> Convulsions, Epilepsies, fierce Catarrhs,
> Intestin Stone and Ulcer, Colic pangs,
> Dropsies, and Asthma's, and Joint-racking Rheums.
>
> [11.479–85]

Such is the scene in Milton's first edition; in the revised edition of 1674 he extended the range and increased the horror by inserting these lines between the last two given above:

> Daemoniac Phrenzie, moaping Melancholie
> And Moon-struck madness, pining Atrophie,
> Marasmus, and wide-wasting Pestilence . . .

It is powerfully done; no wonder Adam weeps and cries out in anguish, asking why life should be given on these terms, and why the Image of God should be subjected to such deformities. But the appalling effectiveness of the scene receives from Michael only the answer of Job's Comforters, an answer that Milton manages to give in a cold, defensive tone:

> Thir Makers Image, answerd *Michael,* then
> Forsook them, when themselves they villifi'd
> To serve ungovern'd appetite, and took
> His Image whom they serv'd, a brutish vice,
> Inductive mainly to the sin of *Eve.*

> Therefore so abject is thir punishment,
> Disfiguring not Gods likeness, but thir own,
> Or if his likeness, by themselves defac't
> While they pervert pure Natures healthful rules
> To loathsom sickness, worthily, since they
> Gods Image did not reverence in themselves.
>   I yeild it just, said *Adam,* and submit. [11.515–26]

Never was submission to a fearful fate so easily obtained. It is all too pat: the problem of sin is no longer being explored: it is being subjected to the easy solutions of the doctrinaire— the very solutions that Milton's earlier books had so successfully avoided. Milton's following account of the gradual decline of the temperate man into old age helps a little to modify the didactic rigor, for Michael here returns to something like the promised balance and poise:

> So maist thou live, till like ripe Fruit thou drop
> Into thy Mothers lap, or be with ease
> Gatherd, not harshly pluckt, for death mature:
> This is old age; but then thou must outlive
> Thy youth, thy strength, thy beauty, which will change
> To withered weak & gray . . .   [11.535–40]

But the recovery is brief. As Milton proceeds into the next vision, where the grave Sons of God are seduced by the "Beavie of fair Women," his writing moves even further into the mode of simple didacticism; the melodramatic ease of the seduction and the sententious harshness of Michael's explanation begin to show the full extent of Milton's departure from his earlier mode of creative apprehension:

> For that fair femal Troop thou sawst, that seemd
> Of Goddesses, so blithe, so smooth, so gay,
> Yet empty of all good wherein consists
> Womans domestic honour and chief praise;
> Bred onely and completed to the taste
> Of lustful appetence, to sing, to dance,
> To dress, and troule the Tongue, and roule the Eye.

To these that sober Race of Men, whose lives
Religious titl'd them the Sons of God,
Shall yeild up all thir vertue, all thir fame
Ignobly, to the traines and to the smiles
Of these fair Atheists, and now swim in joy,
(Erelong to swim at larg) and laugh; for which
The world erelong a world of tears must weepe.

[11.614–27]

Michael's labored sarcasm is perhaps the strongest sign so far that he is losing his "regard benigne," and is beginning to use the rasping voice so often found among the sermons of Milton's day. It does not help the poem to argue that this sort of thing was common: after Milton's performance in the first ten books, we expect a transcendence of the common. Yet in this portion of his poem, Milton's imagination seems to take wing only in delineating scenes of destruction, as in the vigorous scenes that follow here, first of military slaughter, and then of the flood.

As for the promised consolation, for the last third of Book 11 it resides primarily in a series of brief and harsh allusions to the vain attempts of the "one just Man alive," as represented in Enoch and Noah, to stem the tide of evil:

The onely righteous in a World perverse,
And therefore hated, therefore so beset
With Foes for daring single to be just,
And utter odious Truth . . .   [11.701–04]

We may argue that this has been foreshadowed in the figure of Abdiel, but indeed the parallel, undoubtedly designed with care, serves here to show how far Milton has departed from his allegory of the War in Heaven. For in this allegory of the spiritual combat, as fought from the revolt of the angels until the Day of Doom, Abdiel is indeed the only righteous in the perverse band of Satan—but he returns to join the two-thirds of the angels that have remained faithful. Milton's just man on earth has no one to join on earth, for

> all shall turn degenerate, all deprav'd,
> Justice and Temperance, Truth and Faith forgot;
> One Man except, the onely Son of light
> In a dark Age ...   [11.806–09]

In this way life on earth is here explicitly and flatly equated with the life of Satan's host, whereas in the opening books the association of earth with evil has been developed by implication only: implication that provides the setting for a redemptive movement. The strict equation of earth with evil produces a curious effect in Book 11, a feeling that, somehow, nothing much has been accomplished by Milton's beautiful demonstration that the vision of Paradise can be recovered by the mind of man, fallen and redeemed. It is as though the poet had somehow lost hold upon the central, sustaining vision of his journey. Perhaps that is why the reader finds it hard to share in Adam's joy at the ending of the Flood:

> Farr less I now lament for one whole World
> Of wicked Sons destroyd, then I rejoyce
> For one Man found so perfet and so just,
> That God voutsafes to raise another World
> From him, and all his anger to forget.   [11.874–78]

In the circumstances the cry may well strike the reader as the unfatherly utterance of a rigorous doctrinaire, a cry placed in Adam's mouth, not through any poetical decorum or propriety, but rather through the requirements of the remnant-theology that Milton is here fiercely pursuing.

9. *And All our Woe*

Yet perhaps it is unjust to take the visions of Book 11 as symbolical of the whole view of human history presented in the last two books. These scenes, after all, we may argue, deal only with the world up through the Flood; and what else could Milton make of this world, as shown in the Bible? But the

scene of the Lazar-house, the account of old age, and many of
Michael's moral generalizations make it plain that these visions
are designed to represent the world we live in, not some ancient
past. If this is not so, what can we make of Milton's strategy
in devoting 472 lines to the world's history up through the
Flood—and allowing only 551 lines for all the rest of history,
up through the Day of Doom? Milton's design in this division
of events has, I think, been very well explained by Summers
(p. 206), when he says that we are to see "this pattern of
destruction followed by a new and greater creation." As Summers notes, the aim is clearly set forth in the lines that Milton
added when he divided the original Book 10 into two books:

> As one who in his journey bates at Noone,
> Though bent on speed, so heer the Archangel paus'd
> Betwixt the world destroy'd and world restor'd . . .
>
> [12.1–3]

The symbolical visions of the world of sin, we see, are only
half the story: the world of consolation remains. The design
is even more strongly emphasized in the (ex post facto)
Argument to Book 12:[1]

The Angel Michael *continues from the Flood to relate what
shall succeed; then, in the mention of* Abraham, *comes by
degrees to explain, who that Seed of the Woman shall be,
which was promised* Adam *and* Eve *in the Fall; his Incarnation, Death, Resurrection, and Ascension; the state of the*

1. The "Arguments" were first published in the re-issue of *Paradise
Lost* in 1668, when they were printed together before the poem; in 1674
they were distributed to stand at the head of each book, the arguments for
the original Books 7 and 10 being broken up to head the newly divided
books. The above quotation is from 1674; in 1668 the equivalent to this
part of the argument is less precise in its opening portion: "thence from the
Flood relates, and by degrees explains, who that Seed of the Woman shall
be; his Incarnation, Death [etc.]." See the bibliographical accounts and re-
productions of these printings in Milton's *Complete Poetical Works,* ed.
Harris Fletcher (4 vols. Urbana, University of Illinois Press, 1943–48),
Vols. 2 and 3.

Church till his second Coming. Adam *greatly satisfied and recomforted by these Relations and Promises descends the Hill with* Michael; *wakens* Eve, *who all this while had slept, but with gentle dreams compos'd to quietness of mind and submission.* Michael *in either hand leads them out of Paradise, the fiery Sword waving behind them, and the Cherubim taking thir Stations to guard the Place.*

That design, if carried out, might have been magnificently effective, and the bitter visions of sin in Book 11 would be justified by the dramatic surprise and relief in finding the bounty of God poured forth again with so great love upon a race so undeserving of this goodness.

What happens in the poetry is something quite different. First of all, with a rather clumsy explanation, Milton changes the poetic method from vision to narration:

> but I perceave
> Thy mortal sight to faile; objects divine
> Must needs impaire and wearie human sense:
> Henceforth what is to com I will relate ...   [12.8–11]

The basic reason for the change is perhaps clear enough: the process of redemption through the sacrifice of Christ involves the most complex and controversial of theological issues; to provide adequate explanation Michael must be allowed to enfold the action of history within a carefully woven network of accurate and precise theology. There is of course the danger that in poetry the effect of vision will outweigh the effect of explanation; but the risk must be run, since, as Michael says, Reason is essential to "true Libertie." Thus Milton devotes his last book primarily to a rational account of the theology of the remnant, as developed by the protestant reformers under the strong influence of Augustine's later writings on the problem of grace. In other words, Milton is attempting to set together, within the borders of one poem, both the optimistic view of Augustine's *Confessions,* and the less inclusive, darker

156

view of the later Augustine, as found in the last book of the *City of God:*

> Concerning man's first origin, our present life (if such a miserable estate can be called a life) does sufficiently prove that all his children were condemned in him. What else does that horrid gulf of ignorance confirm, whence all error has birth, and wherein all the sons of Adam are so deeply drenched, that none can be freed without toil, fear, and sorrow? What else does our love of vanities affirm, whence there arises such a tempest of cares, sorrows, repinings, fears, mad exultations, discords, altercations, wars, treasons, furies, hates, deceits, flatteries, thefts, rapines, perjuries, pride, ambition, envy, murder, parricide, cruelty, villainy, luxury, impudence, unchastity, fornications, adulteries, incests, several sorts of sins against nature (filthy even to be named), sacrilege, heresy, blasphemy, oppression, calumnies, circumventions, deceits, false witnesses, false judgments, violence, robberies, and suchlike out of my remembrance to reckon, but not excluded from the life of man? All these evils are belonging to man, and arise out of the root of that error and perverse affection which every son of Adam brings into the world with him. For who does not know in what a mist of ignorance (as we see in infants) and with what a crew of vain desires (as we see in boys) all mankind enters this world, so that if man were left unto his own election, he would fall into most of the aforesaid mischiefs?
>
> [22.22]

Inevitably, as the current theology of the remnant begins to dominate the poem's world, its tone and manner move farther and farther away from the poise and tempering of attitudes promised by Michael and God at the outset of Book 11.

Milton proceeds to present the remaining history of the world as a threefold process of corruption and renewal, each part of the process re-enacting the story of the world from Creation through the Flood. First, there is the world from the Flood to the days of Abraham (13–110), a world which begins well enough ("With some regard to what is just and

*Nimrod repeats
the crime of Satan.*

right"), but is soon corrupted, as Nimrod, repeating the crime
of Satan, invents war, tyrannous monarchy, and the divine right
of Kings, and in his ambition tries to build the Tower of Babel.
Milton devotes twenty lines to a vivid account of the folly of
Babel, an account that in its savage way is brilliantly done; it
is in fact another vision of sin, akin to the method of Book 11,
which Milton never completely gives up when scenes of destruction are to be dealt with:

> But God who oft descends to visit men
> Unseen, and through thir habitations walks
> To mark thir doings, them beholding soon,
> Comes down to see thir Citie, ere the Tower
> Obstruct Heav'n Towrs, and in derision sets
> Upon thir Tongues a various Spirit to rase
> Quite out thir Native Language, and instead
> To sow a jangling noise of words unknown:
> Forthwith a hideous gabble rises loud
> Among the Builders; each to other calls
> Not understood, till hoarse, and all in rage,
> As mockt they storm; great laughter was in Heav'n
> And looking down, to see the hubbub strange
> And hear the din; thus was the building left
> Ridiculous, and the work Confusion nam'd.
>
> [12.48–62]

Nothing could be further from the promised sympathy and
consolation; and it is no surprise to find that in presenting the
close of this new cycle of degeneration, Milton seems to have
forgotten Michael's benign and all-inclusive promise that the
presence of God would never be lost to man:

> Thus will this latter, as the former World,
> Still tend from bad to worse, till God at last
> Wearied with their iniquities, withdraw
> His presence from among them, and avert
> His holy Eyes; resolving from thenceforth
> To leave them to thir own polluted wayes;
> And one peculiar Nation to select

158

From all the rest, of whom to be invok'd,
A Nation from one faithful man to spring:
Him on this side *Euphrates* yet residing,
Bred up in Idol-worship; O that men
(Canst thou believe?) should be so stupid grown . . .
                                              [12.105–16]

The banal denunciation is unworthy of Michael and of the
poem. The lines indicate all too well what lies ahead in the next
cycle of decay: the 250 lines relating the history of the Hebrew
people up to the birth of the Messiah. It is a section remarkably
uneven in poetical quality, with long stretches of barren paraphrase:

Meanwhile they in thir earthly *Canaan* plac't
Long time shall dwell and prosper, but when sins
National interrupt thir public peace,
Provoking God to raise them enemies:
From whom as oft he saves them penitent
By Judges first, then under Kings; of whom
The second, both for pietie renownd
And puissant deeds, a promise shall receive
Irrevocable, that his Regal Throne
For ever shall endure; the like shall sing
All Prophecie, That of the Royal Stock
Of *David* (so I name this King) shall rise
A Son, the Womans Seed to thee foretold,
Foretold to *Abraham,* as in whom shall trust
All Nations, and to Kings foretold, of Kings
The last, for of his Reign shall be no end.   [12.315–30]

The deterioration in the quality of the writing is painful,
especially in the clumsiness with which the prophecy of joy
is given in the last few lines above; instead of the promised
consolation, one feels rather a dogged insistence on getting
through with the job. Milton's preoccupation here with a local
and currently popular aspect of theology seems to have drawn
him away from the sources of poetic power that have so magnificently sustained his vision up through the middle of his

eleventh book; he has left behind now the redemptive vision of Paradise and God's Creation, and has turned his mind toward a doctrine of the few that contradicts the implications of his earlier vision of God's universal and creative presence. The principle of God's goodness has now become an abstract test of faith; for the chosen few, it seems, no demonstration of that goodness is needed. Thus the story of Joseph and his brothers, which might have offered a symbol of restoration in its long tale of love and reconciliation, is here passed over in the briefest, barest manner:

> The Grandchilde with twelve Sons increast, departs
> From *Canaan,* to a Land hereafter call'd
> *Egypt,* divided by the River *Nile;*
> See where it flows, disgorging at seaven mouthes
> Into the Sea: to sojourn in that Land
> He comes invited by a yonger Son
> In time of dearth, a Son whose worthy deeds
> Raise him to be the second in that Realme
> Of *Pharao* . . .   [12.155–63]

Yet immediately after this, as he turns to consider the plagues of Egypt and the destruction of Pharoah's host in the Red Sea, Milton's poetic power rises, and he gives another of his potent visions of the ravages of sin:

> To blood unshed the Rivers must be turnd,
> Frogs, Lice and Flies must all his Palace fill
> With loath'd intrusion, and fill all the land;
> His Cattel must of Rot and Murren die,
> Botches and blaines must all his flesh imboss,
> And all his people; Thunder mixt with Haile,
> Haile mixt with fire must rend th' *Egyptian* Skie
> And wheel on th' Earth, devouring where it rouls;
> What it devours not, Herb, or Fruit, or Graine,
> A darksom Cloud of Locusts swarming down
> Must eat, and on the ground leave nothing green:
>   [12.176–86]

Now of course the purpose of relating all these terrors is to show the power of God on Israel's side: "Such wondrous power God to his Saint will lend." And of course this whole section of the poem is interspersed with allusions to the coming victory of the Seed. Near the close of this cycle (12.285–314) Milton has Michael develop with admirable tact and skill the theological method of this coming victory, in a long passage which shows how well at times Milton can set abstractions into ringing verse:

> So Law appears imperfet, and but giv'n
> With purpose to resign them in full time
> Up to a better Cov'nant, disciplin'd
> From shadowie Types to Truth, from Flesh to Spirit,
> From imposition of strict Laws, to free
> Acceptance of large Grace, from servil fear
> To filial, works of Law to works of Faith. [12.300–06]

But in poetry the action of this victory cannot be left to faith, especially if the poet will not trust his readers to remember the ravages of sin set forth in his first ten books, and insists upon bending the best powers of his immense imagination toward the evocation of Babel and the plagues. If Milton is to achieve the promised poise of sorrow and joy, his visions of evil must here somehow be matched by his visions of good, as in his earlier books. One cannot argue that the Bible and Christian tradition forced Milton to refuse this counterpoint; the tale of Joseph, the visions of the Second Isaiah, and the long tradition of meditation on the Gospels might have shown a way. Milton, for reasons of his own, chooses to refuse that way.

Now, as the cycle of Israel's history moves toward its close, the inevitable decay sets in, and Israel's "foul Idolatries, and other faults" "so incense / God, as to leave them" and permit them to undergo the Babylonian captivity. Then, "Remembring mercie," God brings them home again for a brief subcycle of redemption and decay, ending with pollution of "the Temple

161

it self" (12.337–56). At last, over half-way through Book 12, the ground is prepared for the coming of the Messiah, whose whole career from Incarnation to Ascension is dealt with in less than a hundred lines, and these for the most part filled with theological explanation. Milton declines to represent the gospel story in any kind of extended vision: the chief events are simply mentioned, in lines that do not amount to more than fifteen in all, of which these are the most detailed:

> yet at his Birth a Starr
> Unseen before in Heav'n proclaims him com,
> And guides the Eastern Sages, who enquire
> His place, to offer Incense, Myrrh, and Gold;
> His place of birth a solemn Angel tells
> To simple Shepherds, keeping watch by night;
> They gladly thither haste, and by a Quire
> Of squadrond Angels hear his Carol sung.
>
> [12.360–67]

That Carol, we remember, has been sung in Milton's poem by the Angels before the Creation: it is not sung now.

For Milton is not here concerned with celebration or with affectionate meditation: he is "expounding a doctrine," as Madsen has very well said, and the exposition is admirably performed, in lines that "have their own kind of intellectual energy" (pp. 258–59).

> The Law of God exact he shall fulfill
> Both by obedience and by love, though love
> Alone fulfill the Law . . .
> For this he shall live hated, be blasphem'd,
> Seis'd on by force, judg'd, and to death condemnd
> A shameful and accurst, naild to the Cross
> By his own Nation, slaine for bringing Life;
> But to the Cross he nailes thy Enemies,
> The Law that is against thee, and the sins
> Of all mankinde, with him there crucifi'd,
> Never to hurt them more who rightly trust
> In this his satisfaction . . .   [12.402–19]

162

In this account of the method of redemption Milton returns to the inclusiveness of Book 10: this ransom shall redeem "as many as offerd Life / Neglect not, and the benefit imbrace / By Faith not void of workes" (12.425–27). How many this will be Milton does not here predict, but is content with the promise that

> Not onely to the Sons of *Abrahams* Loines
> Salvation shall be Preacht, but to the Sons
> Of *Abrahams* Faith wherever through the world;
> So in his seed all Nations shall be blest.   [12.447–50]

Taken in itself, this hundred-line account of the redemption would be sufficient to justify Adam's glad outcries, first, at the story of the Messiah's birth (372–85), and again, at the close:

> O goodness infinite, goodness immense!
> That all this good of evil shall produce,
> And evil turn to good; more wonderful
> Then that by which creation first brought forth
> Light out of darkness!   [12.469–73]

But the sad question remains: in poetry, can a hundred lines of hopeful doctrine outweigh six hundred lines of visionary woe? Curiously, after the happy outcry here, Milton seems concerned to make Adam feel the encroaching weight of all this earlier woe, for at once Adam adds the uneasy query:

> But say, if our deliverer up to Heav'n
> Must reascend, what will betide the few
> His faithful, left among th' unfaithful herd,
> The enemies of truth; who then shall guide
> His people, who defend? will they not deale
> Wors with his followers then with him they dealt?
>   [12.479–84]

The strange thing is that there is nothing at all in Milton's account of the redemption to evoke this sort of pessimistic query. On the contrary, the question of how many shall believe is left entirely and deliberately open, while the tone of optimism and victory dominates, in line with the promise with which the account begins: that the victory shall be won by the Savior "Not by destroying *Satan,* but his works / In thee and in thy Seed" (12.394–95). And at the close of the account, the Second Coming is presented in a way that should allow the equilibrium promised at the outset of Book 11: the Savior comes

> With glory and power to judge both quick & dead
> To judge th' unfaithful dead, but to reward
> His faithful, and receave them into bliss,
> Whether in Heav'n or Earth, for then the Earth
> Shall all be Paradise, far happier place
> Then this of *Eden,* and far happier daies.   [12.460–65]

But Milton cannot let it happen: those bitter visions of the world before the Flood were indeed symbolical of the world's way, as Milton, the man of his time, now sees the world; and with benign regard far diminished, Michael sets forth the final dark cycle of the vicious world's decay. It is told with a voice of partisan animus, harsh and merciless: the "Oyl of Pitty and the Balm of Lov" are lost in a hatred of blind wretches. At first the Apostles win

> Great numbers of each Nation to receave
> With joy the tidings brought from Heav'n: at length
> Thir Ministry perform'd, and race well run,
> Thir doctrine and thir story written left,
> They die; but in thir room, as they forwarne,
> Wolves shall succeed for teachers, grievous Wolves,
> Who all the sacred mysteries of Heav'n
> To thir own vile advantages shall turne
> Of lucre and ambition, and the truth
> With superstitions and traditions taint,
> Left onely in those written Records pure,
> Though not but by the Spirit understood. . . .
>   What will they then
> But force the Spirit of Grace it self, and binde

His consort Libertie; what, but unbuild
His living Temples, built by Faith to stand,
Thir own Faith not anothers: for on Earth
Who against Faith and Conscience can be heard
Infallible? yet many will presume:
Whence heavie persecution shall arise
On all who in the worship persevere
Of Spirit and Truth; the rest, farr greater part,
Will deem in outward Rites and specious formes
Religion satisfi'd; Truth shall retire
Bestuck with slandrous darts, and works of Faith
Rarely be found: so shall the World goe on,
To good malignant, to bad men benigne,
Under her own waight groaning, till the day
Appeer to respiration to the just,
And vengeance to the wicked . . .   [12.503–41]

And in that mood of "vengeance" Michael alters the charitable view of the world's conclusion that he has given only eighty lines before. Now, we hear, the Savior will come

> to dissolve
> *Satan* with his perverted World, then raise
> From the conflagrant mass, purg'd and refin'd,
> New Heav'ns, new Earth, Ages of endless date
> Founded in righteousness and peace and love,
> To bring forth fruits Joy and eternal Bliss.
>
>   [12.546–51]

The contradiction, the fissure in the poem's last two books cannot be healed; the weight of woe has gradually weakened the epilogue's connection with the poem's center, and here the epilogue at last drops off.

Milton makes no effort to retrieve it. Adam makes no comment on this final cycle of woe, but instead turns to summarize what he has allegedly learned from the angel's whole account of "the Race of time." What Adam says here reminds us of the aim set forth in the first half of Book 11:

> Yet least they faint
> At the sad Sentence rigorously urg'd,
> For I behold them soft'nd and with tears
> Bewailing thir excess, all terror hide.
> If patiently thy bidding they obey,
> Dismiss them not disconsolate; reveale
> To *Adam* what shall come in future dayes,
> As I shall thee enlighten, intermix
> My Cov'nant in the Womans seed renewd;
> So send them forth, though sorrowing, yet in peace:
>
> [11.108–17]

But Michael's sentence has been rigorously urged, and terror has been emphasized, not hidden, in his history of the world. One can feel, in reading Adam's summary of Milton's design, how far Milton has failed here to measure up to the great achievement of his first ten books, in which the promised consolation has already been so well conveyed:

> Henceforth I learne, that to obey is best,
> And love with feare the onely God, to walk
> As in his presence, ever to observe
> His providence, and on him sole depend,
> Merciful over all his works, with good
> Still overcoming evil, and by small
> Accomplishing great things, by things deemd weak
> Subverting worldly strong, and worldly wise
> By simply meek; that suffering for Truths sake
> Is fortitude to highest victorie,
> And to the faithful Death the Gate of Life;
> Taught this by his example whom I now
> Acknowledge my Redeemer ever blest. [12.561–73]

Appropriately, here too Michael recovers his "regard benigne" and prepares the way for the poem's perfectly tempered finale, by recalling that the promised redemption consists primarily in the renewal of man's inner powers: those powers of the soul by which the bard has just pursued his triumphant journey of the mind toward Paradise:

166

To whom thus also th' Angel last repli'd:
This having learnt, thou hast attained the summe
Of wisdom: hope no higher, though all the Starrs
Thou knewst by name, and all th' ethereal Powers,
All secrets of the deep, all Natures works,
Or works of God in Heav'n, Air, Earth, or Sea,
And all the riches of this World enjoydst,
And all the rule, one Empire; onely add
Deeds to thy knowledge answerable, add Faith,
Add Vertue, Patience, Temperance, add Love,
By name to come call'd Charitie, the soul
Of all the rest: then wilt thou not be loath
To leave this Paradise, but shall possess
A Paradise within thee, happier farr.   [12.574–87]

IV

PARADISE REGAIN'D
The Interior Teacher

Concerning universals of which we can have knowledge, we do not listen to anyone speaking and making sounds outside ourselves. We listen to Truth which presides over our minds within us, though of course we may be bidden to listen by someone using words. Our real Teacher is he who is so listened to, who is said to dwell in the inner man, namely Christ, that is, the unchangeable power and eternal wisdom of God. To this wisdom every rational soul gives heed, but to each is given only so much as he is able to receive, according to his own good or evil will. If anyone is ever deceived it is not the fault of Truth, any more than it is the fault of the common light of day that the bodily eyes are often deceived.

. . . when we have to do with things which we behold with the mind, that is, with the intelligence and with reason, we speak of things which we look upon directly in the inner light of truth which illumines the inner man and is inwardly enjoyed.

—Augustine, *De Magistro*

1. The Meditative Voice

MILTON'S nephew, Edward Phillips, tells us that even in the seventeenth century *Paradise Regain'd* was "generally censur'd to be much inferiour to" *Paradise Lost,* though he notes that the poet "could not hear with patience any such thing when related to him." "Possibly," the nephew adds, "the Subject may not afford such variety of Invention, but it is thought by the most judicious to be little or nothing inferiour to the other for stile and decorum."[1] But it is exactly the style and decorum that have troubled Milton's readers. For Milton was given to writing in clearly defined genres: the pastoral elegy, the classical epic, the Greek drama; and for all these kinds of poetry he well knew the appropriate style and decorum. But what kind of poem is *Paradise Regain'd?* Usually, after the hint given by Milton thirty years before the poem appeared, it has been called a "brief epic" modeled on the book of Job.[2] But Tillyard has argued that it has a closer affinity with the old Morality plays; and, more recently, Arnold Stein, in a persuasive book, has made an extended effort to show that the poem is truly a drama, though the stage is set in the hero's mind: a true drama in the usual terms of character, motivation, incident, and dramatic surprise.[3] Now all these epic and dramatic aspects are truly there in the poem; the trouble is that in the actual reading they

---

EPIGRAPH: Augustine, *Earlier Writings,* pp. 95, 96.

1. See *The Early Lives of Milton,* ed. Helen Darbishire (London, Constable, 1932), pp. 75–76.

2. See the famous prologue to the second book of *The Reason of Church Government* (1642).

3. E. M. W. Tillyard, *Milton* (London, Chatto and Windus, 1930), pp. 317–18. Arnold Stein, *Heroic Knowledge* (Minneapolis, University of Min-

seem to be only the vestiges, the echoes, the attenuated sketches of what might have made a true epic or drama; the possibilities of the action are strangely muted, deliberately underplayed, as though the center of the action lay elsewhere.

Yet another suggestion, advanced by Tillyard thirty years ago, has not thus far received the attention it deserves. Tillyard noted (*Milton,* p. 322) that *Paradise Regain'd* and Vergil's *Georgics* were poems of almost exactly the same length, a little more than two thousand lines, and that both poems were divided into four books; moreover, some kind of Vergilian analogy, he thought, must reside in the fact that Milton's opening line, "I who e're while the happy Garden sung," clearly echoes the lines that used to open the *Aeneid* in Renaissance editions:

> Ille ego, qui quondam gracili modulatus avena
> carmen, et egressus silvis vicina coegi
> ut quamvis avido parerent arva colono,
> gratum opus agricolis, at nunc horrentia Martis . . .

—lines, now widely regarded as authentic, which allude to Vergil's earlier works in the pastoral and georgic kinds. It is indeed a happy thought that Milton may thus have concluded his poetical career by publishing three poems in what his age regarded as the three great classical modes: the epic, the georgic, and the drama in the manner of the Greeks.

The more we brood over the possibility, the more fruitful it seems. For *Paradise Regain'd,* as everyone has noticed, is not written in the grand style of *Paradise Lost;* it has its flashes of grandeur, but on the whole its writing is simpler, more subdued, more direct. This is just what the man of the Renaissance was trained to feel in comparing the *Aeneid* to the *Georgics;* in the

---

nesota Press, 1957). See also the presentation of an adverse view of the poem by W. W. Robson, "The Better Fortitude," in *The Living Milton,* ed. Kermode; and the study of the poem from the standpoint of Christ's mediatorial role by Barbara Kiefer Lewalski, "Theme and Structure in *Paradise Regained,*" *Studies in Philology,* 57 (1960), 186–220.

classic definition of "the three styles" handed down from late
Roman critics, Vergil's *Aeneid* was the model of the grand
style, his *Georgics,* the model of the middle style, and his
Eclogues, the model of the low style. As Servius said: "tres
enim sunt characteres, humilis, medius, grandiloquus: quos
omnes in hoc invenimus poeta. nam in Aeneide grandiloquum
habet, in georgicis medium, in bucolicis humilem pro qualitate
negotiorum et personarum."[4] Thus at the outset of *Paradise
Lost* Milton asks the Heavenly Muse to aid his "adventrous
Song, / That with no middle flight intends to soar / Above th'
Aonian Mount"; but now, it seems, in *Paradise Regain'd,* he
chooses to make a middle flight in the georgic style, which
Vergil himself may be said to define at the outset of his second
book:

> non ego cuncta meis amplecti versibus opto,
> non, mihi si linguae centum sint oraque centum,
> ferrea vox.   [42–44][5]

Furthermore, the two works share a common ethical theme:
the praise of the temperate, disciplined, frugal life, as opposed
to the grandeur, luxury, and vice of empires. Thus, as Milton's
Tempter offers Jesus the power and the glory of the Roman
Empire, Milton's hero answers by scorning

> That people victor once, now vile and base,
> Deservedly made vassal, who once just,
> Frugal, and mild, and temperate, conquer'd well,
> But govern ill the Nations under yoke,

4. *Servii Grammatici Qui Feruntur in Vergilii Carmina Commentarii,*
ed. G. Thilo and H. Hagen (4 vols. Leipzig, 1881–1902), Vol. 3, fasc. 1,
pp. 1–2.

5.   "I choose not to enfold
              All things within my verse, not though I had
              A hundred tongues and mouths, a voice of iron."
From the translation of the *Georgics* by Smith Palmer Bovie (University of
Chicago Press, 1956).

Peeling thir Provinces, exhausted all
By lust and rapine; first ambitious grown
Of triumph that insulting vanity;
Then cruel, by thir sports to blood enur'd
Of fighting beasts, and men to beasts, expos'd,
Luxurious by thir wealth, and greedier still,
And from the daily Scene effeminate.   [4.132–42]

It is very close to the warning that Vergil implies throughout
the *Georgics,* and indeed makes openly at the end of his second
book, along with an allusion to the degrading effects of the
theater, Milton's "daily Scene":

But happy
Too is he who knows the gods of nature,
Old man Silvanus, Pan, the sister nymphs.
Not for him "the mandate of the people,"
The royal cloak of kings, not dissonance
Creating civil wars, the swift onslaught
From Balkan coalitions; not for him
The Roman State or Empires doomed to die . . .
Others lash the unknown seas with oars,
Rush at the sword, pay court in royal halls.
One destroys a city and its homes
To drink from jeweled cups and sleep on scarlet;
One hoards his wealth and lies on buried gold.
One gapes dumbfounded at the speaker's stand;
At the theater, still another, open-mouthed,
Reels before crescendos of applause
From the tiers where mob and dignitaries sit . . .
    The farmer drives his curved plough through the earth:
His year's work lies in this; thus he sustains
His homeland . . .
Such a life the Sabines once embraced,
And Romulus and Remus; in this way
Etruria grew strong; thus Rome was formed . . .[6]

6. *Georgics,* 2.493–534, in the translation by Bovie. See the whole
famous passage beginning "O fortunatos nimium, sua si bona norint, /
agricolas!" (2.458 f.).

A georgic form, a georgic style, a georgic theme: everything combines to suggest that Milton, in *Paradise Regain'd,* is following out the same design that he set for himself in *Paradise Lost* and *Samson Agonistes:* to convert the modes of classic poetry into the service of Christianity. In *Paradise Regain'd* he has done this, I believe, by converting Vergil's georgic mode into a channel for religious meditation, with the result that the poem belongs, simultaneously, to the classical mode of didactic, instructive poetry,[7] and to the Christian genre of formal meditations on the Gospel.

From this standpoint we can understand the meaning of the basic style in which the poem is written: a ground-style that Milton carefully announces in his opening lines and maintains with strong consistency throughout the first book:

> I who e're while the happy Garden sung,
> By one mans disobedience lost, now sing
> Recover'd Paradise to all mankind,
> By one mans firm obedience fully tri'd
> Through all temptation, and the Tempter foil'd
> In all his wiles, defeated and repuls't,
> And *Eden* rais'd in the wast Wilderness.

The allusion to *Paradise Lost* here asks us to recall that poem, and to note how different this new poem will be in its theme and hence in its style. We need only recall the latinate suspension and compression of that first enormous sentence of *Paradise Lost* to feel the contrast with the normal movement and scope of educated English speech in *Paradise Regain'd.* This new poem, then, as Tillyard says, "is not an epic, it does not

7. See Addison's essay on the *Georgics,* first published in Dryden's translation of Vergil (1697): "No rules therefore that relate to *Pastoral,* can any way affect the *Georgics,* since they fall under that class of Poetry, which consists in giving plain and direct instructions to the reader; whether they be Moral duties, as those of *Theognis* and *Pythagoras;* or Philosophical speculations, as those of *Aratus* and *Lucretius;* or Rules of practice, as those of *Hesiod* and *Virgil.*" Addison, *Miscellaneous Works,* ed. A. C. Guthkelch (2 vols. London, 1914), 2, 4.

try to be an epic, and it must not be judged by any kind of epic standard" (*Milton*, p. 316). It is a simple "I" who sings this new poem: a plain man without those bardic "robes" that C. S. Lewis sees as characteristic of the high style of *Paradise Lost*. The voice of the narrator now speaks in the middle style appropriate to a personal meditation prompted not at all by emulation of the epic Muse, but purely by the "Spirit who ledst this glorious Eremite / Into the Desert." Reversing the order of Vergil's two great poems, the Christian poet will now "tell of deeds / Above Heroic, though in secret done."

Hence the trappings of *Paradise Lost* recede from view in Book 1 of *Paradise Regain'd:* as the opening lines prophesy, the syntax will tend to display the normal, supple, easy movement of an educated mind. Furthermore, when we recall the vast range of elaborate epic similes in the opening book of *Paradise Lost,* it is significant to notice that the opening book of *Paradise Regain'd* contains not a single simile of this kind; indeed it contains no classical allusions whatsoever, except near the close of the book, where the pagan oracles are mentioned only in order to announce their demise, as Jesus says to Satan:

> No more shalt thou by oracling abuse
> The Gentiles; henceforth Oracles are ceast,
> And thou no more with Pomp and Sacrifice
> Shalt be enquir'd at *Delphos* or elsewhere,
> At least in vain, for they shall find thee mute.
> God hath now sent his living Oracle
> Into the World, to teach his final will,
> And sends his Spirit of Truth henceforth to dwell
> In pious Hearts, an inward Oracle
> To all truth requisite for men to know.   [1.455–64]

The firm and quiet manner of these lines, dignified, yet modest, is representative of the ground-style laid down in Book 1 of *Paradise Regain'd* as a central principle of the whole poem's action. To be sure, the difference from *Paradise Lost* is not complete. The language is less obviously latinate, though there is still plenty of latinity, since this is part of the Renaissance heritage and is also appropriate, in moderation, to a poem with a georgic model. And there are still a good many of those peculiar Miltonic compressions, transcending and defying grammar. The style, in short, reminds us, at a distance, of the manner of *Paradise Lost:* but it is all deliberately muted, thoroughly absorbed into another texture of writing:

> So spake our Morning Star then in his rise,
> And looking round on every side beheld
> A pathless Desert, dusk with horrid shades;
> The way he came not having mark'd, return
> Was difficult, by humane steps untrod;
> And he still on was led, but with such thoughts
> Accompanied of things past and to come
> Lodg'd in his brest, as well might recommend
> Such Solitude before choicest Society.
> Full forty days he pass'd, whether on hill
> Sometimes, anon in shady vale, each night
> Under the covert of some ancient Oak,
> Or Cedar, to defend him from the dew,
> Or harbour'd in one Cave, is not reveal'd . . .
>
> [1.294–307]

We can recognize the voice and the manner as Miltonic: but the language is essentially that of any educated man. This effect, both common and peculiar, is characteristic of Vergil's georgic style, and is also essential to the meditative genre. This meditative kind of poetry consists of "current language heightened" (Hopkins' phrase)—heightened by a voice that is at once that of a unique individual and yet still the voice of a man searching inwardly in common ways for the common bond of mankind. The muted, chastened style thus announced in the first book of *Paradise Regain'd* seems appropriately developed out of Vergil's middle style, in order to pursue a work that is essentially a meditation on the Gospel.

2. The Son of God

From beginning to end of this poem the meditative mind of
the narrator roams freely over the past, present, and future life
of its hero. We begin, after the brief prologue, with a memory
of the scene at Jordan during the baptism of Jesus by John: a
scene that Satan recapitulates only forty lines later when he
addresses his Council and warns them that he has heard "the
Sov'raign voice" at Jordan pronounce this man "my Son." And
only forty lines after this (130 f.) we hear the "Sov'raign
voice" itself, addressing Gabriel in Heaven, and summing up
the whole life of the Son, from the mission of Gabriel at the
Annunciation, through the coming temptation in the Wilderness, where the hero will "lay down the rudiments / Of his
great warfare," in which he will destroy the power of Sin and
Death "By Humiliation and strong Sufferance." Thus prepared
by the Father's own summation of the Son's career, we now
come to "the Son of God" himself:

> Mean while the Son of God, who yet some days
> Lodg'd in *Bethabara* where *John* baptiz'd,
> Musing and much revolving in his brest,
> How best the mighty work he might begin
> Of Saviour to mankind, and which way first
> Publish his God-like office now mature,
> One day forth walk'd alone, the Spirit leading;
> And his deep thoughts, the better to converse
> With solitude, till far from track of men,
> Thought following thought, and step by step led on,
> He entred now the bordering Desert wild,
> And with dark shades and rocks environ'd round,
> His holy Meditations thus persu'd. [1.183–195]

The period of temptation, we see, is primarily a mental retirement—"thought following thought"—and what follows
now (196 f.) is a meditation on the entire life of Jesus, given

in the person of the hero himself, as he meditates on the meaning of his existence:

> O what a multitude of thoughts at once
> Awakn'd in me swarm, while I consider
> What from within I feel my self, and hear
> What from without comes often to my ears,
> Ill sorting with my present state compar'd.

He recalls his childhood, his visit to the Temple, his early aspirations when "victorious deeds / Flam'd in my heart, heroic acts";

> Yet held it more humane, more heavenly first
> By winning words to conquer willing hearts,
> And make perswasion do the work of fear;
> At least to try ...

Then he recalls how his mother had "inly rejoyc'd" at his youthful thoughts, how she had informed him that he was the son of Heaven's Eternal King, how she had told him of the Annunciation and the Nativity: when

> a glorious Quire
> Of Angels in the fields of *Bethlehem* sung
> To Shepherds watching at their folds by night,
> And told them the Messiah was now born,
> Where they might see him, and to thee they came;
> Directed to the Manger where thou lais't,
> For in the Inn was left no better room ...

A Biblical simplicity is thus interwoven with the subdued Miltonic and latinate idiom of this poem. And we learn of the Wise Men, of Simeon and Anna, and how Jesus, pondering these things, along with the Scriptures, came to realize he was the promised Messiah:

> this chiefly, that my way must lie
> Through many a hard assay even to the death,
> E're I the promis'd Kingdom can attain,

Or work Redemption for mankind, whose sins
Full weight must be transferr'd upon my head.

Then finally, after this glimpse of the Passion, he remembers
the central scene at Jordan:

But as I rose out of the laving stream,
Heaven open'd her eternal doors, from whence
The Spirit descended on me like a Dove,
And last the sum of all, my Father's voice,
Audibly heard from Heav'n, pronounc'd me his,
Me his beloved Son, in whom alone
He was well pleas'd; by which I knew the time
Now full, that I no more should live obscure,
But openly begin, as best becomes
The Authority which I deriv'd from Heaven.
And now by some strong motion I am led
Into this wilderness, to what intent
I learn not yet, perhaps I need not know;
For what concerns my knowledge God reveals.

This meditative poem, we see, first of all, concerns the self-
discovery of the hero: what it means to be pronounced the Son
of God. And indeed, as we read and re-read this poem, we are
struck by the way in which that phrase "Son of God" resounds
throughout the poem as the chief title by which Milton alludes
to the hero. The phrase "Son of God" occurs no less than 39
times; 10 times in Book 1 and 21 times in the concluding book.
A few statistics may be in order here to make an important
point. Milton calls his hero Jesus only 6 times; he calls him
Savior 21 times, Messiah 7 times—but he never once calls
his hero by the name of Christ. This is not simply because he
prefers to use the Hebrew equivalent, Messiah, for as I have
said, this term is not used often, nor does he use the translated
title "Anointed" more than once.

Why not use the term *Christ?* I think Milton avoids the term
here because he is not writing only about the life of Christ, that
unique being, Prophet, Priest, and King; he is writing about

a composite generalized being whom he calls the Son of God in such an insistent way as to recall the opening of John's Gospel: "But as many as received him, to them gave he power to become the sons of God" (1:12); or the promise of Paul in Romans 8:14: "For as many as are led by the Spirit of God, they are the sons of God." Or, best of all, the words of John's first Epistle (3:1–3): "Behold, what manner of love the Father hath bestowed upon us, that we should be called the sons of God: therefore the world knoweth us not, because it knew him not. Beloved, now are we the sons of God, and it doth not yet appear what we shall be: but we know that, when he shall appear, we shall be like him; for we shall see him as he is. And every man that hath this hope in him purifieth himself, even as he is pure."

After tantalizing us with the phrase throughout the poem, Milton finally clarifies the issues for us at the very close, as Satan is about to make his last desperate effort: the temptation of the pinnacle. Here, with a wonderful irony, Milton matches the opening meditation of the hero by giving now Satan's own sardonic commentary on the Gospel story, Satan's version of what it means to be the Son of God:

> To whom the Fiend now swoln with rage reply'd:
> Then hear, O Son of *David,* Virgin-born;
> For Son of God to me is yet in doubt,
> Of the Messiah I have heard foretold
> By all the Prophets; of thy birth at length
> Announc't by *Gabriel* with the first I knew,
> And of the Angelic Song in *Bethlehem* field,
> On thy birth-night, that sung thee Saviour born.
> From that time seldom have I ceas'd to eye
> Thy infancy, thy childhood, and thy youth,
> Thy manhood last, though yet in private bred;
> Till at the Ford of *Jordan* whither all
> Flock'd to the Baptist, I among the rest,
> Though not to be Baptiz'd, by voice from Heav'n
> Heard thee pronounc'd the Son of God belov'd.

181

Thenceforth I thought thee worth my nearer view
And narrower Scrutiny, that I might learn
In what degree or meaning thou art call'd
The Son of God, which bears no single sence;
The Son of God I also am, or was,
And if I was, I am; relation stands;
All men are Sons of God; yet thee I thought
In some respect far higher so declar'd.   [4.499–521]

He has not long to wait: placed on the pinnacle and faced with
the final temptation, the hero answers in the words of the
Bible: "Tempt not the Lord thy God, he said and stood. / But
Satan smitten with amazement fell." Into those brief words,
"Tempt not the Lord thy God," Milton has packed a trinity of
meanings: they bear no single sense.[1] First of all, in the traditional interpretation, the words give the answer that any man
might give: that is, one must not ask God for unreasonable
help, one must not ask for unnecessary evidence of divine
favor. But secondly, in Milton's strategic placing of the words,
they show why Satan fell, stupefied, "strook with dread and
anguish," filled with "Ruin, and desperation, and dismay."
Satan is confounded by the revelation that he has been tempt-
ing divinity incarnate. And thirdly, we may take the words to
indicate the full self-realization of the hero: he understands
now what he has not known earlier, or has known by glimpses
only: that he is himself divine.

Certainly the critics are right who have said that this invul-
nerable hero makes it very difficult to produce a dramatic
development in the poem. As D. C. Allen has pointed out,[2]
Satan is "aghast" from the opening and feels his forces shat-

1. For the wide range of interpretations possible here see the study of
the third temptation given by Elizabeth Marie Pope in her valuable book,
Paradise Regained: The Tradition and the Poem (Baltimore, Johns Hopkins Press, 1947), chapter 7. Also the admirable article by A. S. P. Wood-
house, "Theme and Pattern in *Paradise Regained*," *University of Toronto
Quarterly*, 25 (1955–56), 167–82; esp. p. 181.

2. Don Cameron Allen, *The Harmonious Vision* (Baltimore, Johns Hopkins Press, 1954), pp. 110–15.

tered from the outset; his "motivation" for the temptations seems to be the curiosity of desperation rather than any real hope of victory. How, then, can the poem sustain our interest?

I believe the answer lies in watching the movements of the meditative mind as it defines the nature of the Son of God. The whole poem presents a mind that uses the "characters" to explore the problems and besetting sins of any potential Son of God among men: a mind that conveys the process of temptation by creating what might be called a contest of styles. The ground of this great warfare is laid down, stylistically, in Book 1; what we feel here, I think, is the presence of a mind engaged in an immense effort at self-control, a mind held in leash, poised, tense, alert, watching any tendency toward elaboration, luxury, self-indulgence: alert to control any temptation that might lead the meditator far away from the ground that he strikes, ethically, theologically, and stylistically, at the end of Book 1, in answer to Satan's opening maneuvers:

> To whom our Saviour with unalter'd brow.
> Thy coming hither, though I know thy scope,
> I bid not or forbid; do as thou find'st
> Permission from above; thou canst not more.

3. The Contest of Styles

Book 1 is a prelude: it draws the scene; it establishes the middle style; it sets the problems to be explored, and foresees their conclusion. The action proper begins with Book 2, where the life of Jesus is considered from many different perspectives. First, from the viewpoint of the new-born Christians who had been baptized at Jordan—Andrew, Simon Peter, and others, whom we meet in a properly georgic setting:

> Then on the bank of *Jordan,* by a Creek:
> Where winds with Reeds, and Osiers whisp'ring play
> Plain Fishermen, no greater men them call,

> Close in a Cottage low together got
> Thir unexpected loss and plaints out breath'd.
> [2.25–29]

They speak appropriately on the lower edge of the middle style, in language that moves gracefully out of the Biblical toward the latinate:

> our eyes beheld
> Messiah certainly now come, so long
> Expected of our Fathers; we have heard
> His words, his wisdom full of grace and truth,
> Now, now, for sure, deliverance is at hand,
> The Kingdom shall to *Israel* be restor'd:
> Thus we rejoyc'd, but soon our joy is turn'd
> Into perplexity and new amaze . . . [2.31–38]

But they end with simple faith: "Soon we shall see our hope, our joy return."

From these we turn to "Mother *Mary*" (2.60 f.), whom we find pondering in her heart all the major events in her son's life to this point: the Annunciation, the Nativity—

> In such a season born when scarce a Shed
> Could be obtain'd to shelter him or me
> From the bleak air; a Stable was our warmth,
> A Manger his . . .

the flight into Egypt, his acknowledgment as Son at Jordan, the prophecy of Simeon, and that time when Jesus visited the Temple:

> when twelve years he scarce had seen,
> I lost him, but so found, as well I saw
> He could not lose himself; but went about
> His Father's business . . .

And now as Mary "with thoughts / Meekly compos'd awaited the fulfilling," we have a glimpse of her son, at the center of the poem's inward action, as he,

> tracing the Desert wild,
> Sole but with holiest Meditations fed,
> Into himself descended . . .   [2.109–11]

After all these humble, inward scenes, so frequently marked
by a Biblical simplicity of phrasing, the process of temptation
now bursts upon us in the high oratorical style of *Paradise Lost,*
as we hear Satan addressing his host of devils and consulting
with them over how to proceed in the face of such dangerous
self-mastery:

> Princes, Heavens antient Sons, Aethereal Thrones,
> Demonian Spirits now, from the Element
> Each of his reign allotted, rightlier call'd,
> Powers of Fire, Air, Water, and Earth beneath . . .
>   [2.121–24]

That touch of the old fallen oratory leads us quickly down
to the lowest level of sensuality, as Belial moves to suggest that
the Son of God be tempted by sexual appetite. Thus Milton
skillfully manages to include in his poem an aspect of human
weakness that could not be associated with Jesus. Milton has
Satan reject Belial's suggestion in such a way as to remind us
of lust's long history, bringing in the first strong coloring from
classical mythology that has been allowed thus far in the poem:

> Before the Flood thou with thy lusty Crew,
> False titl'd Sons of God—

note how Milton keeps the problem ever before us: what it
means to be a Son of God—

> roaming the Earth
> Cast wanton eyes on the daughters of men,
> And coupl'd with them, and begot a race.
> Have we not seen, or by relation heard,
> In Courts and Regal Chambers how thou lurk'st,
> In Wood or Grove by mossie Fountain side,
> In Valley or Green Meadow to way-lay

Some beauty rare, *Calisto, Clymene,*
Daphne, or *Semele, Antiopa,*
Or *Amymone, Syrinx,* many more
Too long, then lay'st thy scapes on names ador'd,
Apollo, Neptune, Jupiter, or *Pan,*
Satyr, or Fawn, or Silvan?   [2.178–91]

That brilliant cluster of old Ovidian myths, rejected here
even by Satan, prepares us for the meditative combat that will
now develop in a long contest of styles, as the rich, sensuous
coloring and the high rhetoric of the world rises up against the
"frugal" ground-style set in Book 1: that middle, georgic style
which represents the way of temperance struggling against the
self-indulgence of an elaborate style.

. Thus the vision of the Banquet now arises (2.337 f.) in an
effort to obliterate the hero's self-control. It is a step upward
from Belial's sensuality, but it includes a touch of Belial's suggestion in the vision of

> Nymphs of *Diana's* train, and *Naiades*
> With fruits and flowers from *Amalthea's* horn,
> And Ladies of th' *Hesperides* . . .

Its appeal to hunger of course relates back to the preliminary
temptation of Book 1, while the whole scene looks forward to
the following temptations of wealth and regal power; for it is
"A Table richly spred, in regal mode." Milton is offering a
Roman banquet to all the quickened senses:

> And at a stately side-board by the wine
> That fragrant smell diffus'd, in order stood
> Tall stripling youths rich clad, of fairer hew
> Then *Ganymed* or *Hylas* . . .

The worlds of classic myth and medieval romance are ran-
sacked for physical allurement and brought to a climax in
those superbly over-wrought lines of Spenserian motif and
alliteration, carrying the appeal of sound to its furthest poetical
extreme:

186

[margin handwritten notes:] Elaborate ('evil') style vs. middle georgic (temperate) style. in the Banquet scene.

And Ladies of th' *Hesperides,* that seem'd
Fairer then feign'd of old, or fabl'd since
Of Fairy Damsels met in Forest wide
By Knights of *Logres,* or of *Lyones,*
Lancelot or *Pelleas,* or *Pellenore* . . .

We return with a shock to the frugal ground-style, as Jesus rejects the offer, renouncing imagery in favor of irony—except for a brief suggestion of the communion table:

To whom thus Jesus temperately reply'd:
Said'st thou not that to all things I had right?
And who withholds my pow'r that right to use?
Shall I receive by gift what of my own,
When and where likes me best, I can command?
I can at will, doubt not, as soon as thou,
Command a Table in this Wilderness,
And call swift flights of Angels ministrant
Array'd in Glory on my cup to attend . . .

So the central contest, the full excitement, of the poem lies in the movements, the fluctuations, of the meditative mind itself. It is an inward combat created by Milton's brilliant manipulation of styles, a contest in which the flights of poetic splendor are consistently drawn back by the prevailing net of a frugal, georgic style to the ground of renunciation and temperance.[1] The way in which this ground-style represents the controlling ideal of the poem is clearly shown now in the speech of Jesus that closes Book 2, in answer to the temptation of wealth. Here Milton gives, exactly in the center of the poem, a definition of true Kingship, true Sonship. Jesus first alludes to Gideon, Jephthah, and David, and then places them beside certain men "Among the Heathen" who are also "Worthy of Memorial":

1. I believe that this functional view of the basic style of *Paradise Regain'd* was suggested to me by certain remarks of W. Menzies in his essay, "Milton: the Last Poems," *Essays and Studies, 24* (1938), 80–113; see esp. pp. 109–11. A similar view is developed by Jacques Blondel in the introduction (really a sizable monograph) prefaced to his bilingual edition of *Paradise Regain'd* (Paris, Aubier, 1955); see esp. pp. 92–110 *passim.*

"Quintius, Fabricius, Curius, Regulus." This collocation of Roman and Biblical heroes of the simple life points the way toward the association of Job with Socrates that is soon to follow in Book 3, as Jesus rejects the temptation of glory by praising higher conquests won

> By deeds of peace, by wisdom eminent,
> By patience, temperance; I mention still
> Him whom thy wrongs with Saintly patience born,
> Made famous in a Land and times obscure;
> Who names not now with honour patient *Job?*
> Poor *Socrates* (who next more memorable?) . . .
>
> [3.91–96]

Anticipating this open praise of Socrates, the great ethical speech of the Son ending Book 2 proceeds to show how the Socratic reliance on the inner man (Socrates' "discovery of the soul," as Cornford has called it)[2] leads onward into the Christian concept of highest kingship: we note the quiet implication of the "wreath of thorns" and the "burden" of Second Isaiah:

> What if with like aversion I reject
> Riches and Realms; yet not for that a Crown,
> Golden in shew, is but a wreath of thorns,
> Brings dangers, troubles, cares, and sleepless nights
> To him who wears the Regal Diadem,
> When on his shoulders each mans burden lies;
> For therein stands the office of a King,
> His Honour, Vertue, Merit and chief Praise,
> That for the Publick all this weight he bears.
> Yet he who reigns within himself, and rules
> Passions, Desires, and Fears, is more a King;
> Which every wise and vertuous man attains:
> And who attains not, ill aspires to rule
> Cities of men, or head-strong Multitudes,
> Subject himself to Anarchy within,
> Or lawless passions in him which he serves.

2. F. M. Cornford, *Before and after Socrates* (Cambridge University Press, 1950), chapter 2, esp. pp. 50–51.

But to guide Nations in the way of truth
By saving Doctrine, and from errour lead
To know, and knowing worship God aright,
Is yet more Kingly, this attracts the Soul,
Governs the inner man, the nobler part,
That other o're the body only reigns,
And oft by force, which to a generous mind
So reigning can be no sincere delight.
Besides to give a Kingdom hath been thought
Greater and nobler done, and to lay down
Far more magnanimous, then to assume.   [2.457–83]

—"to lay down"—with his careful placing of those words at the end of a line, Milton forces us to pause and complete the phrase in the familiar words of John. And thus the Greek virtue of magnanimity is redefined in terms of Christian sacrifice. It is important that thus, in the middle of the poem, Milton should pay tribute to classic virtue and classic thought, for the tribute helps to qualify the renunciation of Greek culture that follows in Book 4.

4. *The Voice of Milton*

From this steadfast center of the poem, a center defined both by concept and by style, Satan now attempts to move the hero by rhetorical and imagistic elaborations that gradually rise toward the height of Milton's grand style. The temptation of glory begins on a higher pitch of rhetorical insinuation than anything we have seen earlier, especially in contrast with the long, straightforward, temperate speech we have just heard:

I see thou know'st what is of use to know,
What best to say canst say, to do canst do;
Thy actions to thy words accord, thy words
To thy large heart give utterance due, thy heart
Conteins of good, wise, just, the perfect shape.
         . . . wherefore deprive

All Earth her wonder at thy acts, thy self
The fame and glory, glory the reward
That sole excites to high attempts the flame
Of most erected Spirits, most temper'd pure
Aetherial, who all pleasures else despise,
All treasures and all gain esteem as dross,
And dignities and powers all but the highest?

[3.7–30]

In line with such artifice and convolution the first half of the
third book is devoted to abstract argument at a very high level
of rhetorical elaboration and oratorical prowess.

Jesus answers this challenge with a burst of blunt oratory
that has puzzled many readers, since the harshness here seems
out of line with the charity of a Savior, seems rather to voice
the bitter disillusionment of John Milton himself, who had
once tried to win a victory of the Just with the help of the
many, and had seen the whole effort fail:

For what is glory but the blaze of fame,
The peoples praise, if always praise unmixt?
And what the people but a herd confus'd,
A miscellaneous rabble, who extol
Things vulgar, & well weigh'd, scarce worth the praise,
They praise and they admire they know not what;
And know not whom, but as one leads the other;
And what delight to be by such extoll'd,
To live upon thir tongues and be thir talk,
Of whom to be disprais'd were no small praise?
His lot who dares be singularly good.
Th' intelligent among them and the wise
Are few, and glory scarce of few is rais'd.
This is true glory and renown, when God
Looking on the Earth, with approbation marks
The just man, and divulges him through Heaven
To all his Angels, who with true applause
Recount his praises . . .   [3.47–64]

We are right, I think, if we hear in these words the voice of

190

the fierce old Cromwellian, elected even in defeat. But is it a flaw in the fabric of the poem? Is it a flaw like that which Arnold Stein has seen in Milton's later description of the Parthian power, where he feels that "Milton has tampered with the perspective," so that a "narrative voice seems to have intruded without warrant"?[1] But that narrative voice, or that meditative voice, has been in control of the action from the poem's outset, where we met at the first word the meditative "I" whose inward thoughts enact the poem. In such a poem we are bound to hear throughout a personal voice. In a pure drama, properly so called, it would indeed be a flaw if one felt another voice coming through instead of the voice appropriate to a given character in that drama. But in this inward speaking of the meditative mind, all "characters," all speeches, are enveloped within, and suffused with, the controlling voice of the meditator himself. That mind is exploring its own problems, as well as those of mankind, through the speeches of the "characters," who have indeed no separate existence, whose very function is to take upon themselves the meditative voice of the narrator.

That is why the poem never shows any extended effort to present a drama of characters in the usual sense. Satan and the Son of God in this poem speak within the mind of one who hopes to be himself a Son of God; both these actors use the human voice that this particular possible Son of God, John Milton, possesses; for the meditative voice must speak as a particular meditative man himself would speak. So I think it is hardly valid to object that this poem does not present the Christ of the Gospels. For this is not a rehearsal of the Gospels; it is rather (as Hopkins would say) a rehearsal of the self, where the voice of the inner man discovers what a true Son of God ought to reply to such temptations.

Thus earlier we have heard Satan speak, as it might seem,

1. Stein, *Heroic Knowledge*, p. 89. For a discussion of the ways in which Milton "intrudes" throughout the poem, see the adverse criticism by W. B. C. Watkins, *Anatomy of Milton's Verse*, pp. 113–25.

"out of character," when he rebukes Belial for suggesting a temptation through female beauty:

> or should she confident,
> As sitting Queen ador'd on Beauties Throne,
> Descend with all her winning charms begirt
> To enamour, as the Zone of *Venus* once
> Wrought that effect on *Jove,* so Fables tell;
> How would one look from his Majestick brow
> Seated as on the top of Vertues hill,
> Discount'nance her despis'd, and put to rout
> All her array; her female pride deject,
> Or turn to reverent awe? For Beauty stands
> In the admiration only of weak minds
> Led captive; cease to admire, and all her Plumes
> Fall flat and shrink into a trivial toy . . .   [2.211–23]

If this strikes us as more Miltonic than Satanic, it need not worry us: the "characters" of this poem exist, not for their own points of view, but as occasions, as channels, by which the personal meditation can make its way.

Now, after this brilliant battle of rhetoric has ended with the defeat of worldly glory, so, in another mode of temptation, Milton moves onward, in the second half of Book 3, to show a richer, higher style arising out of the temperate ground. It is a significant touch that Milton should have the grand tableau of Parthian power, with its echoes of the grand style of *Paradise Lost,* literally rise up from a georgic plain:

> With that (such power was giv'n him then) he took
> The Son of God up to a Mountain high.
> It was a Mountain at whose verdant feet
> A spatious plain out strech't in circuit wide
> Lay pleasant; from his side two rivers flow'd,
> Th' one winding, the other strait and left between
> Fair Champain with less rivers interveind,
> Then meeting joyn'd thir tribute to the Sea:
> Fertil of corn the glebe, of oyl and wine,

With herds the pastures throng'd, with flocks the hills,
Huge Cities and high towr'd, that well might seem
The seats of mightiest Monarchs . . .   [3.251–62]

And so we come to those grandly over-wrought displays of
proper names that sum up worldly power and empire:

> *Ecbatana* her structure vast there shews,
> And *Hecatompylos* her hunderd gates,
> There *Susa* by *Choaspes,* amber stream,
> The drink of none but Kings; of later fame
> Built by *Emathian,* or by *Parthian* hands,
> The great *Seleucia, Nisibis,* and there
> *Artaxata, Teredon, Tesiphon* . . .   [3.286–92]

> From *Arachosia,* from *Candaor* East,
> And *Margiana* to the *Hyrcanian* cliffs
> Of *Caucasus,* and dark *Iberian* dales,
> From *Atropatia* and the neighbouring plains
> Of *Adiabene, Media,* and the South
> Of *Susiana* to *Balsara's* hav'n.   [3.316–21]

It is appropriate, I think, that near the close of all this splendid
panoply, Milton should bring in (at line 329) the poem's
outstanding example of a pompous and affected latinism:
"Chariots or Elephants *endorst* with Towers." And it is even
more appropriate that at the very end of the vision we should
meet the poem's first example of an epic comparison, one that
clearly reminds us of the allusions to chivalric romance in the
opening book of *Paradise Lost* (582–87, 763–66):

> Such forces met not, nor so wide a camp,
> When *Agrican* with all his Northern powers
> Besieg'd *Albracca,* as Romances tell;
> The City of *Gallaphrone,* from thence to win
> The fairest of her Sex *Angelica*
> His daughter, sought by many Prowest Knights,
> Both *Paynim,* and the Peers of *Charlemane.*
> Such and so numerous was thir Chivalrie . . .
>   [3.337–44]

This great passage on the Parthians demonstrates, as the banquet scene has earlier shown, that this writer is still at the peak of his powers. All the strength of *Paradise Lost* is still there; he can use it when he chooses; but here the Son of God condemns the grand vision as "argument / Of human weakness rather then of strength."

5. The True Image

As the fourth book opens, Milton announces the imminent climax of the grand style by introducing a cluster of similes. They are not quite heroic similes; they are rather subdued echoes of the heroic mode; but they serve to prepare for the epic manner of the following tableau of Rome, where Milton bends his heroic bow still further, carrying the compressed richness of his high style to its absolute and appropriate limit:

> Thence to the gates cast round thine eye, and see
> What conflux issuing forth, or entring in,
> Pretors, Proconsuls to thir Provinces
> Hasting or on return, in robes of State;
> Lictors and rods the ensigns of thir power,
> Legions and Cohorts, turmes of horse and wings:
> Or Embassies from Regions far remote
> In various habits on the *Appian* road,
> Or on the *Aemilian,* some from farthest South,
> *Syene,* and where the shadow both way falls,
> *Meroe Nilotic* Isle, and more to West,
> The Realm of *Bocchus* to the Black-moor Sea;
> From the *Asian* Kings and *Parthian* among these,
> From *India* and the golden *Chersoness,*
> And utmost *Indian* Isle *Taprobane,*
> Dusk faces with white silken Turbants wreath'd:
> From *Gallia, Gades,* and the *Brittish* West,
> *Germans* and *Scythians,* and *Sarmatians* North
> Beyond *Danubius* to the *Tauric* Pool.   [4.61–79]

This vision of Rome is more than the climax of the high style: it is a culmination of all the many threads of temptation that have been weaving their way toward this highest "grandeur and majestic show / Of luxury," of "wealth and power, / Civility of Manners, Arts, and Arms." For the Son's answer recalls the Banquet scene of Book 2:

> though thou should'st add to tell
> Thir sumptuous gluttonies, and gorgeous feasts
> On *Cittron* tables or *Atlantic* stone;
> (For I have also heard, perhaps have read)
> Their wines of *Setia, Cales,* and *Falerne,*
> *Chios* and *Creet,* and how they quaff in Gold,
> Crystal and Myrrhine cups imboss'd with Gems
> And studs of Pearl, to me should'st tell who thirst
> And hunger still . . .   [4.113–21]

It has all been one sustained temptation, from the point where Belial first spoke of sexual appetite, up through the more refined appetites of the banquet, and onward to this moment of final rejection for these kingdoms of the flesh, the world, and the devil.

For this, we must note, is the end of Satan's kingdoms,[1] as Satan himself three times says: first, in concluding his vision of Rome:

> These having shewn thee, I have shewn thee all
> The Kingdoms of the world, and all thir glory.
>   [4.88–89]

Next, in his answer to the Son's rejection, where Milton concludes the whole sequence by bringing in the ending of the second temptation in Luke's account: "The Kingdoms of the world to thee I give . . . if thou wilt fall down, / And worship me"; with the answer: "Get thee behind me . . ." (4.163–67,

---

1. See Allan H. Gilbert, "The Temptation in *Paradise Regained,*" *Journal of English and Germanic Philology, 15* (1916), 599–611, esp. pp. 606–07. Also Miss Pope's book, p. 67.

195

193–94). And thirdly, by way of prologue to the next vision:

> Therefore let pass, as they are transitory,
> The Kingdoms of this world; I shall no more
> Advise thee, gain them as thou canst, or not.
>
> [4.209–11]

But just as he had offered to the meditative mind the sexual suggestion of Belial, before the temptation of the Kingdoms, properly so called, here Milton adds another temptation. What implications lie in this placing of the final tableau of Greek culture outside of the Kingdoms of the World? First of all, we should note, with some relief, perhaps, that these realms of Greek culture do not lie within Satan's gift: he does not control them, he does not offer to give them. Satan can only urge the Son of God to use Greek culture on the wrong terms, that is, to value Greek learning and art beyond the bounds proper to a Son of God. Thus: shall the Son of God concede that Athens is truly "Mother of Arts / And Eloquence," that her Tragedians are "teachers best / Of moral prudence," "High actions, and high passions best describing"? Shall the Son of God concede that Socrates was really "Wisest of men" and that Greek thought is all in all because "These rules will render thee a King compleat / Within thy self"?

The Son has already anticipated his answer in the long speech at the end of Book 2. The Son of God can never rest within the ideal of being "compleat / Within thy self." This, he has implied, is a right beginning, but the Son of God must look beyond himself to the thorns, the burden, the weight of mankind's incompleteness.

The Son's answer at first should cause us no discomfort: he does not at first deny the value of Greek culture: he says only that it is not necessary to the good life:

> To whom our Saviour sagely thus repli'd.
> Think not but that I know these things, or think
> I know them not; not therefore am I short

Of knowing what I aught: he who receives
Light from above, from the fountain of light,
No other doctrine needs, though granted true . . .

[4.285–90]

Milton could have avoided all our modern worries over this
scene if he had only had the consideration to stop here; but,
as in Satan's scorn of sexual weakness, or in Jesus' denunciation of glory, so here the personal involvement of the meditator
runs beyond the bounds of an easy propriety. For the Christian
Humanist and Platonist this is the greatest challenge: can he
be brought to say that truth resides in Greek achievements, in
and by themselves? The Son of God is thus driven to make, at
this point, a judgment more drastic and more violent than that
made by the rest of the poem. For the whole poem qualifies
and moderates this fierce renunciation, while at the same time
this particular episode shows the speaker's readiness to make
the ultimate sacrifice, if it should be demanded. The tone is
tense, vehement, almost savage in places:

But these are false, or little else but dreams,
Conjectures, fancies, built on nothing firm.
The first and wisest of them all profess'd
To know this only, that he nothing knew;
The next to fabling fell and smooth conceits . . .
Alas what can they teach, and not mislead;
Ignorant of themselves, of God much more,
And how the world began, and how man fell
Degraded by himself, on grace depending?
Much of the Soul they talk, but all awrie,
And in themselves seek vertue, and to themselves
All glory arrogate, to God give none . . .   [4.291–315]

And as for learning the "secret power / Of harmony" and
"moral prudence" from Greek poetry:

All our Law and Story strew'd
With Hymns, our Psalms with artful terms inscrib'd,
Our Hebrew Songs and Harps in *Babylon,*

197

That pleas'd so well our Victors ear, declare
That rather *Greece* from us these Arts deriv'd;
Ill imitated, while they loudest sing
The vices of thir Deities, and thir own
In Fable, Hymn, or Song, so personating
Thir Gods ridiculous, and themselves past shame.
Remove their swelling Epithetes thick laid
As varnish on a Harlots cheek, the rest,
Thin sown with aught of profit or delight,
Will far be found unworthy to compare
With *Sion's* songs, to all true tasts excelling,
Where God is prais'd aright, and Godlike men,
The Holiest of Holies, and his Saints;
Such are from God inspir'd, not such from thee;
Unless where moral vertue is express't
By light of Nature not in all quite lost.   [4.334–52]

The violence of the charge, followed by the curt qualifica-
tion, suggests that here is the hardest renunciation of all; but
if necessary, the Son of God is prepared to lay down all. It is
the same action that Milton's older contemporary, Nicholas
Ferrar, performed on his deathbed, where, as the scene has
come down to us, he said at last to his brother:

> When you have measured out the place for my grave, then goe
> and take out of my Study, those three great Hampers full of
> Bookes that have stood there locked up these many yeares:
> They were not many scores but many Hundreths in all kind
> of Languages, which he had in all places gotten with great
> search, and some cost. They were Comedies, Tragedies, Love-
> Hymns, Heroicall Poems, and such like. Carry (sayd he) those
> Hampers to the place of my grave, and upon it, see you burn
> them all: and this he spake with some vehemency and passion
> of Indignation. Goe, Let it be done, Let it be done . . .

And after the books had been burned, John Ferrar returned to
his brother's bedside and "told him, all was done, as he had
required." "Then he suddenly lifting up himself, sat up in his

Bed, gave God hearty thanks, and called for Pen, Inke, and Paper," and wrote out the following document:

> November 28th 1637. I. H. S. In the name of God, Amen.
> In as much as all the Comedyes, Tragedyes, Pastoralls etc: and all those they call Heroicall Poems, none excepted; and like wise all the Bookes of Tales, which they call Novells, and all feigned Historyes written in Prose, all Love Hymns, and all the like Bookes are full of Idolatry, and especially tend to the Overthrow of Christian Religion, undermining the very Foundations thereof, and corrupt and pollute the minds of the Readers, with filthy lusts, as, woe is me, I have proved in my self. In this regard therefore, to shew my detestation of them to the World, and that all others may take warning, I have burned all of them, and most humbly have, and doe beseech God, to forgive me all my mispent time in them, and all the sinns that they have caused in me, which surely, but for his infinite Grace, had carryed my soule down into Hell long ere this. . . . I beseech all that truly feare God, that love Jesus Christ, to consider these things well. Amen, Amen, Amen.[2]

So Milton's Son of God must also enact this final renunciation: a stern demand, but just, in terms of the whole poem; for what has the poem been saying if it has not said that the elaborations of classical literature are unnecessary, dangerous, and unreliable? Milton has constantly affirmed this in the ground-style of his poem, where "swelling Epithetes" are removed, and a basic idiom is achieved approaching the "majestic unaffected stile" that Milton here praises in the Hebrew prophets. "So spake the Son of God" and Satan finds himself now "Quite at a loss, for all his darts were spent."

With those words (4.366) Milton marks the close of his long meditative analysis of human temptation. What remains is prophecy, epiphany, and praise, which Milton gives in three

2. *The Ferrar Papers*, ed. B. Blackstone (Cambridge University Press, 1938), pp. 60–63; I have expanded abbreviations and altered the punctuation slightly.

symbolic scenes. First Satan arouses a tremendous storm which shadows forth the Passion and the Resurrection, as Milton makes clear by having Satan allude to the future sufferings of Jesus immediately before and after the storm (4.386–88, 477–83). Next comes the full revelation of divine power, suggesting the Day of Judgment, as the Son of God stands on the pinnacle, and Satan falls, accompanied to his doom by a pair of true epic similes which drive home the absolute finality of the defeat. And lastly, the "Angelic Quires" sing their concluding hymn of praise, which Milton phrases in a way that allows the Son of God in this poem to suggest the restored Image of God in man, the Paradise within.

> True Image of the Father whether thron'd
> In the bosom of bliss, and light of light
> Conceiving, or remote from Heaven, enshrin'd
> In fleshly Tabernacle, and human form,
> Wandring the Wilderness, whatever place,
> Habit, or state, or motion, still expressing
> The Son of God, with Godlike force indu'd
> Against th' Attempter of thy Fathers Throne,
> And Thief of Paradise; him long of old
> Thou didst debel, and down from Heav'n cast
> With all his Army, now thou hast aveng'd
> Supplanted *Adam,* and by vanquishing
> Temptation, hast regain'd lost Paradise . . .
> For though that seat of earthly bliss be fail'd,
> A fairer Paradise is founded now
> For *Adam* and his chosen Sons, whom thou
> A Saviour art come down to re-install.
> Where they shall dwell secure, when time shall be
> Of Tempter and Temptation without fear.
>
> [4.596–617]

"Now you may see," Thomas Traherne had said near the close of his Fourth Century, "what it is to be a Son of God more clearly. . . . If you ask by what Certainty, or by what Rules we discover this? As by the Seed we conjecture what

Plant will arise, and know by the Acorn what Tree will Grow forth, or by the Eagles Egge what Kind of Bird; so do we by the Powers of the Soul upon Earth, Know what kind of Being, Person, and Glory it will be in the Heavens" (4.70). Under the guidance of the interior Teacher, Milton's poem has moved toward a conclusion essentially the same as that set forth by Traherne at the end of his First Century, where he foresees the goal of all his meditations:

Wisely doth S. John say, We are the Sons of God; but the World knoweth us not becaus it knew Him not. He that Knoweth not the Spirit of God, can never Know a Son of GOD, nor what it is to be His Child. He made us the sons of GOD in Capacity by giving us a Power, to see Eternity, to Survey His Treasures, to love his children, to know and to lov as He doth, to becom Righteous and Holy as He is; that we might be Blessed and Glorious as He is. The Holy Ghost maketh us the Sons of God in Act, when we are Righteous as He is Righteous, and Holy as He is Holy. When we prize all the Things in Heaven and Earth, as He Prizeth [them], and make a Conscience of doing it as He doth after His similitude . . . then are we indeed the Sons of God, a Chosen Generation, a Royal Priesthood, an Holy Nation, a Peculiar People, Zealous of Good Works, shewing forth the Praises of Him, who hath called us out of Darkness, into His Marvellous Light. [1.99]

BIBLIOGRAPHY

The following list includes only books cited more than once during the course of these studies; for other citations see the Index.

Primary Writings

Augustine, *The City of God,* trans. John Healey, rev. R. V. G. Tasker (2 vols. London, Everyman, 1945).

—— *Confessions,* trans. William Watts (London, 1631). This version is strongly influenced by the trans. of Sir Tobie Matthew (St. Omer, 1620).

—— *Confessions,* the Latin text, with trans. by William Watts, rev. W. H. D. Rouse, Loeb Classical Library (2 vols. London, Heinemann, 1912).

—— *Earlier Writings,* trans. John H. S. Burleigh, Library of Christian Classics, 6 (London, SCM Press, Philadelphia, The Westminster Press, 1953). See for *Soliloquia, De Magistro, De Libero Arbitrio, De Vera Religione.*

—— *Later Works,* trans. John Burnaby, Library of Christian Classics, 8 (London, SCM Press, Philadelphia, The Westminster Press, 1955). See for *De Trinitate,* Bks. 8, 9, 10, 14, 15.

Bonaventure, *The Mind's Road to God,* trans. George Boas, Library of Liberal Arts, 32 (New York, Liberal Arts Press, 1953; currently published by Bobbs-Merrill).

—— *Itinerarium Mentis in Deum,* in Bonaventure's *Opera* (10 vols. Quaracchi, 1882–1902), 5, 295–316.

203

BIBLIOGRAPHY

Milton, John, *The Student's Milton,* ed. Frank Allen Patterson (New York, Crofts, 1930; currently published by Appleton-Century-Crofts).

Sterry, Peter, *A Discourse of the Freedom of the Will* (London, 1675).

Traherne, Thomas, *Centuries, Poems, and Thanksgivings,* ed. H. M. Margoliouth (2 vols. Oxford, Clarendon Press, 1958).

Vaughan, Henry, *The Works of Henry Vaughan,* ed. L. C. Martin (2d ed. Oxford, Clarendon Press, 1957).

Vergil, *Georgics,* trans. Smith Palmer Bovie (Chicago, University of Chicago Press, 1956).

Secondary Writings

Barrow, R. H., *Introduction to St. Augustine: The City of God* (London, Faber, 1950). Includes selections from the treatise.

Burnaby, John, *Amor Dei: A Study of the Religion of St. Augustine* (London, Hodder and Stoughton, 1938).

Cayré, Fulbert, *La Contemplation Augustinienne* (2d ed. Bruges, Desclée de Brouwer, 1954).

Ellrodt, Robert, *Les Poètes Métaphysiques Anglais* (2 parts, Paris, Librarie José Corti, 1960).

Gilson, Étienne, *The Christian Philosophy of Saint Augustine,* trans. L. E. M. Lynch (New York, Random House, 1960).

Kermode, Frank, ed., *The Living Milton* (New York, Macmillan, 1961).

Lewis, C. S., *A Preface to Paradise Lost* (London, Oxford University Press, 1942).

MacCaffrey, Isabel Gamble, *Paradise Lost as "Myth"* (Cambridge, Mass., Harvard University Press, 1959).

Madsen, William G., "The Idea of Nature in Milton's Poetry," in a composite volume, *Three Studies in the Renaissance* (New Haven, Yale University Press, 1958).

Peter, John, *A Critique of Paradise Lost* (New York, Columbia University Press, 1960).

Pettet, E. C., *Of Paradise and Light: A Study of Vaughan's Silex Scintillans* (Cambridge, Cambridge University Press, 1960).

Pope, Elizabeth Marie, *Paradise Regained: The Tradition and the Poem* (Baltimore, Johns Hopkins Press, 1947).

BIBLIOGRAPHY

Stein, Arnold, *Heroic Knowledge* (Minneapolis, University of Minnesota Press, 1957).

Summers, Joseph H., *The Muse's Method: An Introduction to Paradise Lost* (London, Chatto and Windus, 1962).

Tillyard, E. M. W., *Milton* (London, Chatto and Windus, 1930).

———— *Studies in Milton* (New York, Macmillan, 1951).

Wade, Gladys I., *Thomas Traherne* (Princeton, Princeton University Press, 1944).

Watkins, W. B. C., *An Anatomy of Milton's Verse* (Baton Rouge, Louisiana State University Press, 1955).

APPENDIX

Traherne's *Select Meditations:*
The Osborn Manuscript

A few days before the galley-proofs of this book arrived, I learned from my colleague James M. Osborn that he had just acquired a manuscript containing meditations arranged in "Centuries", which he thought might have some connection with Traherne. It did not require a very long reading to convince me that these meditations were indeed the work of Traherne, for parallels with his known writings, particularly with the *Centuries,* are everywhere to be found in the manuscript. This represents a different set of Centuries from those already familiar to us, though very closely related in places to the published *Centuries,* as well as to Traherne's *Christian Ethicks.* Since some forty pages are missing at the beginning of the manuscript volume, the first complete meditation is number 82 of the First Century; the Second and Third Centuries are nearly complete, although some gaps occur; and the Fourth Century stops with Meditation 68, which is followed by nine blank pages. Four short miscellaneous pieces are written in the latter part of the manuscript book. The title *Select Meditations* occurs at the head of the last three Centuries (which are carefully subtitled "The Second Century", etc.), and thus was presumably the general title for the work. This title is of considerable interest, since it implies the existence of a larger body of meditations by Traherne, some of which may survive in the published *Centuries*. Since a full account of the new manuscript, by Mr. Osborn, is forthcoming, there is no need to give further details here. My primary aim in adding this Appendix (to the page proofs) is to suggest the nature of the relationship between the *Select Meditations* and the published *Centuries* which form a major concern of the present book.

I shall quote first an important passage from the *Select Meditations* which deals with Traherne's central theme of Infancy; the passage, like those following, contains some of Traherne's characteristic phrasing, along with his characteristic spelling and punctuation (or lack of punctuation):

> Gods Kingdom, His Subjects and Laws are Divine Things, when I Look upon them in the Light of the Citty wherein I Lived. I remember the time when its Gates were Amiable, its Streets Beautifull, its Inhabitants immortall, its Temple Glorious, its Inward Roomes and chambers Innocent and all Misterious, Soe they appeared to the little Stranger, when I first came into the world. As sweet every thing as paradice could make it. For I saw them all in the light of Heaven. And they were all mine, Temple Streets Skies Houses Gates and people. I had not learned to appropriat any thing other way. The people were my Living joyes and moveing Jewells sweet Amazments walking Miracles: And all the place a Grand Hive, and Repositary of Delights.   [3.29]

This passage looks like an early version of the thoughts expressed at greater length and much more eloquently at the opening of the published Third Century (especially 3.2, 3). And there are many specific signs that the *Select Meditations* are indeed earlier than the published *Centuries,* if we accept (as I do) Margoliouth's conclusion that the published *Centuries,* in their present form, date from about 1670, after Traherne had moved from Credenhill to London and Teddington. The evidence for this later dating lies in Traherne's vague reference (*Centuries,* 1.80) to his being "at 100 Miles Distance" from the friend to whom these *Centuries* are addressed, and also in the strongly retrospective tone of the published Third and Fourth Centuries, which seem to place a considerable extent of time between the writing and the discoveries there set forth (see Margoliouth, *1,* 251, 290).

The *Select Meditations,* however, bear strong evidence of having been composed in the 1660s, shortly after the Restoration, when the re-establishment of the Monarchy and the Church still appears precarious. The first extant page of the new manuscript contains the prayer, "Soften our Kings Heart," which seems clearly to date the passage (1.82) after the Restoration. Then Meditations 23–25 of the Third Century present a vigorous defense of the "church of England," a "National church", "Religion Established by Laws, Kings and Magistrates;" and at the same time Traherne strongly attacks "the foolishness of Sectaries": "Ingratefull Pharisies, and Lofty Hypocrites, Disobedient Hereticks, and Selfe Conceited Holy ones; that make Devisions, and are Despisers of union, Peace, and External flourishing." "No Beauty do they see in the Nations union, Much lesse any Benefit in the union of the church. . . . O prodigious and unreasonable Men!"

Along with this evidence, one meditation in the new manuscript seems to suggest a setting at Credenhill, where Traherne resided as priest from 1661 until 1669 (Margoliouth, *1,* xxxvii). Meditation 83 of the Third Century in the *Select Meditations* begins thus: "When I see a Little church Environed with Trees, how many Things are there which mine Eye discerneth not." He proceeds to meditate upon the "Spirituall Beauties" of this church, even though "Perhaps when I Look upon it, it is Desolate and Empty almost Like an heap of Stones:" and then he concludes: "The Services are such that He [any man or minister] should Delight in; and becaus so rejoyce in God for Preparing them to his Hands. Especialy I who have been Nourished at universities in Beautifull Streets and famous Colledges, and am sent thither from God

Almighty the Maker of Heaven and Earth, to teach Immortal
Souls the way to Heaven . . ." One brief exclamation elsewhere in the manuscript (2.38) adds a further association
with Herefordshire: "And cannot I here on earth so Lov my
freinds! O my T.G. O my S.H. O my Brother!" "S.H." is presumably Susanna Hopton, who lived at Kington, near Credenhill, after the Restoration, and became the center of a
religious circle that included Traherne; hence the identifica-
tion of Mrs. Hopton with the friend to whom the published
Centuries are addressed (see Wade, ch. 8; Margoliouth, *1*,
xxxiv–v). "T.G." may be Thomas Good, Master of Balliol
(1672–78), who knew Traherne well, and was in 1660 appointed prebendary of Hereford (see Wade, p. 107; Margoliouth, *1*, xxviii; *TLS*, 27 Oct. 1927, p. 767; and *DNB); but*
the name of Theophilus Gale should also be considered as a
possibility (see Wade, p. 67).

The whole effect of the newly discovered Centuries is in
accord with this early dating: they seem throughout to represent the young minister's self-analysis and self-dedication, his
early efforts to explain to himself the meaning of his life. This
is particularly clear from one meditation (4.3) where he
speaks openly of the mystical experience that he guardedly
implies in the published Third Century (3.59, 60). In the
Select Meditations we find the experience fully declared in
a way that bears out the interpretation suggested in my commentary on the published Third Century (see above, p. 92):

> This Endless Comprehension of my Immortal Soul when
> I first saw it, so wholy Ravished and Transported my spirit,
> that for a fortnight after I could scarsly Think or speak or
> write of any other Thing. But Like a man Doteing with
> Delight and Extasie, Talk of it Night and Day as if all the
> Joy of Heaven and Earth were Shut up in it. For in very
> Deed there I saw the Divine Image Relucent and Shining,
> There I saw the foundation of mans Excellency, and that
> which made Him a Son of God. Nor ever shall I be able to
> forget its Glory.

This evidence that Traherne, during the 1660s, had set together his *Select Meditations* in the form of Centuries also casts some light upon the process of composition that underlies the published *Centuries*. Since Traherne supplied no title for the latter work and gave no heading for the First Century, Margoliouth concluded that "Traherne did not start with the idea of 'Centuries'" but happened upon these divisions as he wrote (Margoliouth, *1*, x–xi, 235). The existence of the other, apparently earlier, Centuries makes this theory now untenable, and suggests on the contrary that Traherne created the book of devout instructions for his female friend with a planned set of Centuries fully in mind. The enigmatic opening of the published *Centuries* is part of a deliberate artistic and meditative design, as I have suggested earlier (see above, pp. 44–45); this design is based upon a theological principle that we find now fully set forth in the newly discovered manuscript (*Select Meditations*, 4.13):

God Hath don more for us than we could find out How to Imagine. All the world is in his Infinity, and His Infinity within us. yet hath He made the Soul Empty, as if there were noe such Infinity within us, no such world, no God, no Being. nay not a Soul till we meditate upon it, to the Intent it might have a Power to Creat these Things and Seat them in it Selfe. as God did by Thinking creat all in Himselfe. They are there but are not seen till the understanding Shine upon them.

Thus the *Select Meditations,* like the published *Centuries,* are derived from the basic Augustinian principle that the Image of God in man is an active, creative, illuminating force: that man, as Traherne says elsewhere in these newly discovered meditations, "is made after Gods Image in respect of Ability capacity and power" (3.43).

INDEX

Adam, symbolism of, 27, 38–39, 54, 60–61, 65–66, 69–70, 76–79, 83–84, 94–95, 105. *See also* Milton, *Paradise Lost*

Addison, Joseph, 175 n.

Alabaster, William, 3

Allen, Don Cameron, 182

Anamnesis, xvi, xviii, 30. *See also* Augustine; Memory

Augustine, St., 54, 73, 75, 78, 156, 211; *beata vita*, concept of, 42–43; *beatitudo,* concept of, 42–43; chaos, concept of, 124–26; concupiscence, doctrine of, 51, 83–85; depravity, doctrine of, 83–85; desire, concept of, 40; illumination, concept of, defined, xiii–xiv, xvii; meditative method, defined, 23–24, 47–49; memory, theory of, xvi–xix, 18–28, 41, 51, 81; mystical principles, 55; Platonism, xv–xvi, 46, 50, 54, 72, 86; powers of the soul, action of, 23, 81–83; repetition, technique of, 43–54; search for truth, method of, 45–49; time, concept of, 52–53.

Anti-Pelagian writings, 83; *De Beata Vita,* 40 n.; *City of God,* xv, 42, 54, 84, 116, 157; *Confessions,* xv–xviii, 18–31, 40–45, 47 n., 49–53, 81, 124–26, 156; style of, 43–44, 49–54; title, meaning of, 41–42; *De Libero Arbitrio,* 71–72; *De Magistro,* 169; *De Musica,* 72; *De Quantitate Animae,* 57; *Retractations,* xvi, 42; *Soliloquies,* xv–xvi; *De Trinitate,* xiii–xiv, xvi, xviii–xix, 23 n., 43, 45–51, 74, 82–83, 105; *De Vera Religione,* 72, 85–87

Barrow, R. H., 42 n., 116 n.

Bastian, Ralph J., 55 n.

Blackstone, B., 199 n.

Blake, William, 103

Blondel, Jacques, 187 n.

Boas, George, 55

Bonaventure, St., 17; *Itinerarium,* 18, 55–59, 67–68, 71–73, 75, 78–79, 81, 83, 85, 87, 90–91, 93, 100–02

Bourke, Vernon J., 55 n.

Bovie, Smith Palmer, 173 n., 174

Broadbent, J. B., 115 n.

Brooks, Cleanth, 112 n.

Brunschvicg, Léon, 24 n.

THE YALE PAPERBOUNDS